Werner Herzog

Contemporary Film Directors

Edited by Justus Nieland and Jennifer Fay

The Contemporary Film Directors series provides concise, well-written introductions to directors from around the world and from every level of the film industry. Its chief aims are to broaden our awareness of important artists, to give serious critical attention to their work, and to illustrate the variety and vitality of contemporary cinema. Contributors to the series include an array of internationally respected critics and academics. Each volume contains an incisive critical commentary, an informative interview with the director, and a detailed filmography.

A list of books in the series appears at the end of this book.

Werner Herzog

Joshua Lund

UNIVERSITY
OF
ILLINOIS
PRESS
URBANA,
CHICAGO,
AND
SPRINGFIELD

Manufactured in the United States of America
1 2 3 4 5 C P 5 4 3 2 1

∞ This book is printed on acid-free paper.

Frontispiece: Werner Herzog with cast on the set of *Aguirre, der Zorn Gottes*, 1972.

Library of Congress Cataloging-in-Publication Data
Names: Lund, Joshua, 1969– author.
Title: Werner Herzog / by Joshua Lund.
Description: Urbana : University of Illinois Press, [2020] | Series: Contemporary film directors | Includes bibliographical references and index.
Identifiers: LCCN 2020001582 (print) | LCCN 2020001583 (ebook) | ISBN 9780252043178 (cloth) | ISBN 9780252085048 (paperback) | ISBN 9780252052057 (ebook)
Subjects: LCSH: Herzog, Werner, 1942—Criticism and interpretation.
Classification: LCC PN1998.3.H477 L86 2020 (print) | LCC PN1998.3.H477 (ebook) | DDC 791.4302/33092—dc23
LC record available at https://lccn.loc.gov/2020001582
LC ebook record available at https://lccn.loc.gov/2020001583

For Sarah, infinitely

Contents

Acknowledgments xi

AMERICAN NOMADIC | 1

Introduction 1

The Small Voice of Conquest 10

Frontier Thesis 51

"I'm planning something geographical . . ." 90

Black God, White Devil 139

Late Work 174

INTERVIEW WITH WERNER HERZOG | 221

Filmography 235

Bibliography 251

Index 265

Acknowledgments

This book would have been impossible without the support, intellectual and emotional, of Benjamin Lund, Natalie Lund, Ingrid Rose Lund, and Sarah Hultgren-Lund. Their insights into Herzog's films inhabit not only my dreams, but also my interpretations; and, as always, the book is dedicated to them.

This project evolved slowly over a period of many years, with suggestions, hints, and inspiration from too many people to recall. Some still stand out; apologies to those I've forgotten. All thanks to Malcolm McNee and the late René Jara for introducing me to Herzog's work, decades ago. Advice from Salomé Skvirsky, Dave Pettersen, and Dan Morgan got the project off the ground; and in sending me to France, Dave revolutionized both the book and my family's worldview. Salomé, too, was a critical interlocutor without equal, patiently ready to help work out a number of the critical turns in this book. Carlos Jáuregui's camaraderie knows no limits, and his generosity of advice around the history of opera, its form and content, put me on the path to be able to write the book: terras e gentes. Peter Hallberg helps me keep the prose smooth (to the extent that that's even possible!) and Anne Garland Mahler helps me keep it real. Lecture opportunities and engaged critique from Ericka Beckman, Dan Nemser, Olimpia Rosenthal, and David Solodkow allowed me to work through key passages of the argument. Thanks to Jonathan Arac and his board at the Pitt Humanities Center, whose well-timed fellowship jump-started the project. A passing remark, certainly forgotten, by Christopher Drew Armstrong allowed me to put the pieces together in the *Fitzcarraldo* section. Same thing from Micol Seigel, Jonathan Risner, and Emma Freeman at the *Cobra Verde* section. Gracias, mil, to Liliana Diaz Castillo for taking the time to tell me about Herzog's pedagogical work on a dramatically windy day in Barcelona (this was a good omen; Herzog loves wind). Too many people showed up with little gifts for me to recall: Ben Lund with an innocent question, Natalie Lund with research assistance and photography, Ingrid Rose with a keen eye for details just at the edge of the frame, S. H.'s jokes and rational advice, Deb Koleski's ethnographic insight, Jon Rubin's *Kritik*, Arpad von Klimo's ear for accents, John Mowitt's bibliographic advice, Philippe Erikson's insight into the Amazonian world, and Roberto Marchi's archival help at the Comunale. To Jorge Azcárate for his rigor working on the filmography and interview: gracias, mi George. Warm thanks to institutions that invited me to present aspects of this work, including the University of Michigan, the University of Pennsylvania, Ohio State University, Indiana University, the Universidad de los Andes, and the University of Virginia, with gratitude to the hosts that extended the invitations and to the forum participants for their attention and their suggestions. Thanks to Karen Redrobe and the Slought Foundation for working with us on the interview. I'm grateful to the University of Notre Dame for both material and institutional support, with special thanks to the Institute for Scholarship in the Liberal Arts. Without the interest, attention, and patience from the team at the University of Illinois Press, this project would not have happened—thank you. Finally, this book consolidated as a coherent project during a visiting professorship in the Film Studies Department at the Université Lumière Lyon 2. The community, solidarity, and critical dialogue from Martin Barnier, Sébastien David, Rémi Fontanel, Raphaël Jaudon, Luc Vancheri, and their students nurtured this book from idea to project and taught me a tremendous amount about work and life.

Werner Herzog

American Nomadic

Introduction

> I have to make one remark. I do not humanize her. I do not make an attempt to humanize her. She is simply a human being. Period.
>
> —Werner Herzog, 2012

To say that Werner Herzog is a major figure of contemporary film is an understatement. While not a name of the household status like his generational peers Spielberg, Lucas, or Scorsese, among even mild cinephiles to say "Herzog" is to invoke a style, an attitude, a mystique, an institution, even something of an industry.

Associated with the New German Cinema in his early career, today Herzog is a transnational celebrity artist, whose themes and narratives spring from landscapes around the globe. Comfortably inhabiting the *auteur* tradition, even while forever attempting to excuse himself from it, he is most fundamentally a film director. But he is also a screenwriter, producer, and actor. He is the author of a few books (essentially published diaries) and he regularly stages and directs operas for some of the most illustrious companies and most prominent stages in the world. Lately he has become something of an educator, lecturing, leading workshops, convening seminars on the lesser-known aspects of filmmaking (from lock picking to permit forging). His first feature film, the critically successful *Signs of Life* (1968), premiered when he was twenty-four years old. Herzog's reputation evolved over time, as critics and the public began to slowly grasp the achievement of his most ambitious early film, *Aguirre, der Zorn Gottes* (*Aguirre, the Wrath of God*, 1972). From *Aguirre* to this day, Herzog has cultivated the reputation of a kind of friendly renegade of the cinema, and his projects are famously marked by some extraordinary detail that links the profilmic to the larger world of production: casting a wayward street musician as the protagonist of two major films, shooting with an entire company placed under the spell of hypnosis (administered by the director himself), pulling a steamship over a small mountain, collaborating with large groups of unprofessional actors, importing two thousand rats to an unexpecting Dutch village, working regularly with Klaus Kinski, and so on. Today he is a good-natured icon, regularly offering unparalleled eloquence on the significance of cinematic images and standing as the object of affectionate parody (see the YouTube shorts "Werner Herzog Reads *Madeline*" or "Werner Herzog on Vegetarianism") and even self-parody (see, for example, his cameos in American cartoons *Rick and Morty*, *American Dad*, and *The Boondocks*). His films come in all shapes and sizes, have won numerous international awards, and span more than sixty titles (and rapidly counting), with a good two dozen since 2000. In short, Herzog's stature as a major filmmaker of our time is well beyond dispute.

But this biographical sketch is not in itself a reason to rethink Herzog today. Everybody wins a prize at some point, quantity is not a virtue, and daring always runs the risk of careening into gimmickry. The reason to consider Herzog today is that his body of work represents a sustained meditation on the modern human condition, one whose challenges resonate ever more clearly in our alarming historical present, a moment in which the world-system is in crisis and the earth, literally, is on fire.[1] The insights that emerge from, and the questions that are asked by, Herzog's films speak to the centrality of the cinema in both producing and provoking our interpretation of the world. If not alone, Herzog is unusual in the courage with which he has staged the most ominous themes of modernity, distilled those themes to the psychological, even melodramatic, norms of contemporary storytelling, and successfully captured this relation within a context of image and sound that consistently leaves the spectator unsettled. The critical and (infrequent) commercial success in this effort has left him in the position of a cult director whose films are now regularly taught and curated at institutions around the world. In considering his output and stature, few systematic analyses of his work exist. His artistic and critical project has not yet been thoroughly explored.[2]

Four major, overarching themes define the bulk of scholarly work on Herzog to this point: (1) The national question, namely Herzog's harried relation with German identity and the multiple studies that take up the topic of his associations with the New German Cinema, German expressionism, German romanticism, the US-based film industry and history, and the like. (2) The intertextual elements of his films, how they relate to other films or to their literary and historical source material. (3) Herzog's cult of personality and its implications for an ethics of filmmaking, such as his relations with actors, crew, possibly vulnerable extras, fragile landscapes, standard industry practices, state policy, and so on. And, (4) perhaps most prominently, his much problematized statements on the relations between aesthetics and truth—what Herzog often characterizes as his commitment to an "ecstatic truth," truth expressed not by an accounting of facts but by the cinematic possibility of expressing a "deeper" truth through stylization—that often lead to philosophical explorations of the nature of the image (especially landscape) in Herzog's work and to the director's controversial use of documentary form.

Any account of Herzog's career trajectory and its importance (artistic, critical, historical) requires attention to all these themes, and they are certainly all at play in this study. None, however, operates as this book's analytical center. Instead, this project takes up a peculiar problem for the interpretation of Herzog's work. In a nutshell, we can call this the *political problem*. And by this I mean political in the widest sense, as the objectification and contemplation of power relations (as opposed to the identification of ideological affiliations or implications).

In turning to the political in Herzog's work, we are immediately confronted with a puzzle, one placed before us by the director himself. It works like this:

On the one hand, in Herzog's ample and unusually authoritative discourse on his own films is a commonly rehearsed refusal of the political: he summarily rejects any identification as a political filmmaker, vigorously resists the discovery of political allegories in his films, occasionally provokes the leftist sensibilities that so often claim a monopoly on political filmmaking as "engaged" cinema, and so on. On the other hand, his films represent a direct and even systematic treatment of blatantly political themes and topics. One obvious, if plain, example: his recent feature-length documentary, *Into the Abyss* (2011), and accompanying series called *On Death Row* (2012–13), are a sustained meditation on and quiet case against capital punishment. But there are subtler and more profound, examples. Take his two most prestigious films, *Aguirre* (1972) and *Fitzcarraldo* (1982). Critics have interpreted *Aguirre* (considered at length in the section "The Small Voice of Conquest" later in this book) as an allegorical or metaphorical reference to the Third Reich and to the US invasion of Vietnam, interpretations that Herzog has variously discarded as unwarranted extrapolations or simply beside the point. But modern allegories aside, taking *Aguirre* solely in the terms of its historical referent reveals a film that could not be more deeply political: it is a story set during, and representing aspects of, the invasion and conquest of the New World by Europeans. *Fitzcarraldo* (considered at length in the section "I'm planning something geographical . . ."), always remembered as the film in which a ship was pulled over a mountain, is a story that rests on—indeed, is impossible without—the formalized primitive accumulation that was the *fin-de-siècle* plunder of America's wilderness and inhabitants. So ultimately we have before us, on screen, for all to see, two of the most dramatic restagings of the historical ground that forges and sustains our political modernity, and yet there is a strong critical resistance to reading Herzog's films politically (beyond, that is, the denunciations of his production practices; a political topic, to be sure, but in another way). It is as if the director's own speech overdetermines the critical treatment of his work. And this weird resonance between political intensity and analytical silence, in turn, makes the aesthetic, narrative, and cinematic dimensions of his work more compelling, more mystifying, more urgent, and more psychologically complex.

In these pages I start from the premise that a central impediment to interpreting Herzog's work is the fact that his navigation of the political defies our basic categories of left-right, progressive-reactionary, liberal-conservative, individualist-collectivist, and so on. Placing the director's commentary to one side, the films in and of themselves are true to this unexpected treatment of the political. It is not so much that the films actively deconstruct the ordering binaries of contemporary social life. It is rather that they simply refuse these binaries and seem to operate outside, or alongside, their discursive conventions.[3] So, in *Aguirre*, we have the most disturbing portrait of fevered conquest ever brought to the screen, and yet the empire (the Spanish Crown) and its opponent (the collapsing indigenous civilizations) are only marginal players, secondary, even tertiary, to the quiet battle between a megalomaniac and a jungle. *Fitzcarraldo*, motivated by capitalist expansion and resource accumulation, turns out to be not a competition over land, but rather over dreams. As with many prominent directors, the center of Herzog's work is power: its circulation, distribution, accumulation, application, negotiation. But his originality rests on the way in which he upsets our expectations of its representation. The protagonist of *Cobra Verde* (1987), a unique, mesmerizing, and profoundly creepy story of the Atlantic slave trade (see the section "Black God, White Devil"), is a slave driver. And his "heroism" (a loaded term, and inapplicable here) does not reside in taking a brave stand against a despicable crime of capital and state, perhaps motivated by some sort of revelation that will lead to redemption. Rather, his protagonism is pure pathos, the fact that he was there to witness the crime's exhaustion; he watched the institution die as it limply gazes toward America, bloated and washed up on an African beach as a maimed figure looks on, ascetic, largely indifferent. Critically, this kind of operatic stylization and narrative collapse is an opportunity to explore the contradictions of the film. And yet, it is simultaneously quite challenging to deal with. My sense is that the surprising lack of critical analysis of the political—not to be confused with the merely controversial—in Herzog stems from the fact that, before these kinds of images, we simply don't know what to say. This is not because there is nothing to say. Rather, the lack of analysis arises from the difficulty of rethinking the foundational themes of our modern political imagination when they are rendered so radically unfamiliar. It is in this gesture that the (ongoing) significance of Herzog's work resides.

Herzog's output is vast, and one day there will be multivolume considerations of his work and life. For now, and as a way of handling the dauntingly prolific material of Herzog's filmography in a single volume, in this book I rest the political question against the idea of America in Herzog's work. Doing so requires two immediate clarifications. First, I invoke "America" in the broad, hemispheric sense. And, second, I do not mean to indicate that I will be preoccupied with Herzog's precarious status as an "American filmmaker." Significant attention has been paid to the Germanness of Herzog's films, and in fact, despite the director's own artistic biography, his identity among film scholars resides largely within that specific national tradition. In the thick and comprehensive *Companion to Werner Herzog* (Prager 2012), for example, 18 of 25 scholarly contributors affiliate with some aspect of German studies. Significantly less attention has been paid to Herzog's sustained problematization of the idea of America and its relation to the consolidation of capitalist modernity. And yet America—as space, discourse, and dream—is central to his most stylistically and thematically ambitious work. In a striking run of films produced over a fifteen-year period, Herzog takes up the big themes of capitalist modernity and forces us to confront them by way of America: conquest (*Aguirre*, 1972); migration, frontiers and economic aspiration (*Stroszek*, 1977); penetration and accumulation (*Fitzcarraldo*, 1982); and slavery (*Cobra Verde*, 1987). From this quartet, America, as both physical landscape and political-historical project, would become implicated directly in the exploration of man's apocalyptic drive that guides Herzog's more contemporary work, including his highly regarded, stylized "documentaries," such as *Lessons of Darkness* (1992), *Little Dieter Needs to Fly* (1997), *Grizzly Man* (2005), *The Wild Blue Yonder* (2005), *Into the Abyss*, and *Lo and Behold: Reveries of the Connected World* (2016). Icarus animates all these films, and it would seem that the idea of America, its status as both dream and limit in the Western imagination, has compelled Herzog to tell and retell his story there. Taking up and reframing the political at these seminal scenes of our historical present, Herzog goes right to the core—the origin stories, the nightmares, of modern consciousness—and then restages it in maddeningly opaque terms. The maddeningness, I maintain, is the politics. It invites us to defamiliarize the world and render its dominant interpretations rethinkable. I've seen this in action in several classroom settings, when I have taught one or another of these Herzog films alongside films governed by much more explicit, even tendentious, politicized narratives (Sayles's *Men with Guns* [1997], González Iñárritu's *Babel* [2006], Morris's *Standard Operating Procedure* [2008], Tarentino's *Django Unchained* [2012]). The immediacy with which Herzog's films provoke notably engaged and controversial discussions that ultimately turn on questions of power is without competition. How does this work? What is the relation between cinematic style and narrative, power and its absence, in Herzog's films? How do these films problematize the privileged categories of Western modernity, especially in their conventional liberal mode? How do they obligate us (or not) to rethink the relations between history, capital, and domination? What are their critical possibilities, and also limits? Not a search for ideological clarity, this book asks: what are the aesthetics of the political in Herzog's work? These are the questions that will guide our consideration of a set of Herzog's most significant films.

When approaching Herzog from a scholarly and analytical perspective, the first and most significant interpretive interlocutor is the director himself. Herzog has directed two autobiographical films (*Werner Herzog: Filmemacher* [*Portrait Werner Herzog*, 1986] and *Mein Liebster Feind* [*My Best Fiend*, 1999]) and is the subject of six largely affirmative biographical documentaries (Weisenborn and Keusch's *I Am My Films* [1979]; Blank's two films, *Werner Herzog Eats His Shoe* [1980] and *Burden of Dreams* [1982]; Gruber's *Location Africa* [1987]; Weisenborn's *I Am My Films, part 2 [30 years later]* [2010]; and Golder's *Ballad of a Righteous Merchant* [2017]). Two volumes of his reflections—*Of Walking in Ice* (2015) and *Conquest of the Useless* (2009)—are widely available in English and several other languages, alongside his amply published literary screenplays that correspond to his individual films. His legendary DVD commentaries are without peer, eloquent, insightful, often hilarious. He has been uncommonly generous with his availability for interviews, a number of which are famous—including one during which he gets shot by a random assailant—and form a kind of Herzog canon on YouTube. The remarkable and extensive interviews conducted for Herzog and Cronin's *Herzog on Herzog* (2002; expanded as *Werner Herzog: A Guide for the Perplexed* in Herzog and Cronin [2014]) stand as a significant work of literature in their own right and are a major source (the single most significant source, I would say) of citation, authority, and affirmation in the scholarship on Herzog's films. An admirable companion, and fascinating to read for its expression of the evolution (or lack thereof) of Herzog's positions over time, Eric Ames has collected many of the most significant early interviews with Herzog in *Werner Herzog: Interviews* (2014). In writing analytical work on Herzog's films, the only responsible way to treat this archive is to know it thoroughly, understand its contours, and remember it as occasionally useful source material and, indeed, as a kind of performance in its own right. Much scholarship takes the bait and, with important exceptions (Davidson, in particular, stands out for his resistance to the interviews as self-evident truth), too quickly treats the director's comments (often opaque, sometimes driven by bombast, and regularly contradictory) as sanctified evidence for the interpretation of his films. Like all who have written on Herzog, I am essentially obligated to draw on the director's own insights. But I use it for what it is: ultimately, literary autobiography and film criticism. Sometimes Herzog's comments are more convincing than others, and I take them up in the spirit of a critical interlocutor. In short, Herzog and I do not usually agree about how best to interpret his films.

Herzog presents the film scholar with the immediate problem of conceptual organization: more than sixty titles in around sixty years of filmmaking. The tendency in book-length studies of Herzog is to organize a selection of these titles into themes.[4] With the repetition of certain ideas, contexts, images and topics in Herzog's films, this certainly makes sense. In part because of the nature of the series for which this book is written—an introduction to the work of major contemporary directors—I have eschewed this tendency in favor of chronology. Of course, chronology is not everything and there are often good reasons to disobey it, but it also presents other conceptual advantages. It can provide a sort of unimpeded arc of the artist's career, where repetitions can be tracked through time, as opposed to bundled together into sections that, ultimately, impose a certain order on the reader that may in the end confine imagination. And this, in turn, allows for the individual films to hang together in something like an organic fashion, allowing for relations to emerge more spontaneously and less from the analyst's impositions. But this, of course, is not to say that this book does not impose. While moving chronologically like a survey, and attempting a realistic level of comprehensiveness (with only a small handful of exceptions, every single Herzog film is at least mentioned in these pages), the book does have a unifying problematic: the relation between the political and the idea of America in Herzog's work. Thus we will be most attentive to those films engaged with that problematic, and in that spirit the chronology does not seek equal time, but is organized around four center-of-gravity films that ground each of the four major sections. Many other films, by both Herzog and his interlocutors, will receive attention within each chapter, and novices of Herzog's work will be able to use the following pages to get a sense of the general evolution of his career.

Through and alongside this film-studies-guided discussion will emerge extensive contextual work that allows us to grasp the critical dimensions of Herzog's major films in new ways. Herzog is fond of paradoxically displacing historical contexts from his keenly grounded historical films and maintains a long tradition of statements that attempt to extract his aesthetic work from the scene of history that it represents and also in which it is made. He argues that his films could be set anywhere, and just happen to be at this or that moment of historical intensity. His argument is a red herring. A basic understanding of the multiple layers of historical processes at play in Herzog's most ambitious films allows us to think them anew, and also to appreciate their provocations, alongside the intellectual ambition that makes them work. In other words, you can't understand the dynamism of these films by placing them into the flow of cinematic history and leave it at that. To deal with *Aguirre*, you need to know the basics of his historical avatar's failed conquest, its situation within the Spanish Empire, and its resonance in Latin American politics of the high Cold War. *Stroszek* requires an understanding of the film's unconscious ogre: not just the American Dream, but the decades-long ideological work that led to America imagining itself as a frontier society and successfully selling that image overseas. To get into *Fitzcarraldo*, you need to get the rubber boom, its economy, and its people and also the history of opera in Latin America, not to mention the vicissitudes of indigenous activism. Nuances of the slave trade, and its contemporary memorialization, emerge in *Cobra Verde* that have simply not been brought to light in other films. A serious political reading of these movies requires us to engage their referents, and their reimagination of them, dialectically. Not to simply witness how they weigh upon the film, but, perhaps more important, to fully understand how Herzog's work intervenes in our received notions about these foundational histories, the building blocks of our contemporary world.

Ultimately, then, this book intends to both introduce Herzog and offer a new interpretation of his work, one that builds on but attempts to go beyond the scholarship that has come before. A nice turn in Brad Prager's *The Cinema of Werner Herzog* (2007) expresses where this scholarship has been and where I hope we can bring it. Here Prager—a prolific scholar of Herzog—is in dialogue with another pioneering interpreter of the director, Alan Singer (1986), specifically his foundational essay on Herzog and the sublime (a basic aesthetic category for Herzog, as we will see). Prager writes that "one should not view the experience of the sublime as trans-historical, something that goes beyond the strictures of history in which it is embedded, but that inevitably emerges out of a historical context. . . . [S]ublimity is more an opportunity to reflect on historical processes than a claim that one is experiencing something authentic, trans-historical or even 'essential'" (2007, 15). While the point is simply left right there by both Prager and Singer, it strikes me as crucial. For I maintain that Herzog's films affect us in precisely this way. With apologies to Herzog himself, his films are windows not to the human soul, but to a possibility: that of seeing the margins of ideological limits and moving beyond self-evidence. Herzog walks us along this path. With Frederic Jameson, we might call it a journey to the political unconscious. Or with Jacques Rancière, simply: politics.

The Small Voice of Conquest

> And then the tyrant said that he would have to kill just the same all the presidents and auditors and bishops, archbishops and governors, scholars and prosecutors that fell into his hands, because he said they and the priests had destroyed the Indies.
>
> —Francisco Vázquez, on Lope de Aguirre, 1561

I am not the Jesus of the official Church, who the police, bankers, judges, hangmen, officers, church bosses, politicians and other powerful people tolerate. I am not your Superstar.

—Klaus Kinski, "Jesus Christ Savior," 1971

A situation always becomes clear with monkeys.

—Werner Herzog, 1973

Shooting got off to a rough start. The scene was the heights of Machu Picchu, a celebrated Incan ruin miles downriver from Cusco, Peru, not by any means the end of the world, but logistically challenging. At dawn, four hundred Indian extras, employees of the film production, prepared for work and somehow slipped out of the barnyard barracks without waking the director, leaving him fitful, with night sweats, mumbling fever dreams, unable to disentangle himself from six hundred thousand coils of mud, moon, and guinea pigs. They loaded up the local train with themselves, the costumes, the animals, and the gear. The machine moaned forward, pulling away from the improvised platform. The director screamed himself awake. Like a barefoot bandit, scattering domesticated rodents, he launched over rails, ties, and shards, an eighth-of-a-mile sprint, finally hauled onto the creeping train, panting, pants unbuttoned, feet bloodied. Years later, the director would explain that this mad dash was the first step of the most important shoot of his career.

The director was met on set by what he remembers as "indescribable chaos." The extras were legion, without experience, and encumbered by period costumes involving armor, heavy weapons, royal gowns, a canon, llamas, chickens in cages, a pig on a leash. The footing was precarious, both steep and slick, the ground saturated by a lady rain and the air was thick, accidents seemed inevitable. Impatient weather, mostly mist with intermittent clearing, surrounded the crew, but the sluggish sun couldn't be bothered to burn off the morning clouds. The extreme long shot, the director's "ecstatic detail" of Machu Picchu, seemed wishful.

And then there was the star. He had arrived to play the title role, Lope de Aguirre, a Spanish soldier from the time of the conquest of the Americas, but he still carried the visage of an angry Jesus (Christ, Superstar), hungover from his combative, and just-terminated, one-man show in Berlin. Parachuting in to highland Peru with a prophet's air and an excess of mountaineering equipment, cantankerous and confrontational (this is the Christ of the Gospel According to Mark) he was prepared for heroic portraits. He soon realized that the opening shot would have nothing to do with him, he would be a speck among others on a jungly mountainside. This did not go over well. The star wanted his human face—"the only interesting landscape," he said—in foreground, with all glorious, postcard, deep-focus Machu Picchu behind. This is neither the point nor the story of the film, the director explained. Aguirre is not yet the leader of the expedition. And Machu Picchu is not a landscape of ruins, but a landscape of ecstasy. Its terrain is its character, and its sacral function, its setting for the divine, flows from this fact, not the other way around. The film begins with "all of the pathos" of this landscape in rebellion, a spirit of revolt that will eventually—but not yet—be transferred to Aguirre himself. The film starts here, down the mountain, into the jungle. The director cut the star from the scene.

The extras are in place—Indians, mestizos, Spaniards, a black slave, a priest, a lady, livestock—they snake down the mountain as tiny, tiny figures trespassing in a land of giants. The shot is ready . . . and there is nothing to see. The clouds form a canopy between camera and cast. Irritation begins to stir, the extras are uncertain in their commitment. The original opening, which would have featured a Spanish army and a parade of pigs atop a mighty glacier, had already been scrapped. Would Machu Picchu also resist its transformation into cinema? And then, the director's gift from above: *And finally, toward eleven o'clock in the morning, everything opened up. And here on the right side, very strangely, the clouds stayed put. And to the left, like a miracle, they parted. And then the file of people came down here. And while we were shooting I had a very profound feeling, as if the grace of God was with this film and with me. And as if I were witnessing something extraordinary which I would never see again. And I can perhaps say that on this day I definitely came to know my own destiny* (from *My Best Fiend*).

Aguirre, der Zorn Gottes (*Aguirre, the Wrath of God*, 1972) is Werner Herzog's breakthrough film, although it took some time for it to actually break through. Loosely based on a historical figure, it tells the story of Lope de Aguirre, a Spanish conquistador who went rogue, declaring himself and his band of companions sovereign, independent from the authority of the Spanish Crown. In Herzog's film, an efficient narrative trajectory follows this Aguirre figure as he is ordered on a mission to find news of El Dorado, stages his coup, and then struggles against his opponents, his sanity, evasive Indians, and the jungle in a failed quest for fame and power. Mostly, nothing happens. First shown on West German television simultaneous to its theatrical release, the film languished for months until picked up by French avant-garde critics in Paris, where it made an extended run of more than a year to increasing curiosity and comment. The laconic, masculine style of its narrative form was not unfamiliar to an arty early-1970s public well versed in the aesthetics of the spaghetti western and cinema novo.[5] But everything from the grandiosity of its scale to the crude urgency of its realism, from the hypnotic body language of the protagonist, played by Klaus Kinski, to the fact that its conquistadors speak German, left audiences with the impression that they had just witnessed something important. Besides announcing the quintessential cinematic portrait of Spanish-era conquest—and an effort that even today has not yet been surpassed—Herzog's film seemed to be indicating something both ineffable and essential, about desire and madness, about the hearts of men at the cusp of a rapidly consolidating darkness, an emergent world-system whose ideological center would be defined by an obsession with gold, but whose ultimate end was . . . nothing. Maybe a doomed raft, spinning in circles, overrun by monkeys. Maybe a dream about an opera house in the middle of the jungle. Maybe a beach, a maimed slave, an exhausted bandit, and an impossibly heavy boat. It's 1972, the fantasies, failures, and crimes of the West in the jungles of Southeast Asia are everyday news, postcolonial critique is just getting on its feet, and the world is ready for this kind of thing.

The opening scene is a good place to begin, both in order to understand the achievement of *Aguirre* and to situate it within Herzog's tendencies, aesthetic priorities, basic themes, and emergent corpus, at that time still only four feature films long (with two of them more recognizable as documentaries). The film begins in silence, with an anachronistically modernist font over a blood-red screen. This script conveys some skeletal backstory information, easy to overlook but crucial: the conquest is over, the Incas have fallen, their empire plundered; in the wake of this destruction "the Indians *invented* the legend of El

Dorado" (my emphasis), the famous lost city ruled by the gold-spangled king, located, auspiciously, at the "headwaters" of the South American river system; and in 1560, an expedition traveling under the authority of Gonzalo Pizarro would be lost in the jungle, an adventure from which only a monk's diary survives. As the titles fade, a choir somewhere between human voice and machine synthesis begins its mournful chorus. Red fades to black, and black opens to reveal the "indescribable chaos" at Machu Picchu.

What looks to be a sheer cliff, punctuated by sporadic vegetation and draped in mist, appears before the spectator.[6] Close attention reveals minuscule human figures traversing the rock downward, a harrowing landscape suggesting man's insignificance before the force of nature, although this detail is easy to miss in the first moment, until the shot zooms to reveal soldiers' helmets, one carrying a flag: this must be the expedition. A cut transitions to an even closer shot, and the descent through the clouds becomes more palpable, with a rather minimalist voiceover—it's the monk Carvajal—announcing the itinerary: down from the highlands into the jungle, it is 1560, Christmas day. The camera zooms again, tracing the soldiers as they clamber along a narrow path, details begin to emerge, the silver glint of full battle armor appears clear before us, some in the party wear more colorful costume. Between the monk's flat tone, the ethereal minor key, and the mist-obscured frame, the whole scene treads close to the surreal.

Now cross-cut to the establishing shot and a new perspective, *the* shot, the one that Herzog promises will "stick in the spectator's mind for a long time" (*My Best Fiend*, 1999). The screen appears almost split in half, as though a special effect, with the right side nearly blank, completely cordoned off in a stew of gray mist, and the left side the desired "ecstatic detail" of the promontory—called Huayna Picchu—across the chasm from the majesty of its preening twin, Machu Picchu (which from the camera's point of view would be behind the viewer; but unless you know the setting ahead of time, you would be unaware of this fact). The scale is disorienting, until the spectator notices—it takes a second—the procession of men squeezed into the lower left corner of the screen. The music, at once holy and disquieting, provides a strangely appropriate rhythm for the march down the mountain. And the rhythm is simply masterful. The camera slowly pans down, tracing the cliff's edge that splits the screen between the black-and-white abyss of the mist and the virulent riot of color on the mountainside. In one long take—about a minute and forty seconds—we descend with the expedition almost vertically, and as the trail bends along the mountain face to our right, eventually the men take center screen and details emerge: a tricky pass causes a minor backlog of about a dozen marchers; costumes come into focus; one soldier carries a battle-ax, another a harquebus; some are burdened, others not, individual gaits appear; all the while the gray void looms just to the right, paleolithic, we wouldn't be surprised if a pterodactyl exploded forth from it.

As the camera continues its methodical, downward tilt, dimensions begin to clarify as the expeditionary trail leads directly toward the viewer's perspective. After its sheer drop, the path elevates right up to the camera, and we begin to nearly discern faces as soldiers and Indians—mostly Indians, we can now see—enter the frame in medium shot and pass right below, as if at our feet. The spell of the long take

Figure 1. An ecstatic detail of Huayna Picchu, with expedition party barely visible (lower left). *Aguirre, the Wrath of God* (Herzog 1972).

is broken with an abrupt cut as a cage of live poultry hurtles down the cliff, the birds smashed against the rocks, and now close-ups begin as we are slowly introduced to the party, the camera positioned right on the trail, almost intruding on the procession. Llamas mix with Indians and soldiers, and a quick cutaway reveals that the Indians must be slaves; they are bound together by thick chains, some are also barefoot. A velvet litter and an unlikely damsel—in garments far too pristine—pass by. We catch a glimpse of dramatic, forested peaks, a small concession to canonical Andean landscape aesthetics. One Indian hauls a medium-sized icon of the Virgin, and he is followed by a man in brown robes with a prominent crucifix around his neck, the monk. Finally, Aguirre appears, blond locks embarrassing his helmet, assisting a young woman, who turns out to be his daughter. The entire procession, now behind the opening titles, takes another two full minutes until it is broken by an explosion triggered by a canon that has torn loose and hurtled down the cliff. Three shots transition to the beginning of dialogue and story: smoke rising through jungle foliage; pigs chortling, wading in the water; and Pizarro with Aguirre—low to the ground, eyes upward, like a crab—gazing out at punishing rapids. "No one can get down that river alive!" hisses Aguirre, and it is here that the expedition's forward motion essentially stops. Pizarro will announce a small reconnaissance force to be sent downriver, and in a neat recapitulation of the narrative's total structure, the first day's travel will end with one of the rafts, full of soldiers, stuck in an eddy and spinning round and round. Trapped overnight, daybreak will find the men caught on the raft slaughtered by unseen Indians. Moreover, a flood has swept away much of the campsite; the adventurers are stuck. Repeated versions of this plot structure—stasis, fear, violence, stasis—constitute the rest of the film.

Both the fabrication of this introductory sequence, and its aesthetic representation, can help establish a baseline understanding of Herzog's larger cinematic worldview. The director himself is enlightening in this regard. Herzog is an unrivaled raconteur, and in an entertaining story about the shoot and its conditions—told in the autobiographical documentary about his relationship with Kinski, *My Best Fiend*—we can perceive four basic elements of his films that articulate form to content, and the profilmic to the story world. The first truth of a Herzog production is that there will be struggle. Still a young man (not yet thirty) during the 1972 shoot, Herzog has always framed *Aguirre* as a force of sheer will, produced on a budget of less than $400,000, on location in an uncooperative jungle, with a crew of no more than eight, and condemned to deal with a maniac (Kinski carried a rifle and also handled swords, nearly killing bystanders on set with each weapon, and a legend grew around the image of Herzog eventually directing him at literal gunpoint). As Herzog has famously repeated over and again, film is more athletics than art and filmmaking comes from the thighs.[7] The spectator feels this in the shots that follow the descent down the mountain, now in jungle terrain. The chain-mail-laden expedition sinks into the rainforest mud and the film takes on the improvisational spirit of a documentary, with water spots on the camera lens, the occasional out-of-character smile from an extra, and a cameo appearance by the director's arm stabilizing the damsel's litter as it nearly tips into the muck. Activity is everywhere as a combustible Aguirre pushes, pulls and whips, and yet progress is nowhere: soldiers sink knee-deep, the horse bucks and bridles, twirling in frustration, its rider cursing, tangled up in a vine, helpless. The monk's voiceover offers a quick report, it's grim, a thumbnail sketch of imperial genocide: "Our Indian slaves are useless. The changing climate kills them off like flies, most of them die of colds. We don't even have time to give them a Christian burial."

Second, this form-content logic of hardship that guides *Aguirre*, with the director stylized as expedition leader, yields another basic truth about Herzog's work, this one more explicitly aesthetic. By so consistently confronting harrowing terrain, Herzog's films have come to be known for their ability to stage forbidding landscapes that speak, in their restlessness, to the human condition. That is, the struggle of exploration leads to landscape cinematography unusual in the authenticity of its intensity. Herzog had already broached this topic in his first films, taking the hot, harsh scrub of Kos and remote inland Crete as the setting for *Signs of Life* (1968) and, most prominently, capturing otherworldly mirages in Saharan Africa for the surrealist documentary *Fata Morgana* (1971). But it is the opening shots of *Aguirre* that stamp the special treatment of landscape on Herzog's aesthetic agenda. Most notable in the initial descent down the mountain is the director's approach to Machu Picchu. In his famous story of the shoot, Herzog makes much of his argument with Kinski about the question of "scenic Machu Picchu." But what slips past almost unnoticed is the fact that scenic Machu Picchu—one of the most iconic, and certainly the most glorious, landscapes of indigenous American ruins to be found anywhere—does not appear in the film *at all*. So the sweat, blood, and oxygen expended to ascend Machu Picchu is dedicated to the image of what the director calls an "ecstatic detail" of mountain terrain next to, but not of, the sacred complex Machu Picchu. The ruins never show up. The "ecstasy" of this "detail" is its ability, in Herzog's idea of the image, to stand as a "landscape where all the drama, all the passion, all human pathos became visible . . . a landscape with almost human qualities" (*My Best Fiend*). Whereas Kinski demands a "human face," his face, Herzog replies, "I also had the feeling that this scene without any faces would stick in the spectator's mind for a long time" (*My Best Fiend*). *Aguirre*, rethought in the light of this comment, becomes understandable as a series of landscape details, and from this it gains its hypnotic strength, the relation between character and setting that Herzog regularly calls "inner landscapes." Shot at the foot of the Andes, there would be ample opportunity for panoramic horizons to grace *Aguirre*, but none do. Instead, the film is recorded largely at low angle, constructed by stitching together a landscape of claustrophobia and vortex: an early close-up of river rapids in slow motion lingers for nearly a full minute; the river is never perceptible as system or conduit, but as a labyrinth hemmed in by tangled forest, even the occasional wide shots of the rafts give the impression of stasis, and the rapids themselves seem to flow at cross-currents;[8] the jungle is a flat wall of green slowly gliding by on the riverbank, maybe yielding the glimpse of a hostile Indian, or an abandoned horse; the single symbol of flight—a ship high up in a tree—is just out of reach.

This notion of landscape as character—"a landscape with almost human qualities" (*My Best Fiend*)—runs strong in Herzog and introduces a third basic element of his work. In the critical consensus around Herzog's films it is a convention to note their investment in various notions of the sublime. The sublime is most famous as an aesthetic category developed in Immanuel Kant's *Critique of Judgment* (1790) and commonly refers to the potential for nonnarrative, and primarily visual, art to produce a sense of awe in the spectator. This sentiment in turn is understood, in its traditionally romantic invocation, as the presence of a spiritual plenitude enveloping the relation between man and nature. But the sublime is a source of controversy in the philosophy of art. Alongside its relation to affirmative pleasure, there is a long history of thinking about the sublime in relation not only to wonder, but also to terror: the awe-inspiring landscape that leaves the spectator feeling diminished, shaken. The striving for these kinds of effects through artifice is often proposed—as in Herder's sublime object—as a kind of ideal in post-Enlightenment art, literature, and philosophy.[9] It is precisely on the basis of his regular production of sublime aesthetics that an ample critical corpus has drawn out the relations between Herzog's films and an earlier aesthetic and philosophical era academically codified as German Romanticism. While some of this scholarship suffers from a rather reductionist notion of the relation between nationality, national culture, and artistic production, it is clear that a range of aesthetic tendencies associated with German Romanticism appeal to Herzog and that he unabashedly enters into dialogue with them, despite his occasional disavowals.[10] The sublime stands chief among these, although just as it exhibits several (and often contradictory) aesthetic possibilities in the history of art—sublime pleasure, sublime pain—so does the sublime fold back, against itself within Herzog's films. So in *Aguirre*, at about minute 58, we witness a strikingly sublime image of sunbeams alighting on the river through a veil of jungle leaves, allowing us to forget, for a fleeting moment, that we are witness to a long, slow death trip and luxuriate in wonder at the jungle's aesthetic splendor. More bombastically sublime, the opening descent down Huayna Picchu with fog and chorus is not necessarily a source of pleasure, for it confronts us with a disorienting frame and near breakdown of lines of perspective. Both sets of images, while not reducible to the German Romantic tradition, resonate its dominant aesthetics, and both can be described as sublime, leaving little wonder that the category has generated diverse opinions about the nature of its presence in Herzog's films. Brad Prager (2007), in a book-length study of Herzog that pays systematic attention to the director's dialogue with German Romanticism, brings forth two of the most salient points on the sublime in Herzog. The first is that, whether life-affirming or crisis-provoking, essential to the work of the sublime is its striving to get beyond narrative language: "Herzog's work . . . is a search for that which exceeds language's capacity to express it" (5). Sublime speechlessness is certainly a motif in Herzog's films (they essentially always end on that note) and resonates dialectically with his storytelling project: the common predicament of his protagonists, he explains, is their inability to communicate in the modern world (Herzog and Cronin 2002, 68), a topic not irrelevant to *Aguirre* and also one that we will take up at length in the following section (on *Stroszek*). Prager's second point about the Herzogian sublime, and more immediate here, specifically involves the way in which he "directs landscapes," as Herzog himself puts it. Prager writes, "Herzog's shots . . . hold the viewer's gaze at a disconcerting height or at a distance from landscapes that apparently extend well beyond the borders of the screen. . . . Such compositions refuse to provide the illusion that we are being presented with a stage onto which we might wander" (85). Consider the Huayna Picchu shot: the landscape is vast, its borders unclear, and we gaze at it, a little unsure for a while, certainly not long enough for us to dominate (comprehend) it, but long enough for it to get inside of us. A sense of endlessness (what in Prager's interpretation we might call framelessness) that Matthew Gandy (1996) associates not with romantic sublime but with existentialist alienation: we are all irrelevant figures dangling on the permanent vastness of that frameless, mist-robed rock.[11]

Taking the story and the story about the story as a single narrative by rearticulating Herzog's description of the conditions of *Aguirre*'s Huayna Picchu shoot to the cinematic scene of representation, a fourth, and much less commented quality of the director's project begins to emerge. Herzog's voluble and omnipresent accounts of his filmmaking adventures are famous for their language of excess. This rhetorical style is very much in harmony with an important aesthetic tendency, one nourished not so much by romanticism as by another trajectory central to the contemporary imagination: what Walter Benjamin, precisely in a discussion about allegory and the sublime, called "the rank metaphorical overgrowth" of baroque aesthetics.[12] For Herzog, the epochal struggle of filmmaking, the attempt to stylize spontaneous, aesthetic order from the disorder of real life, has an opponent, one that he regularly comments on and conjures into his films: the proliferation of animate beings, the natural world—whether man, animal, or plant—and its implacability, at once indexed to the impossible exuberance of monsters and the chilling decay of the undead. It is these physical signs of the unconscious, the world of nightmares, against which Herzog's solitary protagonists consistently struggle and that permeate the border between the story's world and the story of making that world. Witness the excesses, straight out of a Dalí (*the* great heir to the visual tradition of the Spanish baroque), that stack up in Herzog's account of *Aguirre*'s establishing shot, as told in *My Best Fiend*: the original screenplay called for a "huge procession of tottering, altitude sick pigs" atop a glacier at "seventeen thousand feet"; this would then transition to a "huge army of Spanish adventurers" to be accompanied by "eight hundred or a thousand Indian auxiliaries"; Kinski showed up on location with "half a ton of Alpine equipment"; the director's lodging was managed by "a hunchback dwarf with nine children" who raised "a hundred or a hundred and fifty guinea pigs," a source of food, but, in keeping with the profligacy of dreams, "at night they crawled all over me, and that was uncomfortable"; so from there "I moved in with the Indians," which meant dorming with four hundred fifty highlanders, "from an altitude of fifteen thousand feet [not likely] who stayed in this big barn"; the context itself is a land where the jungle roams free, a tabula rasa where "in a radius of a hundred miles, no possibility of finding shelter existed"; this, as we have seen, is the platform for the "indescribable chaos" of the film's opening shots.[13] Things continue on this course as filming unfolds: the river overflows its banks, destroying an early set (and incorporated into the film story as a kind of environmental "found object"), converting the surrounding jungle into swamp, and obligating the cast and crew to live exclusively on thatch-roofed rafts during a week of shooting. Taking this cascade of comments—the like of which themselves proliferate throughout Herzog's discourse—not as an entertaining side note, but as symptomatic of a central preoccupation of the filmmaker, we can begin to understand the nature of his films' stoic minimalism.[14] Not a purely aesthetic strategy (although it is, in part, that), the laconic scripts, long gazes, close-up silent faces, and stylized still-lifes stand as a defense against the fanaticism of nature, the excessive overgrowth of the world, whose "obscenity" Herzog nevertheless "loves" but, as he puts it, "against my better judgment" (in Blank, *Burden of Dreams*, 1982). In turn, these scenes of overabundant life are not reducible to the decorative fabric between narrative seams. From the dramatic cloudscape that opens *Heart of Glass* (1976) to the endless horizon that closes it, from the rural idylls that give life to *The Enigma of Kaspar Hauser* (1974) to the breathtaking bear pasture of *Grizzly Man* (2005), the landscape sublime

Figures 2A and 2B. Above, two women on a remote island, a good example of Herzog's interest in the romantic sublime. *Heart of Glass* (Herzog 1976). Below, rats. A good example of Herzog's interest in baroque overgrowth. *Nosferatu the Vampyre* (Herzog 1979).

of romantic poets certainly animates the interior mood of Herzog's protagonists. But roiling just underneath the ego of these contemplative pauses that give shape to his oeuvre, Herzog confronts us, again and again, with the unconscious nightmares of baroque anxiety and obsessions with mortality that seem to find a special referent in the eddies and backwaters of the world-system's main currents. The million rats imported from the periphery of Europe, which overwhelm a vampire's ship and plague a small town in *Nosferatu* (1979); the thousands of bats and crabs that help usher the great *Cobra Verde* (1987) from slavery epic to horror film; the hundreds of bourgeois Europe's others—Indians and Africans, gypsies and shepherds, proletarians and peasants—that stare back, whether upright or deformed, in defiance of the plots of empire, "our future murderers" as one slave driver puts it in *Cobra Verde*. At once waltz and war, this interaction between the serene uneasiness of the romantic sublime and the enthralling nightmare of baroque overgrowth is the structural counterpoint that propels Herzog's stories, tracing the tension between movement and stasis, between ecstasy and horror, and between the affirmation of human will and the negation of nature's indifference.

The spirit of *Aguirre* can already be perceived in Herzog's earliest work. After announcing his own declaration of independence by stealing his first camera from a filmmaking institute, the director honed his technique neither through school nor apprenticeship, but by hurling himself into aesthetic experiments. This began with a series of shorts, obscure little films about bodybuilders posing to a hard bop jazz soundtrack (*Herakles*, 1962), a satire of war games about a group of kids that defend a deserted fortress with random military gear that they discover moldering inside (*Die beispiellose Verteidigung der Festung Deutschkreutz*, 1967), a beautiful little meditation on abandonment (*Letzte Worte*, 1968), and an impenetrable mockumentary that, while containing a number of themes that will reappear throughout Herzog's films, seems to be something of an inside joke (*Massnahmen gegen Fanatiker*, 1969). There is also the legendary *Spiel im Sand* (*Game in the Sand*, 1964), Herzog's *Black Album*, which he refuses to screen (it is rumored to involve children, a box, and a chicken). But the gem of the era is *Lebenszeichen* (*Signs of Life*, 1968), the critically acclaimed feature-length debut, kicking off Herzog's career with a Silver Bear from the prestigious Berlin International Film Festival.

Opposition to institutions within historical projects of abject conquest runs strong in Herzog's work, and his films are consistently preoccupied with the dignity, even paradoxical rationality, of individual madness and folly in relation to the oppressive structures that order capitalist modernity. *Signs of Life* takes up this theme by placing it within the context of World War II, the German occupation of Greece, and then following the travails of a wounded Nazi soldier convalescing on an absolutely nonstrategic Mediterranean island that they forgot to bomb, so sad, lonely, and dry that it can only impatiently wish for Armageddon: "A town of immaculate virginity, just waiting for someone to bombard it," says the narrator. On the ground, nothing happens: the soldiers sit, carry gasoline, sweat, complain about the heat, complain about the milk, complain about the wine, occasionally argue, fight bugs, watch paint dry (literally), play tricks with chickens and knives, meet a gypsy king and mute peasant girl, and trace the perimeter of entirely useless terrain, occasionally invaded by ephemeral partisans who essentially commit acts of light vandalism. The film can almost stand as a war-movie parody: relieved of the demented prison of combat, these Nazi outcasts are now dying of boredom without any orders to receive. One could perhaps extrapolate (with Herzog; see DVD commentary) from the insecticide scene, but there are no overt references to the Holocaust.

While the rhythm of the film is one of tedium punctuated by images of memorable originality, the action of the plot unfolds in the protagonist's head. Stroszek is his name, wonderfully rendered by Peter Brogle, the Swiss actor. (In one of those vertiginous turns that seem to abound in Herzog's filmography, years earlier Brogle had acted in a television movie as the character of Kaspar Hauser, the feral child of the Enlightenment, a historical figure that Herzog would later make famous in his own eponymous film, and that would be played by Bruno S, a once-institutionalized street musician that Herzog went on to cast in another movie called, precisely, *Stroszek*.) After signs of his emotional distress quietly compound over the course of a week, one day Stroszek is on patrol when he and his partner ascend a crest and confront an otherworldly landscape that in a single shot encapsulates Herzog's twin appreciation for romantic sublime and baroque vertigo. The soldiers march uphill, the camera circling them from back to front in handheld close-up, recording the scene in black and white to the extra-diegetic chords of a young Stavros Xarhakos's intensely beautiful guitar-driven soundtrack. With Stroszek looking increasingly distressed, the music jarringly cuts out for a moment, the camera whirls, and finally our perspective settles on a panoramic landscape: a parched valley full of ten thousand turning windmills.[15]

Now driven mad—the windmill needs no baroque elaboration here—Stroszek tears off his shoulder strap and begins to fire his rifle erratically into the horizon. As he and his partner struggle for control of the weapon, the camera settles on the windmills, turning as the guitar plays. Stroszek is eventually subdued, the churning landscape shot holds, and the music fades to leave us with nothing but an extraterrestrial wind and mysterious creaking, the screen tracing the valley for a full minute. Sublime indeed, it's one of those scenes that can give you chills. But simultaneously, there is a sense of quiet terror as the windmills seem to proliferate before us in their perpetual motion. Like the work of the jungle landscape on Aguirre and his men, this confrontation with man's disillusion before the dispassionate circularity of the world—he's literally tilting at windmills—pushes Stroszek to his story's eventual denouement. After returning to base for a conflictive dinner with his wife and compatriots, he freaks out, chases them from the compound, and subsequently occupies the harbor fortress, armed with fireworks and proclamations: "I've taken up the cause of man!" he cries, and the narrator adds, "He even rebelled against the orbit of the sun at dawn." The rest of the film alternates between extreme long shots of this very small figure perched on a very large fortress, and absurd crisis management as the local squad leader has the village evacuated in the face of this wartime threat. Popular excitement ensues, a donkey falls: finally, war has arrived! The film ends with the great rebellion: that wonderfully nostalgic guitar, now accompanied by cello, and a somehow wistful firework display (melancholic fireworks, it's a nice counterpoint, very baroque) exploding over the fortress; and then a road, and a narrator explaining the universality of Stroszek's failure: "In his rebellion, he had undertaken something titanic—for the enemy was far superior. Thus he had failed as miserably as all others of his kind."

A similar trajectory animates Herzog's follow-up feature, *Auch Zwerge haben klein angefangen* (*Even Dwarfs Started Small*, 1970). Notoriously interpreted as an aggressively reactionary film, even Herzog himself has characterized it as something of an angry movie.[16] But whether or not certain

1968 revolutionaries felt themselves interpellated by the confederacy of dwarfs that stage an impotent rebellion against their asylum overlords (also played by dwarfs; the entire cast is made up of little people), the ideological possibilities of the film are more ambivalent than a counterinsurgent screed would allow.[17] Indeed, the film operates on a narrative plane similar to that of the majority of Herzog's most famous films. As with *Signs of Life*, the film's setting is governed by an oppressive institution, and against this overwhelming force there is a rebellion. More overtly political, here the rebellion's protagonist is not a lone figure gripped by an ecstatic motivation, but rather a group apparently (it's unclear) attempting to change the terms of their confinement. But like the more congenial *Signs of Life* and its tortured protagonist Stroszek, the rebels of *Even Dwarfs* don't express goals beyond a vaguely expressed platform of denunciation. The rebellion of course fails to usher in any transformation in the order of things, but it does produce something that Herzog, and we his audience, like quite a bit: a surreal terrain of defiance rife with images spinning round and round. The uprising in full swing occupies the last third of the film and features a bacchanalian feast of noodles and wine, chickens engaged in acts of cannibalism at every turn, the slaughter of a large pig, and a passion procession featuring a live monkey lashed to a crucifix. A general ambiance of destruction reigns as stones are thrown, and all signs of civilization—the barn, a chair, potted plants—are doused with gasoline and set aflame. Smoke envelopes a lurid cock fight, the cock nearly as large as the dwarf that manhandles it. The rebels turn against themselves, pummeling one of their comrades and abusing others, animals are mistreated, and the film famously ends with the asylum's warden issuing stern orders to a dead tree, a shot that ultimately transitions to a two-and-a-half minute sequence of one of the rebels laughing maniacally before a camel kneeling on its forelegs. All the while, a driverless car spins circles around the scene of man-in-revolt. Despite an opposition of one—the warden—the inmates never even make it out of the courtyard and end up booked for processing in the local police station. The whole thing is pretty disturbing, also darkly funny, and essentially impossible to not keep watching.

Perhaps we can read all of this pessimistically, with Herzog's critics, as a reactionary metaphor about the childishness, and ultimate futility, of organized resistance to systems of oppression: the rebellion of the dwarfs is as successful as Stroszek's lone-wolf declaration against the state. But this

Figure 3. Passion procession with monkey and driverless car. *Even Dwarfs Started Small* (Herzog 1970).

strikes me as a tendentious interpretation, especially within the context of an artist who has brought us an entire film corpus of dreamers who not only dream of defying convention but actually act on those dreams. It makes sense to look closely at the acts of rebellion here, and when we do, something we might notice is not a failure of politics but a total absence of any coherent politics at all. Viewed in this key, the violence of the inmates is the violence of the repressed, who return in the form of nightmares to visit destruction on a world that deforms them, that stands before them completely outsized: the chair is not fit for dwarfs, they burn it; doorways are too large, beds are too high; the monkey crucifix is merely one more example of "natives" seizing the signs of their oppression, rearticulating them as a symbol of defiance. A black comedy about the limits of protest, to be sure, but *Even Dwarfs* is also a riot, and riots, even when blind, always exude a politics *in potentia*. But before potentiality has become actuality, the human condition lives in fever dreams, stewing, spinning, and this is Herzog's terrain. Taken together with the windmills of *Signs of Life*, in the serpentine march of the crucified monkey and the driverless car relentlessly tracing a circle, we can sense something of an artistic preoccupation. Here looking forward to four decades of representations of schemes, grand and small, spiraling out of control, an iconic image and contours of a project begin to take shape; in short, whether reactionary or radical (and it truly could be either) the uprising scene of *Even Dwarfs* becomes a grammeme within Herzog's language of the cinema. A search for the politics of Herzog's obsessive circle can be maddening and is not reducible to anything easily recognizable within the span of our received ideological categories, from left to right, from progressive to reactive. It's worth saying again: the maddeningness *is* the politics. But to begin to suggest the weight of this intervention, its dimensions would need to be made world-historical. And in order to do this, Herzog will look to the formative moments of this history of rebellion, its political unconscious, a time when humankind suddenly occupied a globe and articulated a project upon it. That is, he will look to the world of Lope de Aguirre.

Herzog frequently tells the origins story of *Aguirre*: waiting for a friend to finish a long telephone conversation, he scans his host's library and his gaze comes to rest upon a children's book about Spanish conquistadors. By chance he opens the book to an account of Lope de Aguirre, the mad adventurer who, in flagrant defiance of King Philip II—the Prudent, and emperor over the House of Habsburg's greatest period of geopolitical expansion—declared himself sovereign over the land, a large section of South America: a long-distance and highly performative coup from the middle of nowhere, at the end of a futile attempt to discover a lost city of gold deep in the rain forest, the mythical El Dorado. This is enough for Herzog, who brings his typewriter along on a football excursion and pounds out the script over two days, on the bus, between matches. He builds the context around the script by drawing in figures from this or that story of the era but without great concern for the minutiae of the historical record. Regarding Aguirre, he is fond of reminding interviewers, we have little to go on, "just a few scraps" (*Aguirre*, director's commentary), most spectacularly his hostile letter to the king.

Depending on what we understand by "scraps," Herzog's statement isn't exactly accurate. From documents recognized as emanating from Aguirre's own hand or voice as dictation, it is true, we have a total of three letters, with a possible fourth letter whose authenticity is a source of controversy.[18] Moreover, the central texts of this group—the secession from Spain and Aguirre's screed against the king's management of empire—that so engaged Herzog are transcriptions of proclamations whose original composition seems to be lost to the historical record.[19] But even this is more than we have for the vast majority of middling conquistadors who pushed the boundaries of empire by prosecuting the invasion and pillage of the Americas. And beyond these brief letters, Aguirre is certainly a special case: nothing less than a centuries-deep archive of material has grown up around his adventures, plots, and legend. Indeed, it is safe to say that, relative to the untold thousands of foot soldiers, officers, and mercenaries—from all walks of life: serfs, nobles, slaves, merchants—swallowed into the black anonymity of the conquest, Aguirre is one of the best known. As the eminent scholar of colonial culture Beatriz Pastor puts it, the expedition commandeered by Aguirre lends us an "exceptional" trove of materials both "rich and heterogeneous," unusual in exhibiting a "spatial and temporal frame so clearly defined and that demonstrates such narrative coherence" (2011, 25). From soldiers that survived his incredible El Dorado escapade, we have no less than seven firsthand, if not disinterested, accounts of his rebellion.[20] From these and related sources, significant retellings of that adventure punctuate the long history of Spanish *crónicas* that provide the raw material for much of our understanding of the conquest.[21] Aguirre's accomplishments allegedly pop up here and there in nineteenth-century discourses of independence in South America, including commentary by Humboldt (see Southey 1821) and an unlikely paean ascribed to none other than Simón Bolívar.[22] And beginning with Ricardo Palma's massive folkloric compendium, *Tradiciones peruanas* ([1872—1910] 2007), which includes the section "Lope de Aguirre, el traidor," Aguirre has proven to be an inexhaustible muse for literary exploration in the modern Spanish-speaking world from both sides of the Atlantic. This is not an insignificant bibliography: names like Baroja ([1911] 2010), Valle-Inclán ([1926] 1987), Uslar Pietri ([1947] 2004), Sender (1964), and Posse (1978) leap from the page.[23] Herzog is in good company, and it is a testament to the power of his portrait that today, even in the Hispanic world, it is practically impossible to imagine Aguirre without mentally conjuring the ragged blond locks, transparent blue eyes, and menacing German diction of Klaus Kinski.[24]

To understand the significance—not only historical, but also critical, political, and aesthetic—of Herzog's film, it is important to comprehend the historical specificity of Lope de Aguirre's own, parallel significance: the perennial resonance of Aguirre's politico-historical intervention is precisely the condition of possibility for Herzog's aesthetic project, a prime mover behind its continued relevance today. It is thus worth spending some time with this history, but not, I'd like to clarify, toward the end of citing where and how Herzog deviates from the established set of facts (for this kind of reading, see Waller 1981, Fritze 1985, Stiles 1989, and Stone 2005). Rather, the aim is to trace how Herzog, with or without historical accuracy, draws on the Aguirre legend in order to at once intensify its narrative power and deepen the psychological impact of a world-historical portrait whose political implications go well beyond the historical figure himself. In short, I argue that the continued appeal of *Aguirre, the Wrath of God* is the fact that it tells us something meaningful about the world in which we live.

Here, in outline, is what we know. Lope de Aguirre was likely a petty noble, an *hidalgo* without fortune from a backwater of the Basque region. Fate and ambition took him across the peninsula to Seville, where he worked days busting broncos and spent nights enchanted by reports of glory from across the Atlantic. He made his way to the New World as early as the 1530s, where he engaged as a soldier in a number of projects of conquest on behalf of the Spanish Crown, including the depredations of Bartolomé Sánchez Torreblanca, gainful employment which included some grave robbing on the side. He seems to have developed an early appetite for conspiracy, and historians have implicated him in a couple of rebellions against the colonial authorities, although all this is a little murky.[25] At some point he fathers a child, a daughter named Elvira. By the time he lands in Peru, the Inca empire had already fallen years prior, thoroughly plundered by Spanish mercenaries, and so Aguirre's world is dominated by the politics of resource accumulation (namely, mining) and wars of position, internecine conflicts that proliferate as the imperial project begins to stagnate. He fights against Gonzalo Pizarro's intransigencies and ends up on the losing side of a viceroy, unpopular among the conquering set for his attempt to install the so-called Nuevas Leyes de Indias, new protections for Indian workers; ironically, a few years later in the fabulous silver boom of Potosí, Aguirre is subsequently charged with and convicted of abusing Indians. He is strapped to a donkey (not sure why this stylistic flourish is part of the punishment) and publicly flogged. He pursues the judge that sentenced him—three years, on foot, legend has it—to Lima, Quito, and finally Cusco, where he surprises the erstwhile officer of the court napping in a library. Eventually pardoned for the murder, he suffers a musket wound in battle, leaving him with a limp, a well-honed Richard III aura for the *cronistas*. He ends up on a dangerous expedition in search of El Dorado, standing as an officer in the middle of a multicultural army of flinty conquest veterans from across Europe, and slaves of indigenous and African descent. For reasons unclear, he brings his daughter along. This adventure sets in motion his famous rebellion.

The expedition is led by Pedro de Ursúa, a fellow Basque noble (of higher rank and significant military achievement) several years his younger, who also brings a female companion, Inés de Atienza, his lover. Early on the men lose faith in Ursúa's leadership, and Aguirre conspires to have him killed, establishing the middling noble Fernando de Guzmán as a puppet leader. A letter explaining and justifying the mutiny is drafted by the officers of the expedition; Aguirre signs it "por traidor" (of the traitor).[26] Many die and many of Aguirre's rivals are murdered—eventually including Guzmán and Atienza—leaving Aguirre in charge of the expedition and free to steer it to his ultimate objective: take a hard left at the top of South America, hack his way across the swampy isthmus, rally a free army by liberating the slaves of Panama, and return southbound to the crown jewel, Peru, through the Pacific back door in order to take it.[27] Something like Cortés against the Aztecs, but with open menace: for here the conquistador has not only gone rogue, but has turned his energy against his handlers. Having exited the river for the Atlantic outlet (the mouth of the Amazon), the expedition becomes a forced march, seaborne for seventeen days until it reaches Isla Margarita, which Aguirre sacks and takes, killing many. The trail of destruction continues on Tierra Firme, where, with events turning against him, he composes his famous denunciation of King Philip II, declaring himself "rebel until death" ("yo, rebelde hasta la muerte"). Between threatening letters to local administrators, the march presses on all the way to Barquisimeto (today a large, and famously dangerous, city in Venezuela) where Aguirre, cornered, executes his own daughter. Betrayed by his few remaining associates, he is shot twice, decapitated, and quartered, with his head placed in a cage for public display, his extremities sent to neighboring towns as a warning against rebellion, and his entrails fed to the dogs. Today, several sites, streets, geographical formations, and local legends, in South America and Spain, bear his name or make reference to his exploits.

Herzog doesn't hew too closely to this historical script. There is no backstory, Aguirre appears fully formed, conjured like Macunaíma, dropped armor-clad into the middle of the jungle. The expedition dates are roughly accurate, but its association with Gonzalo Pizarro is fabricated (he had long since been hung for rebellion), and the narrative device of a "found document," the diary of a historical figure, the monk Gaspar de Carvajal, is both fun and funny: Carvajal was indeed a *cronista* but wasn't on Aguirre's adventure, and of course the conceit raises the question of how we come to be in possession of the diary of a dead man whose expedition is consumed by Indians deep in the jungle.[28] It works, though; we suspend disbelief. The daughter and the lover are along for the ride, making historical the seeming inversimilitude of their presence, although they each perish—Atienza walks off into the jungle; Elvira (called Flores in the film) is pierced with arrows—in ways that contradict the accepted history, in which both are murdered by Aguirre. Finally, the expedition doesn't come close to tracing the outlines of its history. In reality, the force was much larger than in Herzog's version, with hundreds of soldiers and slaves, and, most significantly, its objectives and conquests were different. The historical Aguirre abandons the quest for El Dorado in favor of a military project quite early and quite strategically, whereas in Herzog's tale El Dorado never fades from the project, and the military conquest is only suggested as a rambling fantasy, told most explicitly to an audience of monkeys. And the historical Aguirre threads the needle of the Amazon river system, successfully navigating his irregular army to open water, and eventually confronting the Spanish imperial state. For Herzog, the whole thing founders in the jungle, never to escape.

All these disarticulations are to be expected. To nitpick Herzog about historical accuracy would be a fool's errand, and that is certainly not the idea here. The whole point of Herzog's engagement with history is not to reproduce it, but to invoke it, even provoke it, in the attempt to confront us with a deeper truth, what he has long called an "ecstatic truth" to be mobilized against his much-loathed "truth of accountants" (along with chickens, accountants don't fare well in Herzog's personal semiology). As he puts it in an interview with Stephen Colbert, the Manhattan phone book is full of truth, as fact; there we can learn about Jonathan Smith; but the point is not to know that Jonathan Smith lives at 628 Kirtland Street; the point is to know "does Mr. Jonathan Smith cry in his pillow at night?"[29] And to be true to Herzog's working method, we should take the notion one step further: in order to understand the full dimensions of Jonathan Smith, he *must* cry into his pillow; whether he actually does or not is irrelevant. With Nietzsche ([1873] 2008), Herzog is more than happy to lie in the name of truth and, moreover, confront us with the lie—as fabrication, or Herzog's oft-cited commitment to "stylization"—that in fact deepens our relationship with the actually existing world. All this is amply studied and theorized in the critical corpus around Herzog.[30] But there's a detail, rarely noted, something worth introducing here, and that later we will come back to more systematically. Herzog's method is not so simple as taking the outline of a compelling story and then advancing it wherever it needs to go in order to satisfy the director's vision, an impression that Herzog himself often leaves us with in his interviews. Much more significantly, and problematically (in the productive sense), there is something of a paradox between Herzog's indifference before the facts of history (the truth of accountants) and his simultaneous commitment to methodically capturing a historical climate (his term) that clearly resonates not just representation as reenactment (appropriately stylized past events), but as *enactment* of the modern human condition as we know it. In short, Herzog's historical portraits get under our skin and, if we're willing to listen, ask us to rethink the terms of modernity itself. And they seem to do so by drawing on a certain set of themes, situated in moments of deceptive historical intensity of world-formation, and set in motion by a particular kind of protagonist.

Herzog's Aguirre, as the director himself notes, shares a distant family relationship with *Signs of Life*'s Stroszek: both effect a rebellion of one against all, and both fail, Aguirre falling even harder because his opponent is so much bigger, an entire structure of empire. A similar resemblance is apparent with *Even Dwarfs Started Small*: the dwarfs' rebellion is "without end" just as Aguirre "rebels until death," both abide the curse of Sisyphus.[31] More abstract, we can even perceive the distant echo of *Fata Morgana*, as the truth of the world—desert, jungle—reveals itself not in its representation as fact (maps) but as dream (mirages). But if the early films represent the slow coalescence of Herzog's storytelling project, *Aguirre* is something of a watershed and becomes the immediate forefather of his most memorable male protagonists: military entrepreneurs on suicide missions, based loosely yet dramatically on real-life figures whose obscurity cannot completely conceal their world-historical activity. Alongside Aguirre, the two most momentous, not coincidentally, are both also played by Kinski: Brian Sweeney Fitzgerald, the would-be rubber baron Fitzcarraldo; and Francisco Manoel da Silva, the bandit slave driver also known as Cobra Verde. Pivoting to an entirely different register, we can place Bruno S (*The Enigma of Kaspar Hauser* [1974]; *Stroszek* [1977]) in the same family tree, with his impossible adventures of land and mind, set against the implacable institutionality of modern life, and that end in quiet failure. But what is the trick here, what is the relation between psychological intensity and the historical—political, even—intervention that Herzog effects with these figures teetering on the edge of a world?

Aguirre offers a starting point for thinking about these issues. Scholars, critics, students, and cinephiles around the world consistently recall the deep psychological impact of watching a group of unhappy adventurers, in the thrall of a madman, on a death trip down an endless, swampy river. In many ways, this is an iconic story, channeling Conrad and inspiring Coppola, and still provoking distant inspiration to this day (see, for example, Nicolas Winding Refn's *Valhalla Rising* [2009] and, to a lesser extent, the second half of Lucrecia Martel's masterpiece, *Zama* [2017]). The pace, rhythm, sound, mood, together they produce an unforgettable portrait of modern human drives for accumulation and self-destruction. At the same time, and clearly, well beyond the film, generations have been equally hypnotized by Aguirre's story, which has been around since the 1560s. And it's worth repeating: to understand its deep psychological function that Herzog captures with such grace, we need to understand the historical function that gives Aguirre life, as long and as influential a life, I would suggest, as that of the story of Cortés. But Cortés, in the most literal sense, was at the military vanguard of a changing world. Aguirre is essentially a minor incident within the context of that turbulent geopolitical paradigm shift. Conquistadors were a restless class—Cortés himself broke rank—and rebellions of various intensity were not unknown and, by the time of Aguirre, even common.[32] Most of them have been forgotten. Aguirre's has inspired stories and studies, productive of both literary themes and historiographical theory. Clearly, it possesses special narrative possibilities.

In the popular versions of the story of Ursúa's ill-fated expedition—from the old *cronistas* to the new novelists and everything in between, a span that includes Herzog—the representation of Aguirre is schizophrenic. Everyone agrees on his calculations, his paranoia, his volatility, his vindictiveness, even his sadism. But the interpretations of the political meaning of the actions that give shape to these rather unflattering qualities move in two opposite directions. The traditional portrait, which descends to us from the politically motivated first accounts of the rebellion—composed by soldiers attempting to avoid implication in Aguirre's crimes against the state—paints the picture of the great traitor, a monster of ambition, cruelly skilled manipulator and quite clearly mad, eventually led by demonic hubris to disrupt the natural order of dutiful men in the service of kings.[33] Even with the historical fall of monarchism, this image sticks hard, and if in modern times Aguirre's identity as traitor has receded, his status as tyrant (its association with usurpation making it always already a kind of traitor) has been amplified, as in the account of a writer no less than Valle-Inclán, *Tirano Banderas* ([1926] 1987), which would become a narrative model for the great Latin American autocrat. A second, politically progressive interpretation, while not denying the sociopathology of Aguirre's violence, sees in the rebel conquistador the meteor of revolution, specifically, America's secession from the maritime empires and its epochal project of erecting modern liberal republics on the backs of the various wars of independence. While nobody really makes an impossible case for a sixteenth-century liberal-progressive Aguirre (although Uslar Pietri [1947] 2004 gives it a go), we could, of course, say the same thing about the priest Hidalgo in 1810 and his inspirational *Grito de Dolores* that sparked the Mexican war of secession. The idea is that Aguirre declared a kind of independence, in writing, and couched his declaration in a rhetoric that becomes a prominent salvo in the emergent discourse on imperial corruption, what Foucault (2003) would call the kind of "counter-history" that will eventually consolidate as the language of "race war." The king is asleep at the wheel; the priests are out of control; the bureaucracy is exploding; and the loyal workers—that is, the conquistadors—are getting screwed. This, in essence, is Aguirre's argument.

It's a good case. By 1560, the Spanish Empire had fully turned the corner toward a condition of increasingly obvious decline, pummeled by pirates on the sea, by the Hanseatic League and the incipient United Provinces on the trade and financial markets, and by what we could call imperial malaise on the unexplored margins of its precious viceroyalties. The world of active conquistadors was grim. While failure and death were always more common than success and wealth in the conquering business, ideologically the New World had become dissonant, unable to keep up appearances and bridge the gulf between a potentially perceived reality and the desire of the perceiving subject. To paraphrase Roberto Schwarz (1973) writing about a distant context, the truths of medieval honor that grounded Spanish imperial ideology were increasingly thwarted in their capacity to represent a recognizable reality, even falsely. Or as Pastor and Callau put it, "disillusion and discontent represent the disappointment felt before frustrated hopes and dreams; but they are also a particular experience of the crisis of the imperial American dream" (2011, 35). All the first-wave conquering based on a model of heroic (even holy) war was finished, with the massive proto-bureaucratic states of the Americas having been dismantled and plundered, the protagonists of those projects—Cortés, Pizarro, Pedro Alvarado—now the heroes of *lieux-dits* and children's songs. With little left to be despoiled of, beyond their bodies and souls, indigenous groups—who always understood the conquest for the genocide that it was, the historiographical fetishization of blond gods notwithstanding—took to sending as many Spanish expeditions as possible to their certain doom, by coaxing them "just a little further" to impossible lands of impossible riches, El Dorado, Omagua, the River of the Immortals, and so on.

All this presented real problems for proto-proletarian conquistadors. The violence work of conquering requires an initial debt of both transport and equipment (e.g., weapons) and pays off only at the moment of conquest. There is plunder, and the conquering subject receives his share of booty according to nobility and rank. By the 1560s, plunder had dried up, creating a crisis for conquest work. Take Aguirre's own adventure, led by Ursúa: even *before* embarking, still at the staging ground, the expedition ran dangerously low on food; a reconnaissance party was sent on a mission to resupply; and a couple of that party's members *starved to death* before they could return to base with a basket of turtle eggs.[34] Landless conquistadors—Aguirre is archetypical here—were legion, a kind of excess labor pool, armed, with military training and experience, angry, disillusioned, restless, and undercompensated. Moreover, they were forever badgered by the beneficiaries of the spoils of empire: the clergy and the clerks. In many cases, they took compensation into their own hands. The conquest had begun to cannibalize itself.

Aguirre seems to perceive this, and his letter to the king reports, without flinching, this state of bureaucratic decay. Cleverly turning the tables, Aguirre concludes that it is Philip the Prudent who is guilty of treason: betraying his loyal servants in favor of the machinations of bureaucrats, whose shamelessness extends to placing a rent on the fishes in the stream.[35] In this he is by no means looking forward—toward the meritocracy of a modern liberal order and the output-structured financial machinery of a capitalist world-economy—but rather back, like a New World Quixote, toward a medieval ethos of chivalry and honor where knights did the king's bidding and were privileged in kind. But if he's truly mad, as opposed to simply marginalized, it is certainly not in the delusional sense. Even as reactionary and sociopathic as he is (he's implicated in around sixty murders), and while descending into Counter-Reformation paranoia (he turns out to be fond of quartering suspected Lutherans), his prose is clear, his critique is rigorous, his aim is true, capturing the spirit of its time.[36] As Neira et al. (2006) point out, his military strategy—itself impressive—had to be underwritten by a political strategy that allowed him to take and maintain command over a large group of heavily armed men in difficult terrain. Clearly, his counterhistorical discourse of royal betrayal resonated.

This is where a third potential reading of Aguirre comes in, one that resists the binary character sketch based on motivated interpretations of political schemes animating the monster-versus-meteor debate and one that begins to introduce the lasting power of Herzog's portrait. The biographical description of Aguirre's qualities must nourish itself on certain tropes of discovery and conquest, most significantly and recalling Herzog's penchant for baroque aesthetics, the thick catalog of statements about European man overwhelmed by American nature (an aestheticized object that includes American man, the Indians). Even in the most laudatory accounts positioning Aguirre as a revolutionary avant la lettre, his psychology is rounded out by drawing on this trove of metaphors. Here's Uslar Pietri, from 1947, for whom Aguirre represents nothing less than the emergence of Venezuelan independence; and yet, nevertheless, "All the mystery and tragic fascination of nature seem to have melded into his persona. The sensations of fear, of unease, of disquiet, that had emerged from the river, from its savage and antagonistic immensity . . . from the war-painted and implacable Indian that launches his arrows . . . the delirium of sickness, the constant presence of death . . . all of this now incarnate . . . in those restless eyes, that suddenly become translucent and fixed on something, or someone" (Uslar Pietri [1947] 2004, 103). This is obviously Herzog's environment as well (and one, as we saw, that the director physically places himself in the middle of), but he turns away from Uslar at the crucial narrative point, the jungle itself. And this jungle is not merely the source material for the psychological portrait of a man that becomes symbol of a political project. For Herzog, the jungle resonates an entire world-historical context. Rather than convert Aguirre into a partisan (republican saint or royalist traitor?), the critic of the truth of accountants offers an account that mobilizes America in its deepest sense. In consonance with Latin America's self-fashioning before the world (from Vespucci to García Márquez), Herzog's Aguirre is reducible to neither history nor myth but intensifies each by participating in both. There is the human pathos that is the sustenance of myth and that makes for watchable movies: ambition, greed, madness, violence. And then there is the historical world that makes the myth come alive: a conquest project in a land with nothing left to conquer; an imperial project in which the empire is bankrupt; a would-be world-historical project in a world-system rapidly turning away from nobles and knights executing deeds as chivalry and toward merchants and bureaucrats executing deeds as contracts. It's not the jungle that drives Aguirre mad; it is the world of the clerks. Neither monster nor meteor, Herzog's Aguirre is reduced to historical man: the small voice of conquest, a baroque subject for his time.[37]

Neither history nor myth, but both. The deep psychological function that is so consistently ascribed to *Aguirre, der Zorn Gottes*, "all human pathos" as Herzog puts it, only actually functions through the dialectical rigor that it exhibits with its broad historical context: the modern world. Lope de Aguirre, like his not so distant cousin a half-century younger, wants to confront giants and be heralded by kings. But the jungle, it turns out, isn't a source of dragons; it is instead a source of disappointments. The historical Aguirre is explicit about this: "Marching down our path, with all of these deaths and misfortunes on this river Marañón, we arrived at its mouth, at the sea, more than ten and a half months: we traveled one hundred days, one thousand and five hundred leagues. Great river, fearsome, it has a mouth of eighty leagues of fresh water, and not, as they say, because of its many tributaries. It has great depth and is deserted for eight hundred leagues without village. . . . Along the path that we traveled it has more than six thousand islands. God knows how we escaped this fearsome lake! I implore you, King and lord, do not consent or attempt that any armada take this ill-fated river, because in Christian faith I swear to you, King and lord, that even if one hundred thousand men come, none will escape, because the report is false, and on this river there is nothing but despair, especially for those arriving from Spain" ("Carta de Lope de Aguirre a Felipe II," in Pastor and Callau 2011, 77–78). Aguirre wants monsters, but what he gets is windmills, a jungle indifferent to his struggle, six thousand islands and cross-currents swirling round. His conquest becomes farce, "nothing but despair." The jungle, it turns out, can bore you to death, and in so doing, confront you with the worst monster of all: your uselessness. The theater of history is a central theme of the film, and on this venture down the Marañón, Lope de Aguirre, quite consciously, constructed his stage. But the staging of history is artifice ("the report is [perhaps 'reports are'] false") by its very nature, written in sand. And in poor Aguirre's case, the mendacity at the heart of his project is literal. With the conquest petering out and way too many men with guns and bad attitudes lying about, suddenly a new wave of royal commissions appeared, sending large expeditions to explore the deepest regions of the continents, in search of all the little Dorados out there, way out there. None of these succeeded, and many never returned. This, it appears, was one method for removing insurrectionist threats, for thinning the herd. In other words, Ursúa's expedition was a suicide mission in the actual sense. All evidence suggests that this fact wasn't lost on Lope de Aguirre, the man.[38] And it isn't lost on Aguirre, the character in *Aguirre*, either. Indeed, let's recall that it frames the entire film: "No one can get down that river alive!" he says, prophetic, in his first line of dialogue.

By evoking the climate of a lost world with ingenious subtlety, Herzog intervenes in our own. I won't make the case that it's allegorical: Aguirre is to Vietnam what one fruitless project of conquest is to another. But I will make the case that it's historical: Aguirre resonates all Vietnams as the fraternal echo of late-systemic malaise, a moment of clarity where we can see the certainty of god's will (duty, honor, grace) overwhelmed by the punishing overgrowth of doubt, the secular world (opportunity, betrayal, decay). The reason that *Aguirre* sticks in our minds is because the world whose climate it captures is not in fact lost to us at all. It's strange, but familiar, because it's us, as a kind of primordial memory, one that ought to have remained forgotten, the formation of a world that simply can't contain the avarice of its fundamental violence, and, ultimately, bad faith. Herzog translates this as the power of inner landscapes to unsettle the human soul, and he is poetically correct to put it in those terms. I would translate this kind of statement as the provocation of confronting us with the history of accumulation, in other words, of modern societies and their contradictions. The significance of *Aguirre* is not that it captures the reality or even spirit of Lope de Aguirre. Its achievement is the universalization of Aguirre's struggle, from a backwater of conquest to the center of an emergent order. A world whose basic terms, in the wake of 1968, had been again cast into doubt.

When contemplating *Aguirre*, it's important to situate the film, simultaneously, in its two most immediate historical points of reference. First, the story world of late sixteenth-century America. Second, the material world of early 1970s Cold War cultural politics. While historically resonating neoimperial adventures and all they represent, there is no need to say that the film is "about Vietnam." It's more than enough to say that it's about the European assault on the interior zones of the Americas. In *Aguirre*, as I've argued, this scene is not studied as historical fact but made theatrical as the emergence of a state of mind, a worldview, an incipient world-system and its attendant political economy. And this project, Herzog's project, is advanced at a moment of critical distress to that system. The world revolution of 1968, accompanied by global economic shocks in 1967 that would persist through the 1970s, nourished a general sense that the dissonance in the system was becoming unmanageable. It led a generation of cultural producers, in many fields of knowledge production, to contemplate the historical unfolding of the world-system in new ways, from activist protest to historiographical revisionism. Herzog takes up the question on cinematographic terms.

Herzog's position—easy to cobble together through his decades of interviews—seems to be that the essential world-historical quality of the rise of capitalist modernity is precisely its lunatic nature. Both *Signs of Life* and *Even Dwarfs Started Small* revolve around aspects of this theme. As a way of deepening this contemplative project, *Aguirre* brings together an ambitious and fascinatingly conflictive trio of historical objects. First is the Spanish Empire, moribund protagonist of the emergent world-system. Second, Lope de Aguirre and his team of rebels, a restive margin and prescient critic of that historical project. And third, the sixteenth-century jungle, as physical obstacle, historical construct, and, moreover and more important, an inner landscape of the unconscious mind. There is a notable absence here: the Indians. Now, before taking one step further, let's clarify that the film is in fact full of indigenous characters. As the opening titles explain, the story's very raison d'être flows from indigenous agency because "the Indians invented the legend of El Dorado." There is a large group of extras playing indigenous slaves, and three of these characters accompany Aguirre's expedition. One of them, Balthasar, acts as translator and offers a prominent discourse on *lesa civilización* early in the film.[39] Another, a scene-stealing flute player, represents nothing less than the "decisive figure" of the film, according to the director.[40] Tribal rain forest Indians (recruited from local Yagua communities), shadowy figures sometimes glimpsed from a distance, harass the expedition without respite and a large number of the party is killed by their arrows. Indians populate the margins of the screen and even once hoot at the explorers ("meat, meat, meat is floating by!" they cry, at least in Balthasar's translation) from the shore. Their traces are on display too, as the Spaniards sack and destroy two riverbank villages. And finally, the adventurers are approached by a canoe carrying an indigenous couple, whom they interrogate about potential sources of gold and then promptly murder, for blasphemy. So yes, there are many indigenous figures in the film. But for better or worse, the subjectivity of the rain forest Indians within the logic of the film only exerts itself as natural man, that is, insofar as it is subsumed within the much larger antagonism of the jungle as totality.[41] Herzog is explicit about this: one Indian in the canoe refers to their world as the place where "god didn't finish his creation"; but then, slyly, he sidles up to his ally, the jungle, and points the conquistadors *just a little further along* (a mute gesture, index finger extended: that way), upstream, keep the river on your right, that's where you'll find the gold. As for the second group of Indians, the direct descendants of Inca hegemony, this civilization now lives as bound labor. The historical referent highlighted by this aesthetic dynamic lends a subtle, but crucial, ambient element to the film. The possibility of any conquest narrative that takes place between identifiable warring camps, in which the victims of conquest tragically, inevitably, lose, is foreclosed. The war is over; or better, the new terms of its slow grind have been established. What we have before us now, in 1561, is systemic transformation, in which the Incas are swept up into a new historical order. Leaving them out as a civilizational opponent—no monumental sites to be desecrated, no enemy army, no Atahuallpa—Herzog creates a climate simultaneously unusual and epochal. What we are left with is a story that doesn't pit man against man (Spaniards versus Indians), but rather fractured man (Aguirre's proto-baroque rebellion) against jungle; that is, man against himself, the inner landscape; and at the same time, man against environment, not just natural but more importantly historical.[42] This is how Herzog is able to lend his conquest film such an uncanny tone: it's a military conquest without war, at least, like *Signs of Life*, no war that in any way meets our cinematic expectations. And thus the received notion of action that should propel the plot is pure interiority: once they are finished shooting at each other, Aguirre and his men, like Stroszek, shoot at nothing. A soldier, to Aguirre, "What are we to aim at?" Aguirre, to his soldiers, "Just shoot, you asshole!!!"

The kabuki battle scenes are emblematic here. It's halfway into the movie, about minute 47, and our conquistadors have yet to directly confront a single hostile force (excluding the nighttime assassination on the foundering raft, early in the film, which happens off-screen). The tortoise pace has slowed down almost impossibly, and a rare panoramic long shot, with near imperceptible soundtrack, reveals the quiet twisting of the rafts with very little impression of progress. Indeed, the seductive camera angle makes it difficult to tell whether the party is moving toward us or away from us; the river seems to flow at cross-purposes. More than half a minute of this, and then a large fire ahead: a battle beckons! The expedition approaches the bank while a village burns above them as on a stage; they close ranks on shore, wary of ambush. For those paying diligent attention, we notice that the birds are singing, a sign that the Indians have abandoned the site. The men assume battle formation, and the assault begins like this: "strip the negro!" Okello, the slave, is duly stripped and prodded out front, "to frighten the Indians," the narrator explains.[43] And this comedy of Europe producing its others degenerates into the battle itself, unfolding between absent Indians (they are long gone) and a reluctant African (he's clearly not into it). The main action revolves around the corralling of the half-naked slave to keep him in front of the soldiers. The only actual fighting, with sword, is between the men as they grapple for green bananas. Somebody plunders a pig, a mummy turns up, and signs of cannibalism (including remains from another Spanish expedition, obliquely alluded to early in the film) scare the adventurers away. A half-hour of film time later, the water is now glass and the party confronts another village, here occupied by actively confrontational Indians. This time there is a real fight, but again, it's a bit silly, a war of flowers: the Spaniards lug an outlandish canon up the riverbank, useless in its heft for the task at hand, as nimble Indians immediately retreat into the jungle perimeter and pick off soldier after soldier. Aguirre orders the village burned as his men grovel on the ground over a stash of salt, in pathetic prostration. Again, it couldn't be a more uneventful battle, until the real action asserts itself. Suddenly everything seems to go still as we confront Inés de Atienza in formal gold-and-white gown, walking toward the camera, now in close-up, then passing by, determined, and straight into the jungle accompanied by a weird synthetic dirge. The men all stare as the jungle swallows her whole. It's surprisingly eerie. The incident reenacts a scene from eight minutes prior, when Don Fernando ejects the horse from the raft. Whereas the historical expedition ended up roasting all the horses and dogs relatively early, in the cinematic grammar of *Aguirre*, the horse, the quintessential sign of military advantage and also (like the mistress) of economic power, must simply fade away, deteriorate, consumed by overgrowth, one more victim of the implacable jungle. It's another uncanny shot, cross-cut with

Aguirre's disquieted stare, as the horse, a statue all tangled up in swampy overgrowth, glides out of view while the raft creeps downriver.[44]

The fact that this war is grounded in legal documents only aggravates its outlandishness, lending a kind of magic realism to its performativity. The kingdom of literacy and its attendant imposition of paper over fugitive landscapes—a process of territorialization that Angel Rama (1984) calls "the lettered city"—in the political history of modern America becomes a wry symbol of ideological disjuncture as imperial property is at once registered as script and dissolved into nothingness through the activities of the conquistadors. The first instance comes early in the film, it's straightforward enough, Pizarro's formal orders to send a small reconnaissance group downstream, to find news of hostile Indians and the location of El Dorado. Already both historical (state policy) and mythical (a quest), the document that Pizarro signs could just as well be a death warrant, a point on which he is explicit: if the men aren't back in a week, they will be considered lost. The second document exaggerates further the mute theatricality of the situation. After mortally wounding Ursúa, and now well downriver, the men elect Don Fernando de Guzmán—a Sevillano noble and impressive glutton—emperor of El Dorado, in the process declaring the House of Habsburg "overthrown." As Aguirre escorts Don Fernando to the royal seat—"what is a throne but a plank covered in velvet?"—he rolls up the writ and jabs it into Don Fernando's reluctant fist. Tears roll, the group turns to look directly at the camera in painterly portrait, bringing into focus the groundlessness of the modern world's formation, with contracts, declarations, and deeds affirming sovereignty in theory where there is none in fact. Finally, late in the film with the plague of delusion infecting the entire expedition, Don Fernando sits with the self-satisfied smile of a degenerate prince, scribbling a map and, recapitulating the historical Aguirre's critique of sacerdotal excess, declares "all the land to our left and all the land to our right now belongs to us."[45] As he "solemnly and formally take[s] possession of all this land" he estimates that "our country is already six times larger than Spain and every day we drift makes it bigger." Aguirre's rejoinder—"is there solid ground that would support your weight?"—points up, a little heavy-handedly, the precariousness of the very notion of sovereignty within this overgrown landscape and moreover the comedic gap between signifier and signified in the parceling of conquest writ large.[46] The political-historical logic of the film, then, revolves around a chain of delusions: the war of shadows is certified through documents without ground, the leader possesses demons in his gaze, his followers hypnotized by his inevitability, and imperial expansion rests on drifting and shouting while its vehicle, the rafts, are slowly taken over by slimy river moss and small animals. A quick cutaway appears to show a raft-borne mouse eating another mouse. If all this makes a mockery of the Spanish imperial project, and it does, we should remember a couple of aspects of the film and its referent before reducing its intervention to that *particular* critical impulse. First, as we've detailed, this is the rebellious periphery of the Spanish Empire, a group of mutineers "playing conquistador," as it were.[47] And second, the empire itself isn't much of an object of critique. It's 1972, what will eventually be called postcolonial discourse is up and vigorously running, Eduardo Galeano's *Venas abiertas* (1971) stalks the bookstore display tables, and the relations between Spanish imperial plunder and US interventionist accumulation is well honed: in short, at this point, nobody loves the Spanish Empire anyway.

There is, in fact, a more explicit object of critical engagement here, one much more immediate, suggestive, and problematic than the perverse violence of imperial adventures. As his autobiographical narrative has evolved over the years through his copious interviews, Herzog has increasingly distanced his films and his vision from any kind of historically engaged critical intervention. He put it succinctly in 2002: "Simply, I do not care about themes, I care about stories" (Herzog and Cronin 2002, 67). But he wasn't always so circumspect about open participation in political critique. In a 1973 interview with Peter Schumann, days before the German premier (on television) of *Aguirre*, Herzog mentions Brazilian cinema—the implicit reference here is the *cinema novo* generation—as a kind of ally in producing historical films, "highly political films, just like *Aguirre*" (Herzog 2014e, 13). He continues, "as a theme, this horde of imperialistic adventurers performing a great historical failure, this failure of imperialism, of the conquerors, is really quite modern" (13). Its modernity rests on the fact that to retell its tale today is to reflect not only on an imperial past but also on a political (national) present. And it ain't Vietnam: "How do you shake off the last vestiges of this imperialism, of Spanish conquest, to achieve a sense of 'Peruvianness' [sic]. *And that's the theme of my film.* It shows that the strong and the enduring are the Indians and their culture" (15, my emphasis). While I'm not so sure that the film "shows" this about the Indians, it certainly deals with the world-historical condition of a hemisphere. "It is largely meant for Latin America. But the topic may be of interest everywhere" (15–16).

At the center of *Aguirre*, propelling its engagement with both Latin America and the world ("interest everywhere"), is not so much history as statecraft (states here are essentially echoes), but rather history as stagecraft (and on this point, see also Davidson's pioneering work [1993]). Again, Herzog explains, "The method by which history was then [in the historical setting of *Aguirre*] made is actually one that can still be found today in many Latin American countries. History there is staged as theatre, as theatrical coups" (13). We'd probably like a little less exoticism here (contemporary Germany is, of course, well known for the depth of its commitment to "staging" history), but the next line is crucial: "What's fascinating is that their theatre tricks made world history" (ibid). Cortés stages history—the ample theatricality of his five *Cartas de relación* ([1519–26] 2005) communicating his epic play to Carlos V—and Aguirre takes up his myth in both theory and practice. And as it turns out, so does Herzog. *Aguirre* was shot in 1972 Peru, during the middle years of the leftist dictatorship of Velasco Alvarado.[48] This yielded a meeting of the minds: "A big panel of officials read the script in advance and was extraordinarily moved by the story. . . . They noticed very clearly that my story revolves around the same problem of identity for the Peruvian people, the identity they're searching for, as well" (15). As Carlos Páramo Bonilla (2009) explains, both trajectories of the Aguirre binary exert themselves here. If, for Herzog, Aguirre the man is largely a monster of Spanish depredation, its militarist descendants in Latin America, and the delusions of empire, then for the Alvarado clique, *Aguirre* the film resonates a revolutionary national character (138), Herzog's "sense of 'Peruvianness.'" A couple of years later, after the rise of Pinochet in Chile and the regionwide neoliberal counterrevolution, and as Alvarado was about to fall in Peru, Herzog links the hazy ambience of Aguirre's mythical river run to contemporary history in even more explicit terms: the delirium of avarice, the "senseless dream of gold and power," is the same obstacle that a figure like

Salvador Allende must confront in his attempt to "transform the painful life of the poor into something dignified" and "this struggle against delirium is arduous and carries the weight of centuries."[49]

Staging history, Herzog, like a different baroque Lope, participates in his own object of dialogue by sustaining his spectacle on the ambitions of a state: moved by the possibilities of Aguirre's story, the Alvarado administration mobilized its armed forces in support of the production—including logistical and infrastructural work in the area of shooting—and negotiating the participation of the indigenous cooperative at Lauramarca, the workers on set, some of whom would become the famous Indian extras that give the early scenes their cast-of-thousands flair (see Páramo Bonilla 2009, 138). If, as I've maintained, *Aguirre* operates between myth and history, belonging to neither but participating in both, there is a specific site—at once mythical and historical—for this operation: America. Myth and history meet on America's stage, reacting and exploding into an emergent world, born both of conquests and nightmares, of negotiations and assaults, of empires and their others.

Late in *Aguirre* there is an important transitional scene, one that provides an interpretive key to the film. We're not ten minutes from the end, and the raft, now whirling in what appear to be accelerating circles, carries living dead men. Aguirre has just murmured his loathing for his soldiers who prefer to "measure riches in gold" over "power and fame." History has ceded to the unconscious, as the monk's narrative voice announces, forebodingly, "I can no longer write." He's out of ink, a confused soldier drank it. Abandoned by our narrator, we must now give ourselves over to a dream. Okello the slave, framed in medium close-up with Carvajal the monk, gazes off into the distance. "I see a ship with sails, in a tall tree, and from the stern hangs a canoe." The monk corrects him. "The ship is in your imagination. . . . We all have the fever." Cut to a panoramic long shot of the shoreline and there it is: a modest ship, high in a tree, with ragged sails and canoe dangling below. Set perpendicular to the vertical line of the tree, it forms the shape of a cross. The monk's words hang heavy: "It is only a mirage."

Mirages are of course real, an atmospheric effect, it is only our perception that turns bent light waves into oases, the heat radiating off sand dunes into the outlines of fantastic desert cities. And in this particular case, the mirage is historical. The ship must be real, as object of ambition. This is America, after all, founded and foundering on Europe's desires: like Cerca del Cielo, the place where dreams go to die, a land of failures only fanning the flames—in the German imagination, from Hegel to Arendt, the release valve of Old Europe's demographic pressure cooker—of frontier desires, of the transcendence promised by open, unconquered space, another kind of mirage. In *One Hundred Years of Solitude* (García Márquez 1967), with the village Macondo trapped in interior American isolation, José Arcadio Buendía rounds up the town's elders and sets out across the swamp on a dangerous expedition to find a passage to the sea. They traverse an enervating jungle in a melancholy route reminiscent of Aguirre's eight thousand leagues, "like sleepwalkers through a universe of grief . . . overwhelmed by a suffocating smell of blood" (12). Late in the journey as the jungle canopy has fused with the starless sky, they wake one morning, refreshed, and find themselves before a hulking Spanish galleon, covered in barnacles, moss, and orchids. They are deep in the forest, nowhere near the shore. Is the ship real? You don't ask: this is the power of magic realism, and to pose the question is to reject out of hand its resonant connection to America and its political culture, between myth and history. José Arcadio Buendía certainly doesn't ask: the good soldier of magic realism, he simply shrugs and continues another four days' march until they reach the outskirts of the sad Sargasso Sea, "that ashen, foamy, dirty sea, which had not merited the risks and sacrifices of the adventure" (13).

The fact of the ship is not the point; the point is the ecstatic truth churned up by human desire and the ruins of history that act as its notary. As spectators, we see the ship (in Herzog's account, built high in a tree over the course of a week by twenty-five workers), and in the next shot we are now behind Aguirre, gazing with him at the ship in the distance, and we feel his admonishment: "Shut up, monk! We'll get that ship! It is real! We'll sail the Atlantic with it." These are the expedition's death throes, lucid in their confusion. Carvajal protests—"we are weak and hungry"—Aguirre delivers yet another withering look of disdain, we cut back to the ship momentarily, and now Okello again: "That is no ship. That is no forest." Thwack. An arrow pierces his thigh. He looks at it, in sleepy curiosity. "That is no arrow. We just imagine the arrows, because we fear them." Aguirre, still rabid, fires the canon. Cut to Carvajal the monk, shot through with an arrow to the chest and everything now covered in rain (the editing gives a hypnotic sense of disjointed timelessness; a frame ago, it was sunny). "This arrow can't harm me." Extending his hand and looking skyward: "This is not rain." We know that we are nearing the end, in prelude to the film's conclusion, our perception at cross-purposes with that of the adventurers, and it's not entirely clear what's real.

But the monkeys are real. As Herzog himself puts it, "a situation always becomes clear with monkeys" (1973 interview with Noureddine Ghali, Herzog 2014f, 18), and in this case, he unleashes a boatload of them, a scene of baroque overgrowth in which the raft has been overwhelmed by chattering creatures and with it man's reason before nature. In a memorable series of shots, Aguirre, his daughter dead and his men dying, lurches around the raft pronouncing a discourse to an audience of squirrel monkeys (or "frailes" as Herzog calls them in the local vulgate). Early in the film, Aguirre delivers a wild but rational speech, justifying the mutiny by citing Cortés and the relation between glory and disobedience. Later, now with full command over an obviously doomed expedition, he resonates the paranoid delusions of the tyrant on the cusp of his fall, declaring "ich bin der Zorn Gottes"—"I am the wrath of God"—and promising an eternity of morbid suffering for all those who would defy him, including nature itself. In the former discourse, he addresses the men, directly and lucidly. In the latter, he speaks aloud to a paralyzed audience, but his gaze is elsewhere and he seems to be equally addressing himself, spewing epithets at a profane divinity. Now with the nonhuman primates, we are fully inside Aguirre's head, his final soliloquy delivered largely through internal monologue. A situation always becomes clear with monkeys, and this clarity leads us to the center of the film. Neither a legendary doomed quest for a lost city, nor a comment on the history of conquest, *Aguirre* most centrally confronts us with a new world order and the historical production of its own myths, its commitment to nightmares. With promises to bring his fight to the fortresses of the imperial state itself, marry his own daughter and form the "purest dynasty," Aguirre declares, "We'll stage history, like others stage plays." In other words: we'll stage a play that will resonate historical truth, the political unconscious. Much of this scene was improvised, with Herzog's instruction to Kinski simply to "follow

Figure 4. "We will endure": Aguirre (Klaus Kinski) delivers his final soliloquy. *Aguirre, the Wrath of God* (Herzog 1972).

the monkeys" (*Aguirre*, DVD director's commentary). Aguirre staggers toward a large cluster, plucks a creature from the corner of the raft, holds it to his face. Now speaking aloud, the monkey wriggling and staring back, mouth agape, Aguirre insists one last time. "We will endure. Ich [an important dramatic pause here] . . . bin der Zorn Gottes!" Looking completely distraught in a way that only Kinski can, he flings the monkey away and utters the final words of the film, "Who else is with me?"

Cut to the sun, and now the choral music that opened the film, for a closing shot that rivals the opening for atmospheric drama. Circling the adventurers for a final iteration of Herzog's infinite spiral, we get a lasting impression of this doomed expedition, with moribund soldiers strewn about, an impotent canon mute in its station, and clusters of monkeys colonizing the raft. The raft is very clearly now a stage. And in the middle stands a lone figure, perfectly still: hunch-chested, mismade with one arm longer than the other, one leg stiff and the other leg limber, the small voice of conquest exploding with desire, held together by leather straps.

Frontier Thesis

> The people who watch this and laugh are right to laugh. Those who do not are right, too.
>
> —Werner Herzog, 1978

> The stubborn American environment is there with its imperious summons to accept its conditions; the inherited ways of doing things are also there; and yet, in spite of environment, and in spite of custom, each frontier did indeed furnish a new field of opportunity, a gate of escape from the bondage of the past; and freshness, and confidence, and scorn of older society, impatience of its restraints and its ideas, and indifference to its lessons, have accompanied the frontier.
>
> —Frederick Jackson Turner, 1893

> Today they do it differently. They don't thrash you, beat you, or step on your hands. They do it ever so politely, and with a smile. It's much worse.
>
> —Bruno, in *Stroszek* (1977)

Between and around Aguirre's scheming, plotting sociopathology, there's the surprising quiver of vulnerability. His unpredictable rages and barbed declarations of menace (before his wrath "the birds will drop dead from the trees," he whispers) stand in defiance, as we saw, against his *de facto* historical marginalization. A conquistador with nothing to conquer, an obsolete cog in a sputtering historical machine, a class of violence worker no longer readily employable, Aguirre occasionally reveals cracks in his shell of megalomania, and therein Herzog and Kinski plant fleeting images of man's distress before the world he has created. There's a nostalgia to Aguirre's interactions with his daughter, a kind of *tristesse tropicale* as he observes the flute player, an expression of stunned grief as he holds the dying Flores, and flickers of anxiety that punctuate his terrifying speeches. His eyes constantly shifting, even more than hubris, his desperate project seems motivated by fear. For all his crimes, we can perceive in this spaghetti-western antihero a quiet fragility, world-historical victimization, a quality absent, for example, from Clint Eastwood's "man with no name" character.

As Herzog moves through the wake of 1968 and deeper into the riptides of the chaotic 1970s, this subtextual portrait of world-historical victimization will be forged into something like a unifying theme. The secret vulnerability of his conquistador speaks to a larger preoccupation, one that Herzog will take up quite systematically in his post-*Aguirre* work of the 1970s, an astonishingly creative decade by any standard, during which he would be the outlier within and internal critic of the talented generation of directors that compose the so-called New German Cinema.[50] In his Cronin interviews, Herzog explains, "I have always thought of my films as really being one big work that I have been concentrating on for forty years. The characters in this huge story are all desperate solitary rebels with *no language with which to communicate*. Inevitably they suffer because of this. They know their rebellion is doomed to failure, but they continue without respite, wounded, struggling on their own without assistance" (Herzog and Cronin 2002, 68, my emphasis). A facile interpretation might take this as a celebration of crude individualism, but Herzog's narrative project is far subtler than that, even, in fact, something like the opposite of individualism as we know it. The individual, in its ideological sanctity within modern liberal society, stakes its coherence on a set of interests that ultimately revolve around not just survival but, more important, accumulation. People are individuals insofar as they pursue interests, ultimately, profit. Thus the essence of "inalienable rights" in that foundational document of modern liberalism, the US Declaration of Independence (1776), can be summarized as "Life, Liberty and the *pursuit* of Happiness" [my emphasis]. These are the things that the state is ordained to protect, that is, the basic context (life, liberty) that cultivates the right to get in on the game (pursuit) of accumulation, not necessarily any essential right to the happiness itself that might come from a range of human activities outside and beyond social relations of accumulation. The rebel without a cause, as celebrated Hollywood outsider, fails to adequately perceive the hypocrisy and contradictions embedded in this social contract that equates the violence of pursuit with the ill-fitting condition of happiness. He thus shouts into the wind, he has no cause. The rebel with a cause, as revolutionary, adequately perceives the internal contradictions of liberal ideology and inspires the people to take part in its dialectical reversal. She thus shouts manifestos to admiring crowds, she draws them to her cause.

Herzog's "desperate solitary rebels" are located somewhere in between: their diagnosis is clear-eyed, but they have no clear path forward, no revolution to advance. That is, they have no language with which to enter into pacts of solidarity with the other. Acutely they feel and perceive the malaise of capitalist society, but its adequate expression eludes them. This is the dramatic tension that animates Herzog's 1970s films. The inability to "communicate" isn't literal; indeed, one of Herzog's great underdogs, the magnificent Fini Straubinger from *Land des Schweigens und der Dunkelheit* (*Land of Silence and Darkness*, 1971), is nothing less than a champion of communication, floating life rafts to those most immediately cut off from the social world because of their physical disabilities. By "communicate," Herzog seems to be indicating the possibility of making oneself understood and felt—the possibility of evoking empathy—from the losing end of world-historical development, that is, the historical unfolding and institutionalization of capitalist society. Take Aguirre: finding himself historically useless and without means to productively enter into the course of history, he rebels, not without a cause, but uselessly, now a self-fashioned protagonist of history, a nostalgic history of his own making, in the end a theater play with a simian public. Instrumentally, this is absurd, that it would all end on a boat full of monkeys hardly even surprising. But subjectively, critically, it's devastating, opening up discursive cracks that expose the contradictions of a world-system whose deranged violence makes Aguirre's rebellion look timid by comparison. The Herzogian protagonists that we will meet throughout the decade are far quieter than Aguirre, effecting little revolts in a range of forms, but not less rebellious in their posture toward normative society: Fini Straubinger, deaf-blind teacher to the deaf-blind in *Land of Silence and Darkness*; the damaged and defiant ski-flyer Walter Steiner of *Die grosse Ekstase des Bildschnitzers Steiner* (*The Great Ecstasy of Woodcarver Steiner*, 1974); the monumental Bruno S. in his role as the foundling Kaspar Hauser in *The Enigma of Kaspar Hauser* (1974); the mystic Hias and the hypnotized monks of *Herz aus Glas* (*Heart of Glass*, 1976); the haunted solitude of the Vampyre, *Nosferatu* (1979); the hunted cuckold played by Kinski in *Woyzeck* (1979); and most of all, Bruno Stroszek of *Stroszek* (1977).

While passion-play sadism looms just under the surface in the exhibition of all this suffering and failure, what some have described and even denounced as Herzog's "pessimism" (e.g., Rentschler 1984, 615) and "virulent fatalism" (e.g., Rentschler 1981, 30) do not, in fact, capture the defining mood of these films. As we saw with *Aguirre*, *Signs of Life*, and *Even Dwarfs Started Small*, Herzog's portraits of those on the losing end of history are full of pathos, ecstasy, and exhilaration. These figures, without language, express their dire predicaments and their heroic attempts at liberation with a startling eloquence. Evoking their poetry is Herzog's aim, the illumination of what he commonly refers to as their "radical dignity," the essential humanity that explodes through their post-traumatic distress, "I learned so much from my time with them and I think the radical dignity they radiate is clearly visible in the films" (Herzog and Cronin 2002, 69). It is these marginals, wandering the periphery of capitalism, that for Herzog offer the clearest insights into the politics of being human. These men and women (but mostly men) are Herzog's secret mainstream, revealing in their oblique perception not just the contradictions but the bald eccentricity, the ethnological strangeness and abstraction, the methodical dehumanization wrought by bourgeois society.[51]

Herzog's 1970s films, portraits of aching marginalization and its (sometimes fleeting) transcendence, can be grouped into three general types. First are the ambitious, historical sets, lushly inventive feature films that consolidated Herzog's reputation as an auteur of the first order. They are period dramas, set in idyllic central European towns that take place during the high times of Romanticism, the late eighteenth and early nineteenth centuries: *The Enigma of Kaspar Hauser* (more colorfully known as *Every Man for Himself and God against All*), *Heart of Glass*, *Nosferatu the Vampyre*, and *Woyzeck*.[52] While told in a range of styles and grounded on different narrative conceits—the relatively straightforward cinematic storytelling of *Nosferatu* and *Kaspar Hauser*; the almost theatrical, deep psychology of *Woyzeck*; the challenging abstraction of *Heart of Glass*—each of these films deals, in one way or another, with an overwhelming sense of alienating loss, even bondage, that seems a direct corollary to the freedom promised by bourgeois modernity and its will toward institutionalization. In each, tortured characters strive to see the world behind the veil of social convention, or even to simply enter into its pacts as an invested participant, only to be beaten back time and again: the heartlessness of formal education; the sadism embedded in the scientific method; the social disintegration that ensues as craft rapidly transforms into industry; the depredations of modern regimes of care, from mental to public health; real-estate transactions.

Alongside these art films stand the second and third categories of Herzog's work in the 1970s, a set of documentaries, all produced for West German television, which we can split into two loose groups. On the one hand are three intimate portraits of the inner lives of characters whose relations with normative society are, in one way or another, fraught. Two of these deal explicitly with the challenges facing the physically or sensorially disabled (*behinderte*) in early 1970s West Germany. *Behinderte Zukunft* (*Handicapped Future*, 1971) is the most explicitly polemical, a critical examination of the institutional treatment of the disabled in the wake of the thalidomide scandal and the political struggle to create a more inclusive society. The echoes with Germany's still recent experiments with National Socialism are hard to miss. For Herzog, it's strikingly straightforward—a *Gebrauchsfilm*, or classroom film—"dangerously conventional" (Herzog and Cronin 2002, 73), Herzog calls it, noting that it is "one of my most directly politically aware films" (ibid.).[53] While *Handicapped Future* focuses more on institution than individual, its production led Herzog to make the acquaintance of Fini Straubinger—the extraordinary deaf-blind activist for disabled rights—and thereby direct what is often lauded as his finest documentary film, the 1971 feature-length masterpiece, *Land of Silence and Darkness*. Among other reasons, the film is notable for its codification of some of the basics of Herzogian film language, not least his heterodox use of narrative fabrication within the documentary form, a practice that mirrors the extensive documentary elements of his fictional films. The opening lines spoken by Straubinger, for example, were scripted by Herzog; the memorable closing shot of a developmentally disabled man embracing a tree was directed; and so on.[54] Worth noting here is the fact that the entire film is structured around the dialectic between the near total marginalization of absolute incommunicability—the challenging long take of the severely retarded young Vladimir, or Straubinger's poignant attempts to evoke sentient reaction from a deaf-blind individual who has essentially given up—and its contradiction as this stigmatization collides with Straubinger's will, her lust for life, and her fierce generosity with those who could be easily lost to the possibility of sociability. The shots of Straubinger and her deaf-blind friends at the zoo, where an ape must be touched rather than seen, are some of the most joyful of Herzog's oeuvre.

If these two films confront us with the possibilities and limits of the mind's liberation from physical bondage, then *The Great Ecstasy of Woodcarver Steiner* takes the question from something like the opposite angle: an extreme ski-jumper—better, ski-flyer—whose exuberant, world-champion flights stand at odds with an almost painful humility as he eloquently describes his social anxiety, profound fears, childhood traumas, and regular confrontation with death. The fact that *Land of Silence and Darkness* opens with a set of images of ski-jumpers hurtling through the air that would later be restylized for *Woodcarver Steiner* amply suggests the immediacy of the universal contradiction between the limits of the human body and their transcendence through technique—skis, tactile sign language—or dreams. "I wish *you* could see that" [my emphasis], says the blind Straubinger as she describes her vision of these winged humans, in words composed by the director. Later in the film she will literally fly as she accompanies a deaf-blind friend on her first trip in an airplane.[55]

On the other hand, a different set of documentaries describes the third category of intervention that marks Herzog's 1970s films: in a very loose sense, American capitalism. It might be better to say the *eccentricities* of American capitalism. In three short television documentaries (each about 45 minutes) Herzog offers meditations, without any clear theses, on some of the surprising manifestations of the American dream. Coinciding with the US bicentennial is *How Much Wood Would a Woodchuck Chuck* (1976), a portrait of cattle auctioneers in spirited competition that Herzog has characterized as a testament to "the last poetry possible, the poetry of capitalism" (director's commentary, *Stroszek* DVD). In long sequence shots of mesmerizing repetition, a technique that Herzog mobilizes with some regularity across his films, we are greeted by auctioneer after auctioneer (the folkloric type, who bark their wares with extraordinary speed) as they plow through several million dollars' worth of cattle. It's highly entertaining. Five years later, as he was ramping up to the marathon shoot of *Fitzcarraldo* (1982), Herzog inaugurated the Reagan years with two surprising straightforward portraits, each consisting of long shots of a very different form of American preaching. One is *Glaube und Währung: Dr. Gene Scott, Fernsehprediger* (*God's*

Angry Man, 1981). It focuses on the televangelist and scam artist Dr. Gene Scott, as he pleads and menaces his audience to send money in support of his cheap theology. It's essentially a montage of long takes, intercut with interviews and shots from Scott's own production team. The German title is blander but gets directly to the point, translating literally as *Faith and Currency*. Its inverted twin is *Huie's Predigt* (*Huie's Sermon*, 1981), mostly an extended long take of Bishop Huie Rogers, the minister of an African-American Pentecostal church in Brooklyn, as he excites his congregation with an increasingly rousing sermon founded on a set of overlapping paranoid screeds—against gender-reassignment surgery, against the government, against artificial insemination (that's right), against exchange rates, and so on—alongside some brief cross-cuts of urban poverty and blight (notably, at the moment that Rogers cries "Gaaaaawd! . . . is in control!"). The whole thing crescendos to an inspiring gospel jam, complete with near-ecstatic congregants, the laying on of hands and an immersion baptism in an interesting balcony-level pool with a transparent wall making the ritual visible to the congregation. Placed next to one another the obsessive focus that all three films demonstrate vis-à-vis their speaking subjects provide a captivating, if also perplexing, portrait of American folk cultures in their commitment to communion through dollars: salesmanship as entertainment, exploitation as entrepreneurship, and faith as defense against privation. Implicit, ambiguous comments on social class and race swirl through the films as well.[56]

It is important to emphasize that the red thread of these three portraits of American eccentricity is the relation between language and money.[57] Each film dwells on the intensification of speech, phenomena that emerge at the edges of a cultural system as its relations of production become rote, with Herzog comparing this kind of "extreme language" to the "ritual chants of the Orthodox Church" (Herzog and Cronin 2002, 140). So on the one hand, it is very hard to ascertain the extent to which these forms of address actually communicate: the effective content of the utterances seems to disintegrate into their formal intensity. On the other hand, the ambiguity melts away as we realize that all are bound up with a logic of a confused financial and spiritual transaction (whether immediate—"Weeeeeee're gonna sell some cattle . . ." begins one auctioneer—or forestalled—I'll strike my bargain with a higher power and thus later deliver myself from this suffering). More than entering into the active mind of dialogue, their common quality seems to be one of hypnosis. The mesmerized ecstasy of Rogers's congregation, the trance-inducing cadence of the auctioneers, the menacing gaze of Smith as he separates his victims from their wallets. Through these films we are confronted with some of the more garish practices of capitalist exchange, where use- and exchange-value melt into the performative rigor of the salesman preacher. What is the critical action here? Is the strangeness of the spectacle an oblique form of distantiation, confronting us with a space to question ideological naturalization? Or is it an aesthetic of absorption, pulling us into the logic of the spectacle itself in order to experience it, entranced, alongside the cattle shoppers, Rogers's congregants, Smith's victims? Besides his seemingly genuine expressions of affection for all his protagonists, from the nimble auctioneers to the ghastly Smith, Herzog gives us little to go on. The gap between his ambivalent admiration for America—"I like America," he says in the director's commentary on the *Stroszek* DVD, "but in some sort of an ambivalent way"—and his impulse to explore its spaces of greatest contradiction, which is ours to fill.

This deluge of words, their hypnotic power, and their immediate relation to late-capitalist malaise is what rearticulates these American vignettes back to the seemingly unrelated historical dramas and disability documentaries. All contemplate the limits of vocal speech—whether as extreme presence (e.g., *Woodchuck*) or extreme absence (e.g., *Silence and Darkness*)—in the context of modern social relations and the institutionality that mediates them, where the authority of technocratic segmentation scores increasing triumphs over the affirmation of human community. These problems are staged with considerable rigor in the period pieces. *The Enigma of Kaspar Hauser* revolves around a foundling, the historical personage of Kaspar Hauser, raised in a dungeon without human contact, whose mysterious appearance in the town square of Nürnberg with a letter of introduction and subsequent socialization beguiled the 1830s continental literati. In other words, we are invited into the world of the individual as literal blank slate, a pure human, non- or prerational, the film revolving around the passion play of his suffering, the assaults of reason as he moves from prison, to circus, to bourgeois home, to school, to church, to sickbed, to morgue. Dialectically, the film's action operates through the space between Kaspar's subjective collision with a social structure that he can only obliquely comprehend (making his observations about it deeply poetic) and that same society's reception of him as a kind of instrumental experiment. Whereas we can imagine worlds in which he would be received as guest of honor, god, proconsul, slave, or witch, in late-Enlightenment Bavaria he stands as *evidence*: a proof submitted to prevailing theories of mind, with the last scene of the film portraying a bureaucrat skipping with joy to relay the results of Kaspar's autopsy (the report: some vaguely defined cerebral deformation and a swollen liver). Adding to the ambient intensity in *Kaspar Hauser* is the fact that the lead role was played by a real-life foundling of sorts, the ineffable Bruno S., who spent an entire childhood and early adult life in and out of institutions, a victim of systematic abuse whose trauma becomes visible the moment his outsized gaze appears before the camera.

Further intensifying this exploration of the interaction between language, communication, and modern society is *Heart of Glass*, a story of social class relations in rapidly industrializing Bavaria during which Herzog placed the cast under literal hypnosis for many of the shots. The result is as strange as it sounds, producing one of the more *unheimlichen* moods ever brought to the cinema. The important point here is that not every character in the film acts under the seemingly foggy spell of hypnosis. While the peasant villagers, aristocrats, and domestic servants—in other words, the subjects of a moribund set of social relations—seem to sleepwalk through a rapidly changing historical landscape, the two motivating protagonists retain their lucid perception of the world. One is the clairvoyant, Hias, a figure pulled from Bavarian folk culture, whose prophecies—their regular intercalations providing the architecture for the film—announce repeated allusions to popular rebellion. The others are the workers themselves, the glassworks laborers and craftsmen who clearly perceive the impending crisis of production, take action to preserve their own livelihoods (for example, by smuggling their wares to a black market), eventually seize the glassworks owner, and may or may not enact the revolution that Hias *perhaps* predicts.[58] This immediacy of experience, of direct exposure to the buffeting winds of historical upheaval, is where Herzog places his characters. The heroic striving for an adequate language to articulate and resist the violence on which these social conditions rest is what links Kaspar, Hias, Fini, and Huie (and Nosferatu, and Woyzeck, and Steiner, and so on). These are Herzog's rebels. As we have seen, his inexhaustible curiosity follows them to a variety of contexts and represents their struggles through a range of forms: in period dramas of striving against institutions, in documentary portraits of the inner lives of the traumatized, in arcane observations of the strange rites of American capitalism. One film, Herzog's definitive 1970s statement on America (as United States), ties these threads together. Let's turn to *Stroszek*.

Herzog loves a rebel, but the passage from rebellion to revolution is something that he leaves outside his cinematic frame. Thus we are not surprised that, at the end of *Heart of Glass*, Hias's vision of man-in-revolt has transformed into something else, one of those "wizardly curveballs," to borrow Tom Bissell's (2006, 70) expression, the strange codas that almost always close Herzog's films. After spending the story predicting uprisings and fire, Hias's final vision seems to look back, or somewhere else entirely. It's another rebellion, to be sure, but one that confronts not the vampirism of capitalists but rather the contingencies of history, geography, imagination, and will. A man stands alone, on a rock, thousands of feet above the sea, and stares into the abyss. For days, weeks, months, years. This is hope, Hias's vision tells us, and also doubt: perhaps the world is round, like an orange. The object of rebellion is unclear, it fades into mist, and is nothing less than the arc of the earth itself, an infinite horizon hovering somewhere between human consciousness and the physical world. The object is full of risk, an open question: it is, in short, the frontier. Other men join the solitary man, they vow to step into the mist, but even in solidarity, the outcome can't be known. Revolution, whether political or geographic, is the step toward this frontier. And let's face it—Herzog is a realist—the chances are slim: songs of deliverance are sung, the men push out to sea, . . . but the boat, it's far too small. And yet the film ends with a glimmer: a sign of hope, reads an epilogue, was perceived as the birds follow the overwhelmed sailors into the void.

In the modern world, no political imagination trades on passages into the frontier like the idea of America, specifically (although not exclusively) the United States, whose very identity consolidates as a frontier society in the late nineteenth century. *Stroszek*, Herzog's 1977 portrait of America, features a frontier image that recalls the man on the rock from *Heart of Glass*. Shot from the back in wide horizon portrait, the protagonist Bruno Stroszek looks out into the frozen November abyss of a Wisconsin plain, made extra cold by the absent snow. The shot holds for a long time, Bruno perfectly still, his stocky form made shapeless by a heavy coat, with all the midwestern sex appeal of a garden gnome statuette. Were it not for a black Labrador retriever stalking the horizon, it could be a still. Like the man on the rock, Bruno stares into an infinite plane, but the mood is in a different register. Where the man on the rock sees a future of what might be, with the possibility of hope suggested by the swooping helicopter-mounted camera, Bruno can only contemplate what might have been. He gazes into a frontier landscape not full of promise, but full of regret; not a space of solidarity, but of abandonment; not a future of possession, but a present of the dispossessed, in Bruno's case, literally repossessed. The empty space before him was filled, an instant earlier, by his mobile home, purchased on credit, and now auctioned off and hauled away as collateral for bad debt. It's the central, and pivotal, shot of the film, a frontier landscape saturated in disappointment. In its aftermath, Bruno will attempt a bank robbery, assault a barber, steal a frozen turkey, and take flight in a battered getaway tow truck on a cross-country trip that will end in his doom.

Generically, *Stroszek* is a hybrid, opening up lines of dialogue with a number of cinematic traditions. Most broadly, it is a melodrama, tracing the rise of the romance and eventual fall into domestic disintegration between Bruno Stroszek, played by the inimitable Bruno Schleinstein, also known as Bruno S., Herzog's "unknown soldier of the cinema"; and Eva, played by a coy Eva Mattes, performing at the very height of her considerable talent. But, at the same time, the film treads the terrain of the bio-pic, focusing, often in documentary realism, on aspects of the life of Bruno S.: his institutionalization, his apartment, his neighborhood, his daily routines, his musical vocation. It is also a road movie, an immigrant epic, and, of central importance, even a deformed western, with oblique references to cowboys and Indians at every turn.[59] Part of the film's genius is to defamiliarize all these elements by placing them within a narrative and a setting that become exotic precisely through their banality. Bruno is a marginal in the truest sense, not a *pícaro* or trickster, simply a lost soul trying to get by; Eva is a sex worker in essentially the same spirit, brutalized and opportunistic, no redemption, no pathos, no heart of gold; and their odyssey takes them from the everyday small-mindedness of the peripheral spaces of the European city and its extortionate thugs to the same small-mindedness of the American country town and its extortionate bumpkins. There is nothing epic in Bruno's quest, it's just a sad little story of human failure, and this quality, paradoxically, lends it a feeling of being somehow an essential document of our time. It's one of Herzog's very best films.

The plot structure of *Stroszek* is familiar, in that it governs several of Herzog's stories, and, perhaps surprising when we consider the vast historical gulf between, essentially updates *Aguirre*. A European man, here Bruno, finds himself on the losing end of history. He faces tribulations in the form of physical (local thugs) and political (repeated institutionalization) obstacles until he finally takes matters into his own hands with a dramatic gamble. Leaving (almost) everything behind, he goes in search of his El Dorado, America, and its guiding dream, in which, his friends tell him, money can be made and the livin' is easy. There is a sense of tentative progress upon arrival in Wisconsin (compare *Aguirre* and the early days of the rebellion)—everybody gets a job, he and Eva take out a mortgage on a mobile home—although not without the faint whiff of lingering dread, even violence, in the background. Soon the dream stalls, the objective becomes illusory as payments can't be met, and the quest descends into darkness (compare *Aguirre*'s slow unraveling on the rafts). Things fall apart, collapsing into a set of infinite spirals, and in a majestic closing sequence, Bruno, out of options, puts a gun to his head (cf. *Aguirre*'s monkey-infested conclusion). There are even Indians. And while, unlike in *Aguirre*, none of these picturesque natives are harmed along the way, their obstinate presence provides a contextual counterpoint that lends an intensified air of absurdity to the narrative of easy money that propels the Eurocentric plot.

Now, between the two films, we are of course in different worlds. About four hundred years separate the historical settings of *Aguirre* and *Stroszek*. But I would submit that this chronological leap isn't the important difference in and of itself. Landscape, so central to Herzog's grammar of filmmaking, is the essential point that distinguishes Bruno's quest from Aguirre's. Aesthetically and metaphorically, they operate on different planes. Aguirre's mysterious float down an unknown river into thick jungle is also an exploration of the dark corners of human desire, as the jungle resonates the implacable bewilderment of the unconscious mind. And Bruno's equally bewildering encounter with the open horizons of a rural modernity conjures more immediately the contradiction between a wish for solidarity and the fundamental loneliness that underwrites capitalist society. Beyond metaphorical suggestion, however, at work in Herzog is the historical production of space, the chronotopic pressure that narrative storytelling can exert on form and content, and the determinate role that historical context plays in crafting the sociocritical possibilities embedded in the story. We saw this with *Aguirre*: the delirium of rain forest jungle only takes critical shape as we reposition it within its world-historical logic, an object of not just any desire, but of sixteenth-century *imperial* desire, a site of conquest, pillage, plunder. In spatial terms, *Stroszek* is divided in two, its quest moving from the intolerable pressures of the modern city to the release-valve land of opportunity. While Herzog's story makes sense only by placing the latter in dialogue with the former, it is the second context, America, that holds the key to *Stroszek*'s critical intervention. To understand how, we need to situate it within its very specific landscape, the terrain that propels its narrative: America, yes, but more precisely, the frontier.

Persecuted by local toughs—a pimp and a thief—Bruno escapes the claustrophobia of working-class Berlin by way of ship. (This is in deference to one of his traveling companions who doesn't believe in the structural integrity of airplanes.) We suspend disbelief, because it's important for the historical resonance of the story: it's the immigrant passage, old school. He travels with the prostitute Eva, who seems like his girlfriend although it isn't totally clear, and Herr Scheitz, an eccentric elderly neighbor whose contact, a distant nephew, is their ticket to the promised land. They disembark in the old New World, New York City, where they ascend skyscrapers and buy a used vehicle, not a stagecoach but a station wagon, cash in hand. They head west, across miles and miles of hills and plains and mountains and sunsets, Chet Atkins provides the soundtrack, and eventually they arrive at their country town: Railroad Flats, Wisconsin.[60] Ed, the distant nephew, is there to meet them, and we know that we are not only in America, but *America*, the frontier, because Ed has an Indian sidekick, his largely mute employee, Eli.

The story couldn't be better known. It's the great pageant of immigration, to be sure, but beyond that it's a story that plays on the very cultural identity of America, at once celebrating and defamiliarizing its mythical relation to space. The subject of countless cultural artifacts, both high and low, the frontier's canonization as the center of American identity wouldn't coalesce until it was essentially exhausted as political space, as an object of accumulation, closed to further expansion. In convenient harmony with *Stroszek*, the writer who would establish the framework for the hegemony of the frontier in the American psyche was a Wisconsinite, the titan of American historiography at the turn of the century, Frederick Jackson Turner. In 1893 Turner delivered an address before the American Historical Association at the World's Columbian Exposition in Chicago. It was called "The Significance of the Frontier in American History" ([1893] 1921) and so massive was its impact in setting the agenda for historiographical explorations of the nature of American political culture that it took on a succinct nickname: "frontier thesis." In this extraordinary paper, Turner argues that what makes American history essential, and its cultural identity exceptional, isn't merely the frontier in and of itself, as a constitutive fact of the cartography of the country. Rather, it's the way in which the frontier penetrates American civilization. The Hegelian model of historical movement saw in America a kind of escape hatch for the population pressures of Europe, a space in which that civilization could further unfold and reinvent its internal logic, and this notion would be translated by generations of historians and race scientists throughout the nineteenth century as the foundation of various "germ" theories of national identity as a kind of essence of spirit. The movement west, then, is implacable, dominant, and white. Turner's dialectic comes off as more rigorous, and less jingoistic, proposing that the essential point of frontier space is not the way in which European civilization fills it up, pacifies it. Instead, the political and cultural fact of the frontier is to be found in the new forms of sociability that emerge there, negotiated between disparate cultural groups, and how they double back, in their turn making demands on the "old Europe" ethos of the eastern seaboard. In short, he argued, American democracy relies on the renovating function of the frontier for its progressive elements. Decades prior, Tocqueville had been enchanted by a version of this idea, and Turner's reelaboration of it has been seducing

American exceptionalists ever since: as William Appleman Williams put it, the frontier thesis "rolled through the universities and into popular literature as a tidal wave" ([1955] 1992, 383).[61]

The popularization of the frontier thesis rests on a neat formula that misreads half the essay and ignores its dialectical power. The frontier is about freedom, that freedom is grounded in the figure of the individual, and it is this free individual divorced and liberated from old Europe that turns back to make claims against the state and leave its mark on the national psyche. But all this, Turner reminds us again and again, is hemmed in and made national by the actions, precisely, of a state. So, even if the history of land grants is a way of keeping up with an actually existing frontier reality protagonized by a vanguard of trappers, prospectors, and pioneers claiming lands, that reality is always recontained, quickly, by both state authority and capitalist accumulation when these claims are given sanction as property. For Turner, the state is in the position of just catching up with the reality on the ground; but that is not to say that it does not catch up ([1893] 1921, 25). A double paradox emerges around the myth of the frontier as sacred space of American individualism. First, the frontier, as "the West," resonates freedom as liberation from state power, but it is in fact founded on some of the most thoroughgoing state regulation on the continent, a reality that continues to govern "frontier" life to this day. Second, the frontier as the space in which the individual struggles against nature to carve out sustenance (self-reliant, free from sovereign interference) masks both the origin and destination of this historical process of accumulation and enclosure that we know as property, that is, land made manageable by parceling it into units corresponding to an owner who can then place this title into a market of exchange. The West was made by men, but this land development project becomes a social relation in its conversion into something else: real estate. What Turner describes as an epochal *social* pageant of will, violence and resource extraction—the great "middle West" circuit of Pittsburgh, Cleveland, Minneapolis, and St. Louis, where Chicago "reigns" as imperial "center" (126); the "Indian trade" (14) in beaver pelts wherein first commerce then war push the transformation of indigenous paths into trails, then roads, then turnpikes, then railroads—converts into an ideological truth as the grammar of the frontier: individual, freedom.

The opening narrative arc of *Stroszek*—about the first half of the film—traces the popular trajectory of man's flight to frontier freedom. Herzog injects a strong dose of real-world situation into this narrative by casting Bruno S. in the title role. Bruno S. (or Bruno Schleinstein; he died in 2010) was an often institutionalized factory worker whom Herzog first spotted in a documentary about the marginalized street musicians of Berlin.[62] Captivated, Herzog soon placed him in the title role of the critically acclaimed *The Enigma of Kaspar Hauser*. Second only to Kinski in Herzog's legend of director-as-lion-tamer, Bruno S. proved to have an uncanny screen presence whose evocation required significant patience from the crew: Herzog and other witnesses describe him as sweet and friendly, but also highly paranoid, often opaque, erratic, and prone to fits of rambling denunciations. While certainly independent (he had a job and an apartment), Bruno S. nevertheless also had to be cared for at some level during shooting: hygiene was an issue, he would sleep fully clothed on the floor at his hotel door, he refused to deposit his salary into a bank, and the like. Famously, when he would enter into one of his long screeds, Herzog would instruct the crew to listen attentively, regardless of the duration. Of course he had no professional training as an actor. As Herzog tells it, after *Kaspar Hauser* he had originally wanted to cast Bruno S. as *Woyzeck*, the troubled cuckold (eventually played by Kinski) harried by a set of modern institutions—medical, military—who murders his fiancée Marie (Mattes), but then decided that it would be a mistake. Upon learning of this decision, Bruno S. was so devastated that Herzog made an on-the-spot commitment to cast him in another film, promising him the script ready in a matter of days. The screenplay turned out to be *Stroszek* and its opening story revolves around significant aspects of Bruno S.'s life: key scenes are shot in his apartment; a long interlude features him performing in an urban Berlin courtyard; and there are institutions.[63]

The film begins in full claustrophobia, with the titles opening over the interior space of a prison, the bars in close-up and then unlocked to allow passage to Bruno (the lead character's name is Bruno Stroszek) and a prison guard. It's release day and Bruno is being subjected to a series of interrogations and admonitions. First the return of his possessions, then a farewell to his cellmates—"I don't want to leave," he confesses—and finally a tedious lecture on the dangers of alcoholism from the administrator. This latter scene is one of Bruno S.'s finest, introducing us to an actor who moves haphazardly in and out of frame as if by improvisation (Herzog confirms this), his unusual prosody, distant gaze, and eccentric interruptions of his interlocutor immediately endowing his character with an attractive and yet slightly mystifying sense of detached alienation. When the administrator addresses his beer drinking and warns that "If you don't stop . . ." Bruno cuts him off with "Who can stop?"; as the administrator pontificates on the virtues of work and hygiene, of the straight and narrow, Bruno mumbles, "It goes in circles." As we will see, both these rejoinders stand as something like the working theses of the film. Most significant, these opening shots set the scene of oppressive spaces crammed full of objects and emotions. The takes are long, but the shots are tight, we feel crowded in with the characters. The symbolic, almost desperate, gestures to open spaces only add to the sense of confinement. In order to glimpse the outdoors, the inmates have hung a half-full water bottle in front of a high window, allowing a view of refracted reflections. One cellmate gives Bruno a gift of freedom, a ship: made of folded paper, it is as tiny as a fingernail. And in the same cell we see our first indications toward the frontier: a poster of the cast of *Bonanza* (1959–73) a famous American western television series starring Lorne Greene, hangs in the background, and a second cellmate wears a ten-gallon cowboy hat. He bids goodbye to Bruno by farting into a lit newspaper, creating a small explosion.

With the exception of a couple of streetscapes, the entire Berlin sequence of the film is shot in similarly cramped settings. The bar, the breakfast joint, the stairwell, the apartment, all offer no quarter, no space to breathe. Added to this is the overwhelming presence of street-life political and economic violence. Upon his release from prison, Bruno rekindles his friendship with the abused Eva, but this immediately makes him a target of two brutal delinquents, one of them Eva's pimp. Well cast, they look somehow mismade, their faces always a little too close, overlarge in relation to their bodies as they fill up the screen, entirely absent of any Scorsese-style thug charm.[64] "It goes in circles" as a theme of unbearable stress is made palpable with the thugs, as they threaten Bruno in public not once but twice and then invade Bruno's apartment not once but twice—first dragging Eva up the stairs by her hair, later humiliating Bruno in forced prostration atop his piano as they hurl

Figure 5. Bruno (Bruno S.) asks the warden, "Who can stop?" Note the averted gaze. *Stroszek* (Herzog 1977).

anti-Muslim epithets (he's not Muslim; but in keeping with the centrality of historical-political space to the story of the film, he resides in the Muslim quarter, the Kreuzberg neighborhood, subtitled "Turk town" in the local vulgate of the thugs). All this intensifies through repetition, an overarching mood of oppression, a doubling of trauma that will become the film's leitmotif.[65] Even the spaces of quiet reflection are hemmed in. When Bruno takes his accordion and xylophone out onto the street, his performance happens in a grim tenement courtyard, garbage cans providing the backdrop, narrow and with high walls scaling up a low gray sky.[66] When he finishes, a single child stands, face against the wall, weeping (Herzog reports that this was unscripted). When Bruno seeks counsel from his former doctor, a wonderful little set piece unfolds as the doctor demonstrates that even premature babies have a prehensile ability to grip and, amazingly, sustain their own weight. It's a touching scene and an important metaphor of the relation between survival and community (the baby, essentially, needs to grasp at *another*), but of a piece with the aesthetic of claustrophobia that dominates the film's Berlin narrative: the babies are contained in small boxes, wired to EKG machines pinging all around.

The line of flight points to America. It's rare for a Herzog film to feature a female protagonist, but *Stroszek* turns out to be as much about Eva as Bruno. After the encounter with the apish baby grip we cut back to the apartment where we find Eva, her face swollen after a beating from her pimp and his sidekick. She announces the struggle that will propel the story forward: "we'll go away from here, Bruno." Bruno is skeptical: you need money to get away. America always comes up in the context of home economics, and an attentive viewer may recall a transition from twenty minutes prior, when Eva and Bruno are discussing financial difficulties and then cut to Herr Scheitz with the first mention of America and his contact there. Now in a charming scene, the band of misfits gathers around an atlas and a plan starts to come together. "Where is Wisconsin, anyway?" "I don't think it's on there." They seem to be looking at South America. They get on the correct page, pointing: here, "right near Canada." The romance of the frontier runs strong in German culture up to this day, even with its own, massively popular subgenre of literary westerns canonized by the nineteenth-century novelist Karl May, but beyond these fantasies from another world, the film's referent is, of course, in reality material.[67] Eva: "Everyone makes money there and we can too." Bruno: "How are we going to pay for the trip, and get visas? We don't have that kind of money" Eva: "I'll get it, don't you worry about that." She gets it the old-fashioned way, through work, returning with an impressive wad of cash after an excursion to what appears to be a back-of-the-warehouse meeting with a band of twitchy Turks, declaring, "We're going to start all over again." Plans begin to get specific: Bruno can work with Herr Scheitz's nephew as a mechanic's assistant; a truck stop up the road has a waitress position for Eva; there's even a "red Indian" employed at the garage; a prefabricated house can easily be purchased; unlike Berlin, "there's plenty of room." Next stop: America.

The gateway to the frontier explodes onto the screen with a wide horizon shot of New York's arrogant skyline, Babylonian in its arch toward the heavens. The aesthetics of space hit hard: while the soundtrack, in keeping with the protagonists, is modest, eccentric, and introspective, we are almost blinded by the light of icy blue winter. From this skyscraper's view of future possibilities, recognized by Bruno as he blows a hymn to "freedom" on a primitive horn (another of the film's infinite, doubled repetitions: he also blew his freedom horn when released from prison), the immigrants quickly embark on their American experience by purchasing a car and widening these already wide spaces by heading for the open road. Chet Atkins ushers them through Appalachia (the original frontier) to Railroad Flats and, the next thing we know, there's Bruno, wearing a cowboy hat and gainfully employed. Ed, the nephew, is a little weird, and doesn't waste any time before moving on Eva, kissing and grabbing, but the following scenes—at work in the shop and the restaurant; at home doing dishes and watching American football; frolicking on a frozen lake; arranging furniture—represent the story's romantic interlude, Bruno and Eva's arcadian days on the frontier. There's something light there: friends, community, work, opportunity, freedom from political interference, freedom from stress. They easily get a loan (a low mortgage rate in the mid-1970s would be about 9 percent, and theirs would not be low) and immediately buy their dream home, and it's mobile.

So there's something light here in America, but even from the beginning, there's something dark here too. Ed's wolfish grin is the least of it. Words, but also the quiver of violence and threat, hang in the air. In the land adjacent to the garage, two farmers plow their fields in wary détente, each armed with a 12-gauge shotgun lest the one venture onto property disputed by the other. A rash of murders haunts the countryside, with reports of one farmer disappearing, tractor and all, never to return. And there are guns: scenes of rifles move from good-humored hunters to the hands of Bruno and Herr Scheitz as they close out the film with their crime spree.[68] There are no thugs striking, pulling, beating, and stomping. But there is that loan.

Turner's thesis on the frontier is remembered for its effusive expression of American exceptionalism, the republic's ability to realize a malleable set of democratic practices as forged in the experience of capitalist penetration. But hovering just between the lines and, often crystalizing right in front of us, is the historical fact of epochal violence that underwrites the frontier project. The "free land" (3) of the west was, of course, a world of sacked indigenous tribes, entire societies "honeycombed" (13) by inroads from the East, pried loose from one rival state preoccupied with its own project of imperial violence (France) and expropriated from another (Mexico) through a war of expansion. If, in Turner's citation of an "Italian economist" (it's Achille Loria), "the land which has no history reveals luminously the course of universal history" (11), then the basis for the revelation of this *course* is "colonial settlement" (ibid.) and its constant return to a condition that, as Marx would remind us, is always linked to accumulation: the "primitive" moments of "European development" (ibid.). All around the multicultural ebullience of the colliding cultures through which would arise "the formation of a composite nationality for the American people" (22), structuring and restraining the apparent freedom of movement and progressive horizons, is the blunt fact that the frontier is also one big "military training school" (15). The dominant relation to community and land is transience, desire yields an opportunistic nomadism, there is a propensity to the fake, what Lévi-Strauss ([1955] 2012) would notice a half-century later as the constant temporary of American architecture, always on the verge of being blown away by a stiff wind.[69]

The settled formation that would constitute the nodes of this expanding web of frontier trade routes is the country town. It is important that Bruno and Eva's American sojourn happens in one of these, the fictional Railroad Flats, as its name suggests, a once-busy junction for train commerce toward points west (explaining this is a scene in the film). Structurally, the counterpoint to the permanence of Berlin—founded in the 1200s and outlasting modern social catastrophe and political division with a bored yawn—is of course significant. But more centrally, the barren and flimsy space of the town that appears in the frame, and the fact of its nominal relation to commerce and movement (products and people on the way to someplace else), assert the specificity of the American country town as it intrudes upon and orders the sad story of Stroszek. A would-be center of commerce—and not, as Bruno craves, of community—the country town stands as an icon of American capitalism, a distribution point for the frontier, its front line of accumulation, and its enduring legacy as a social formation.

As Turner's expression of insight and nostalgia settled in and became a guiding thesis of American historiography, not everyone was as sanguine about the role of the frontier in the formation of an affirmative American identity. Thorstein Veblen, Turner's contemporary and another Progressive era son of the Upper Midwest, ditched the romanticism of frontier spirit and instead took a more material approach by focusing on the nature of American capitalism in the hinterlands. His laboratory (one that he knew intimately from his Norwegian immigrant childhood in southern Minnesota) was, precisely, the country town. A man about town of the Jazz Age (his most important work is from the 1910s and 1920s), Veblen makes the case that this community formation should be understood as an institution, one that "has had and continues to have a greater part than any other in shaping public sentiment and giving character to American culture" (1923, 417). Bastion of quaint values, plain speech, and whiteness, the country town's sway over the American imagination is still identifiable today, blandly conjured by politicians, columnists and the man on the street as the "real" America, in preposterous disdain for the reality of an intensely urban national culture ("country" music is made in Nashville, population seven hundred thousand). The historical emergence of this formation, for Veblen, has little to do with any sort of ethos absorbed from frontier heroism and do-it-yourself pluck. Rather, the country town stands as the point of capitalist accumulation for frontier expansion, ultimately a "product of the American land system" (Veblen 1915, 317). In formulaic terms, the country town complex effects a productive balance between rote (and enforced) expressions of "patriotism, public spirit, civic pride, and the like" in the service of "a businesslike endeavor to get something for nothing by engrossing as much as may be of the increment of land values due to the increase in population" (ibid.). So, "as an institution and engine of cultural discipline," the country town "never (hitherto) loses this character of real-estate speculation" (ibid.).

The country town system consolidates, with the frontier (to whose nomads and settlers it sells retail and logistical services), during the nineteenth century, reaches its "fullest efficiency" in the "north middle region" most effectively during the "period of large immigration from northern Europe" (Veblen 1915, 317–18), whence it stabilizes a labor-business model constituted by two groups, both at play in *Stroszek*. First, the new immigrant "tillers," that is, labor. And second, old American "businessmen" (318), that is, "men well at home in the common law of the land and directed to getting something for nothing at the expense of the foreign immigrants who were unfamiliar with the common law" (ibid.), in other words, newcomers "who could with great uniformity be relied on most meticulously to avoid all litigation under a system of law with which they had no acquaintance, before local magistrates (businessmen) whom they had no reason to trust, in a language which they did not understand" (ibid.). *Stroszek* will quickly become the twisted descendant of this historical boondoggle.

Like Turner, Veblen describes a system at its point of historical exhaustion. But even if "the material conditions are progressively drawing together into such shape that this plain country-town common sense will no longer work" (1923, 443), historical and cultural obsolescence are notoriously uneven processes. Just as the frontier, well closed by 1893, would continue to nourish cultural attitudes and underwrite aesthetic subgenres for another century and counting, so would the country town persist as a foundation of American ideology even as its population dwindles to a vast minority. Between the two, frontier and country town, we can perceive the tragic cultural-historical frame of Bruno's ballad and Eva's flight. Both spaces promise dreams, but their dreams are equally dead, or perhaps better, undead, living nightmares, always a little strange and here made stranger by relocating them in America's mid-1970s economic and cultural malaise. On the one hand, Bruno and Eva seek the freedom of the frontier, only to find simulacra, confinement, and menace. On the other hand, they seek the community of the country town, only to be taken in by slick grins and real-estate schemes. *Stroszek* is conventionally read as a comment on the American dream, the ethical platitude that equates hard work with economic advancement. The audience is always right, and this conventional interpretation is certainly correct. What's unconventional is how rigorous Herzog's portrait turns out to be.

"How are we going to pay for this?" It's an hour into the story, Bruno and Eva linger over morning coffee, looking slightly dejected, and Bruno's quiet question announces a narrative shift. A whimsical adventure with Ed and a metal detector has just closed off the narrative arc of immigrant optimism and now the reality of privation is beginning to set in. It's not a long way down, but the psychological exploration of the fall will be methodical, defining the final third of the film. A remarkable series of dialogues between Bruno and his interlocutors—his lover, his banker, and his friends—will trace this process and consolidate the grandeur of Bruno S.'s evocation of Wisconsin on the periphery of capitalism.

So "how are we going to pay for this?" and Eva attempts to cut him off. Bruno persists, patting the table as he rattles off in rhythm: "The TV set . . . the house . . . and then those contracts." It's the country town: "All in English, and the small print." Eva attempts to reassure, her English is "all right." Things are clearly going south and Bruno's tick, his tendency to talk, in a sort of declamatory manner, with his eyes closed, begins to take on symbolic portent. Soon he will begin to speak, with regularity, of being shut out in a number a senses. But here he continues, "I thought America would be different, and we could get rich quick." Eva interrupts, "Cut it out. . . . I can't listen anymore. . . . you can earn money here. . . . It's no problem at all. I'll take care of it, you'll see." Bruno, his eyes shut tight: "All right, you take care of it then. . . . For sure."

It's important to notice the complexity—libidinal, domestic, economic—of the interaction here. Bruno and Eva's migration, while motivated by financial distress in the broad sense, is inspired in the immediate sense by a desire to escape the depredations of overregulated sex work. But within months (probably weeks; the timeline is unclear), these same depredations return with a new face. Eva's promise to "take care of it" cuts to a scene at her waitress's job in the truck stop. A goofy, slightly wooden encounter takes place between her and a diner, a cowboy, er . . . trucker, Al, who propositions her to meet at his big rig—emblazoned, he explains, "Slippery When Wet"—after her shift.[70] She accepts. Back in the sex trade, Eva must now again produce the capital to liberate herself and Bruno from financial entanglement. And with foreclosure looming, this threat, if less directly than in Berlin, is also material: they are only a payment or two away from sleeping in a parked car.

The loan officer pays a visit. Eva's on the couch, grouchy, eating store-bought chips right from the bag, she's put on some weight. The banker knocks: a thin man in humongous 1970s glasses, feathered hair, astonishing cheap suit, somewhere between pinstripes and pimp. The actor has been recruited from another of Herzog's meditations on American capitalism, Scott McKain, the emcee of the auctioneering competition from *How Much Wood Would a Woodchuck Chuck*.[71] He's perfect for the role. All smiles and with saccharine flattery about their "beautiful" home, he quickly gets to the point. The point is money and the fact that they haven't been able to make payments. He's on their side—"we want to know if there's anything that we can do" and, while it pains him to deliver the news, it may come down to reprisals: "for example, your nice TV, um we, would, may have to, ah, come *remove* it," and "as a last resort, as the *very* last resort, um, we may have to take the home away." All this is put in the terms of help (Veblen: "the meritorious appearance of thrift" [1915, 318]), all of it as a way of lending time to delinquent borrowers. "We want to help," he affirms, and yet lest there be any misunderstanding, he immediately clarifies "but frankly, we *need* the money." The meeting comes to a surprising conclusion when Eva swoops in. Handing over several high-currency bills, she queries, with eyelashes and coquetry, "maybe this is enough?" and, while "usually we take checks or credit cards," the officer assures them that "this will do!" Bruno, declaring the visit "a pleasure and an honor," sees him out, thanking him again for the "friendly visit."

The domestic dynamic is depressingly familiar, an echo of Berlin, but clearly it's a repetition with a difference. Physical violence, the threat (and reality) of being kicked in the eye is now removed. But the extortionate and predatory elements of the relation between use value and exchange value remain. Complicating matters, this low-intensity conflict has taken on a more personal tone. The American dream assumes a nuclear family, and Bruno pays homage to this when they move into their home, happily singing about "the country life, without storm or strife, where the billy goat dances with his wife." In this context, Eva's informal profession is suddenly more productive and less tolerable than it was in their old life. This is the situation that frames the watershed moment of the film, Bruno's soliloquy, where his disappointments come crashing down and the failure of his striving is laid bare. Again we find him alone with Eva, in declamatory mode, the coffee replaced with a can of Old Style, and this time the issue isn't household expenses, but rather his soul. Money, in fact, seems to be symptomatic of something deeper. The discourse of making money and the fantasy of material security through affluence to be cultivated from the American country town was always Eva's. Bruno has followed Eva to the frontier in search of something that has clearly eluded him: solidarity, camaraderie, community. Not in the name of any political or material project, simply in the name of survival. We can perceive the distant silhouette of his longing, from the very beginning of the film, when Bruno bade farewell to his cellmates, declaring, "I don't want to leave." This desire looms large

Figures 6A and 6B. The Berlin pimps extract cash from Eva (Eva Mattes) (above). The Wisconsin banker extracts cash from Eva (below). *Stroszek* (Herzog 1977).

now. "They're closing all the doors on him [in keeping with his out-of-frame gaze, Bruno often refers to himself in the third person], and oh so politely." America is an illusion: here "Bruno's getting pushed aside as if he didn't exist." A more serious problem begins to come to the fore as he accuses Eva of keeping a cruel distance from him. She reminds him that here he is free from attacks and now nobody kicks him. His response is devastating (also, says Herzog, largely improvised), worth quoting at length: "No, not physically. Here they do it spiritually. . . . In the reformatory it was just like here. If someone wet his bed—this was under the Nazis—instead of hanging the sheet on the clothesline, they used to make the person who did it stand holding it up like this [raising his arms and standing] all day and the teacher would stand behind him with a stick. And boy, if his arms started getting tired from standing so long, he got a beating. . . . They hurt you openly then. Today they do it differently. They don't go like this [kicks], or like this [strikes]. [Now whispering] They do it ever so politely, and with a smile. It's much worse. You can smell it in the air, and you can see it too. Who knows what fate will bring. . . . The prison doors are wide open, and we're not in Germany any more. You've got to be careful here."

A relation of problematic economies is now in the open. On the one hand, there is a sexual problem. Any exchange of intimacy between Eva and Bruno has evaporated, he accuses her of despising him, and the fact that they aren't sleeping together is revealed. On the other hand, linked to the first but, perhaps of greater structural significance, there is a productivity problem. The disintegrating exchange of intimacy is overdetermined by another imbalance: the fact that Eva can earn a living and Bruno cannot. While it's never clear whether Bruno earns more than complimentary beer as a mechanic's apprentice with the goofball Ed (whose shop features few instances of repair activity, but one memorable scene in which Ed extracts his own necrotic tooth with a monkey wrench), it is abundantly clear that Eva has the skills and the wherewithal to open revenue streams whenever necessary. This new set of conditions shatters their interdependency. If in Berlin, Eva needed Bruno to provide the security of kindness (if not physical protection, for which he was incapable), in Wisconsin the situation is reversed. And this is not a role that Eva is inclined to play. In a concise sociocritical reading of *Stroszek*, Victor Enyutin aptly describes the larger implications of this new dynamic. Bruno, with his hesitations and mistrust before the backslapping and glad-handing of the country town, seems to have instinctively perceived the family resemblance between Berlin and Railroad Flats, where only the style of intimidation and the credentialization of authority has changed: "in a new world it's not direct extortion of money but it is financial trickery of extortion in a masked form (including seduction into financial dependency)" (Enyutin 2011).[72] "Here they do it spiritually," says Bruno, who, Enyutin proposes, "understood the difference pretty quickly, but was shocked by the strength and cynicism of power in the new land not less than he was back in Europe" (ibid.). Thus, while the overarching fact of exploitation represents a continuity between the two societies, the characteristics of this abuse are not the same, and it affects the protagonists in distinct ways.

Eva adjusts nimbly and, indeed, is able to mobilize her skills transactionally (her sociability, her sexuality) within a country town capitalism. She is even able to leverage the puritanism implied by the American dream, playing on its hypocrisies—that is, following Veblen, its greatest strengths—for profit. In Berlin she wore the uniform of a prostitute, and this semiformal work yielded dependency and abuse: she received only a portion of her earnings, risking a beating by going freelance with the Turks in the trick that would pay for their transatlantic journey. Now in America she wears a disguise, a waitress, whose tricks on the side, with no middleman to take a cut, transform her into a consultant, an entrepreneur; in short, a businessman. Free to negotiate her own fees and choose her clients, the revenues from which are clearly enough to maintain a small mobile property, and engaging in the kind of profitable business that the country town ethos must at once denounce and tolerate, Eva turns out be the good capitalist, a minor cog within the American dream machine. And with this, along with the reduction of her masters from fists to feathered hair ("I'll handle him," she says to Bruno of the banker—unimaginable in Berlin), it suddenly turns out that her need for Bruno's companionship has withered. As Enyutin puts it, "But this work for herself made her somehow unable to feel that she cares about Bruno—it made her grow out of the taste for enjoying him disinterestedly, to tolerate his awkwardness, his particularity" (2011), in other words, his marginalization. The next time we see Eva, she is again accompanied by the soft-country guitar of Chet Atkins, making up her face for a night out, then crossing a parking lot, and then locating her truck. Bruno comes looking for her—asking the restaurant hostess in his non-English for "Eva" in a voice that he once used with his pet myna bird—and eventually makes his way to "Slippery When Wet," where cowboy Al invites him to "get a shot of the foxy beaver back here, I got a surprise for ya', look at this!" Of course it's Eva, in the cab's bunk area with another trucker. Terse words are exchanged as she announces she's leaving with the truckers for Vancouver.[73] An American nomadic, and that's the last we see of Eva.[74]

Bruno, on the other hand, has always depended on the kindness of institutions, a social safety net that, however impersonal, even abusive, he mastered at a young age, whose cruelties he fully understood, and whose embrace he could turn to in times of need. This is the meaning of his melancholy goodbye to the reformatory prison, and, more consolingly, his interview with the doctor in the neonatal ward. Life in Berlin left him marginalized, but not out in the cold. As Bruno himself puts it, "today they do it differently," and a central preoccupation of *Stroszek* is the quiet viciousness that underwrites the country-town portrait. Bruno's soliloquy cuts to the garage, where he is being accosted by an Old Style–fueled Ed and a giggling Eli. Ed is in a lather over the desirability of Eva and drunkenly proposing the vulgar terms of a girlfriend-swap to Bruno: "You take Eva, until I find, something better, that is to you. . . . And then I get Eva, and you can have whatever I find," he chortles, all hyena and pervert. It's a set of long takes, filled with profanities, the hardest scene of the film. Ed jerks around, bragging about his sexual prowess and launching into an absurd coital dance: thrusting hips and shouting, "hit the penny! hit the nickel! hit the dime! hit the quarter! . . . hit the quarter, hit the quarter, fuck the small change . . . that's the way she plays that game" and so on (Herzog reports that this was improvised, and, I'll admit, it is pretty impressive to be able to just come up with that; Clayton Szalpinksi—the auto mechanic who plays the character of Ed—is a natural). Bruno spends the length of these shots wedged between the soda machine and the wall, his face in profile and largely obscured by his once-proud cowboy hat, a stressful cigarette between his fingers, his eyes closed shut for the entire scene, essentially cowering, his interjections met by Ed with cruel outbursts of laughter. *Here they do it spiritually* and you can almost feel the beating as he winces. (More doubling: the scene can be productively compared to his humiliation at the hands of the Berlin thugs.) The dialogue is nonsensical, with Ed offering propositions about Eva in English, and Bruno, clearly distraught, essentially shouting, in German, toward the wall "Bruno's on the outside looking in . . . coming to America, just to watch his whole world fall apart!" His romantic partner having exchanged life in a mobile

Figure 7. Ed proposes a swap for Eva; Bruno "coming to America, just to watch his whole world fall apart." *Stroszek* (Herzog 1977).

home for life on the road, chin-deep in bad debt, Bruno finds himself surrounded by a community of individualist depravity, with his American friend (and host) making jokes about Eva-swapping. Up against a wall, Bruno's portrait traces the profile of a broken man.

Like the Berlin street thugs, the banker rings twice, and this second visit will deliver Bruno's coup de grâce. Retreating from Eva's rejection, we cut back to the mobile home, where Bruno sits drunk, alone, belligerent, in the dark, having moved from suspicious to cynical. As the loan officer unfolds the notices of foreclosure and begins a viscous explanation, Bruno interrupts, "I can't say I know the language, but something smells mighty fishy to me." Signing, with a violent flourish, he growls, "Here, so you don't have any more sleepless nights!" He later shares a smoke with Herr Scheitz, concluding, "now he [Bruno] is hanging in the tree, and they'll throw him to the dogs."[75] Those are his last significant words of the film. He hasn't reached bottom, however, as his decline bumps along through a series of indignities. These scenes will represent the film's most memorable images.

First comes the auction. There's a kind of cold that possesses the upper Midwest in late November that defies description to those who haven't experienced it firsthand. This is the climate for the film's denouement.

The horizon is flat, the sky is gray, and people in shapeless coats stand with a lock-kneed, hunched-shouldered posture that is more reflex than strategy (it doesn't work, you still freeze). Breath billows out in vapors and it is important that there is no snow: ugly intensifies the cold. The loan officer stands before a small, unsmiling crowd, several in the group are dressed in the blaze orange costume of deer hunters. Alongside him is a man in a cowboy hat, it's the real-life Colonel Ralph Wade, world-champion auctioneer.[76] As Bruno drifts through the crowd, they present three objects of sale: a console television, a refrigerator, and a mobile home. The colonel's rapid-fire patter quickly sells the items for bargain prices ($5800 for the house; $400 for the television, they cost more back then). Herr Scheitz shakes his fist at the vultures, the crowd dissipates, and Bruno, back to the camera, stands alone before his erstwhile dream home. The film's strategy of doubled repetitions continues, as the same insouciant music—it's an old Edison recording—that greeted the arrival of the home before an ecstatic Eva returns as the home continues its nomadic journey and is pulled away by a truck, exit screen right.[77] The take holds for nearly a full minute as Bruno stares into empty space. It's an iconic shot, a good example of Herzog's interest in "directing landscapes": the inner landscape of Bruno, the frozen plane of his predicament, abandoned and bereft, wedged between frontier and country town.

This humiliation provokes a crime spree. The following shot is an abrupt cut to a full-screen framing of Bruno at the wheel of the station wagon and Herr Scheitz literally riding shotgun, looking militant and brandishing an impossibly outsized 12-gauge (the transition invariably evokes big laughs: the audience is always right). Ammunition is spread across the dashboard. It's not about riches, but rather justice. "We're going to put a stop to this vile conspiracy!" declares Scheitz. But Bruno is a man without a plan: the bank that they expect to rob happens to be closed; a hold-up of the barber next door yields thirty-two dollars; Herr Scheitz is quickly arrested at the grocery store across the street, but Bruno somehow goes unnoticed by the authorities and slips out with a frozen turkey. He returns to the garage, grabs some beers, and swaps the wagon for an old tow truck. A road trip in reverse, he will now retrace the steps of his original cross-country trek.

This cascade of American icons—the bank robbery, Bruno's stubborn cowboy hat, the station wagon, the gun, the bullets, the quintessential Main

Figures 8A and 8B. Bruno watches as his mobile home is repossessed. *Stroszek* (Herzog 1977).

Street, the turkey, the tow truck, the truck stops, Chet Atkins (again), the highway, the frontier itself—spills out into a strange and tragic closing sequence and yet one that is something of a logical step in Herzog's grammar of images, here at some of his aesthetically most powerful. In both suggestion and literal citation we'll catch glimpses of the original Stroszek's windmills and fireworks (from *Signs of Life*), the inmates' rebellion (from

Even Dwarfs), the nightmare of the drifting, spinning raft overwhelmed by monkeys (from *Aguirre*), even an oblique gesture to the oracle (from *Heart of Glass*). Consolidating this Herzogian iconography is the specificity of its American setting, and after a misty drive through the Great Smoky Mountains, Bruno's quest will end at an indigenous village. It's Cherokee, North Carolina, a reservation town that traffics in a tourist-show indigenism as an engine of is local economy.[78] As he pulls up, his noisy transmission startles a mascot, looking slightly tired in outlandish headdress, standing beside a souvenir shop called The Indian Store. The truck now on fire, Bruno ducks into a sterile sandwich counter where he has an inexplicable interaction with a German-speaking American. Reciting Bruno's personal tragedies—no car, no girlfriend, no house—the oracle concludes, "I wouldn't worry about it." Bruno concurs, they raise a toast. Everything, now, will go in circles. Leaving the restaurant, Bruno proceeds to set the tow truck in gear and leave it spinning in the parking lot. Carrying his gun and his long-thawed turkey, he crosses past the mascot chief and enters a kind of fun-house arcade, abandoned, that advertises "Educated Animals." It's one of those tourist traps where you pay a coin and a small farm animal does some rote trick—a duck plays a drum; a rabbit boards a fire engine; one chicken plays a piano, another one dances the barnyard shuffle—for its food and your entertainment. Activating the scenarios and reviewing the animal displays, Bruno makes his way to a closed ski chairlift, which he powers on. He boards a chair emblazoned with the arcane message *Is This Really Me!* and ascends, cross-cut with the educated animals hard at their tasks. After a round trip, a long shot traces the arc of the chairlift cable, following Bruno for a couple of seconds and then moving up the lift, leaving him out of frame. A single gunshot rings out. Back down on the street, it's chaos, sirens blare, squad cars have been scrambled, a fire truck works on the still burning abandoned vehicle, and an indigenous policeman calls for an electrician, uttering the film's immortal closing words "We can't stop the dancin' chicken." The film closes with a montage of the various captive animals, a rousing blues harmonica soundtrack by Sonny Terry, no interruption, no credits, and a long, long take, of the dancing chicken, strutting frenetically for scraps of sustenance.

The crew refused to shoot the scenes of the educated animals. In his DVD interview with Norman Hill, Herzog speaks at length about the negative climate on set, a general pessimism among the crew about the prospects of the film. He confesses to perhaps exaggerating this "bad mood" in his memory (Scott McKain, in his recollection of the shoot, gives the impression of a generally affirmative camaraderie on set), but, whatever the case, Herzog recalls that he had to film the educated animals himself, deeming it "some of the best I ever shot in my life" (*Stroszek*, DVD director's commentary). Like Aguirre's raft overrun by monkeys, it's a great metaphor, although one whose object is unclear. "A big metaphor, without knowing, metaphor for what" (ibid.).[79] There is something about the unfolding of this final sequence, its elegant balance of intersecting circles—the sirens, the truck, the chair lift, the chicken dance—colliding with the riot of sound (the police sirens reverberating off the fun-house bells and whistles morphing into Sonny Terry's harmonica) and color (the muted tones of winter landscape interrupted by the garish primary hues of the arcade) that is at once magnificent (simply "big," Herzog calls it) and disquieting. Its overarching sentiment is very much in the spirit of earlier scenes, such as the dueling farmers with their tractor-mounted rifles, plowing their fields in mutual, glowering hostility: we laugh in amazement—it's common to see *Stroszek* referred to as a comic film—yet also a little on edge, unsure about our laughter. In keeping with Herzog's aphorism on the topic, we are right to be unsure. Indeed, as Daniel Crown points out about the crew's rebellion against these final shots, "by being disturbed by the given metaphor, the dissenters themselves became its supreme, somewhat ironic justification" (2009).

While the meaning of this final sequence is open to interpretation, one certainty is that America is the cultural context that gives it life. We've seen the vast catalog of Americanisms, from the legend of the frontier to the plain-speech sadism of the country town, and now, finally, the educated animals, straight out of Wall Drug, adding a final layer of distortion to this twisted reinterpretation of the American dream. A surreal descent into despair, the closing montage is also weirdly beautiful and paradoxically consoling. While everything points in the direction of failure, *Stroszek* somehow never becomes a feel-bad movie (that said, apparently if it hits the wrong way, it can leave the spectator feeling pretty terrible: Ian Curtis, the lead singer of Joy Division, reportedly watched *Stroszek* shortly before he hanged himself).[80] In Herzog's interpretation of his own film, the relation that Bruno's character suggests between defeat and America is beside the point. Something about *Stroszek* provokes Herzog, utterly sincere in his performativity, to insist on his love for America and assert that the setting is merely casual. The setting is American, yes, but the story could have happened anywhere. As he puts it, "For me *Stroszek* is about shattered hopes, which is clearly a universal theme, and it would not really matter if they had moved from Berlin to France or Sweden" (Herzog and Cronin 2002, 144). And besides, he loves the country town. Veblen's land of bullshit, is, for Herzog, precisely the opposite. "In particular the Midwest, which I consider the best part of America. People are very kind, very big hearts, down to earth, hard-working, no bullshit, nothing like Hollywood, nothing like the crazy New York or whatever. Good people, solidly on the ground, generous, everything that's good about America you find in the Midwest. And always the very best come from there, Hemingway from Kansas [Oak Park, Illinois, actually], Marlon Brando from also the Midwest somewhere [Omaha], Bob Dylan from Minnesota, that's where the good ones come from" (*Stroszek*, DVD commentary).[81] Placing to one side the fact that his entire pantheon of Midwesterners left the region for good as soon as they were able (and the fact that he doesn't name the one midwestern titan who actually stuck around: Prince), this kind of praise makes a regular appearance in Herzog's long history of interviews, and he genuinely appreciates a certain can-do spirit that he perceives in the American Midwest.

And yet there's a strong dose of circumspection there, a fact that Herzog himself notes in the same set of director's commentaries. "I like it, I like the country, I like America, but in some sort of an ambivalent way" (ibid.). While the comments on his filming heap unqualified praise on the everyday people who agreed to help the production through their logistical support and their images (most of the cast are "found," nonprofessional actors), they emerge reconstructed as garish predators in the film: Ed, Al, the banker, the auctioneer, and so on; even the nice guys, the hunters, are out slaying defenseless animals for sport.[82] And if he speaks effusively about the great expanse and energy of the American landscape that he represents with such aesthetic insight, the setting itself—territory conquered in the brutal Indian wars—is a modern workshop in homicide: inspired by neighboring Plainfield, Wisconsin (the actual shooting location was Nekoosa, about thirty miles away), a nondescript country town that happens to be the hometown of Ed Gein, notorious murderer and necrophile.[83] *Stroszek*, the story, reflects this ambivalence too. In a way, and in keeping with the baroque sentiments of Herzog's aesthetics, it's a study of the absent object of nostalgia, a feeling of longing for an American dream that never really was, a desire for community and upward mobility whose impulses cancel each other out, hemmed in by capitalist relations of production and the form of conflict that they assume. We can see it in Turner himself, where the frontier is, on the one hand, freedom from old social hierarchies, and, on the other hand, military training school. And we can see it in the ghost of Veblen haunting Herzog, the way in which his discourse of plain speech and "no bullshit" can't help but reconvert into the depredations of fine print exploitation. As Jonathan Beller puts it, in a study on cinema no less, capitalism has a way of colonizing even our dreams, infecting us with wishes that are always already obsolete (2006, 15, 20). Herzog's act of resistance, the liberation of dreams, is to let the nature of capitalist social relations run their course for all to see.

Enclosed by history's pressure cooker, Bruno and Eva escape to freedom, America, the frontier. But they soon discover that the frontier is a myth, an object of desire, El Dorado (Eva: "everybody makes money there"), its truth not hidden (myths don't lie) but wrapped in veils of gauze, its sharp outlines obscured, edges to be revealed in the social logic of the country town. There's something at odds between making money and making community, and Bruno learns the hard way that the truth of the frontier is not shelter—a home of one's own—but real estate, not cooperation but accumulation. The myth that Bruno pursues was obsolete at its narrative emergence, an ideological structure whose ability to correspond with appearances only could be sustained a century before, during the moment of America's great territorial expansion. In Bruno's America, the ideological structure is of course alive and well, but, in keeping with Herzog's baroque, now repositioned at its moment of unstoppable decline. In the wake of the Kennedy-era's quaint faith in the language of "the frontier" and its ability to shroud the blunt fact of imperial practice—a sentiment that Turner foresaw. "He would be a rash prophet who should assert that the expansive character of American life has now entirely ceased" ([1893] 1921b, 37)—the 1970s would make a mockery of the frontier thesis and its anodyne truths. American frontier expansion, in the literal sense, had just experienced its comeuppance in a failed war of colonial occupation, the downward slide from the Tet Offensive (1968) to its humiliating retreat from Saigon (1975), setting the tone for a grim decade. Smelling blood, oil-producing countries provoked shocks that quadrupled the price of petroleum, inflation shot up from 5 percent to 10 percent by mid-decade, with unemployment sitting at 8 percent and growing. The crime rate climbed one year after the next, hard drugs harmonized with heavy metal, a humiliated president staggered—often drunk—out of office, and the neoliberal revolution began paving the way to a Reagan-Thatcher-Pinochet decade that would gut the working class. By any measure outside metaphysical civil rights, it was a tough bicentennial, the transition from decades of postwar economic and political expansion to a long, slow decline. Truisms of the American dream, such as intergenerational advancement, were falling apart, and the old rural zones of open spaces and country towns were some of the most notable victims.

A still-young Herzog seems to sense this mood, and he captures it in *Stroszek*. If a quarter century later he can reinterpret *Stroszek* as something of a celebration of his beloved America, it is at the same time telling that he regularly calls it a eulogy (Herzog and Cronin 2002, 144; see also *Stroszek*, DVD director's commentary), with its connotations of recent death, and characterizes its mood ("it doesn't have anything optimistic about it," DVD commentary) as a product of story and not context. But the 1970s Herzog was a bit more direct. In a 1979 workshop with Roger Ebert, he states that "Americans . . . believe that they are normal, that they make sense, and that the *rest* of the world is exotic. They do not seem to understand that they are the *most* exotic people in the world right now" (with Ebert 1979, 10). *Stroszek* is his study of this exoticism, this frontier exceptionalism and its effect on a subject, whose marginalization is in fact the sign that he is, like Kaspar Hauser, "the *only* one who makes sense, the *only* one who is dignified, who has a radical human dignity" (ibid., 7). Herzog thus joins those quintessentially American genres of road movie, immigrant epic, and western in an attempt, as he puts it, "to define my position about this country and its culture" (ibid., 11).[84] While it wouldn't be Herzog if this position were definable in any transparent way, the circulation of images in the film has less to do with the pragmatic spirit of plain speech, and far more to do with the fraudulence of dreams that revolve around making money. The cowboys and Indians that populate the film are references not to any lived history, but to hokey, profiteering performances of that imagined history: *Bonanza*, tourist traps. Everything stands rotting, on the precipice of exhaustion: Railroad Flats, Ed explains, *used to* be a center of rail traffic, now just a cluster of decaying outhouses (in the British sense) surrounding a tangle of unused track. Always already exhausted, the living frontier thesis sees everything as transitory opportunities for profit. There's something light there, to be sure, not least the promise of a new start. But there's something dark there too. It's not veiled: Herzog places his country town setting of rural Wisconsin among "those focal points in the United States . . . very strange points in the United States where every line, every thread, everything seems to come together . . . all the nightmares come together" (*Stroszek*, DVD commentary), a family portrait of grim geographies that also includes "Wall Street, Disney World, Las Vegas, and San Quentin" (ibid.).

The chicken that closes the film can mean a lot of things: the treadmill fate of work in capitalist society; the sadistic relation between profit and pain, pain and entertainment; an absurdist take on the condition of Sisyphus; Bruno's predicament (it's hard to miss the parallel between the customer's relation to the dancing chicken and the Berlin thugs' relation to Bruno). Whatever it means, it closes the film and stands at the frontier of a world whose cultural violence and fraud—Cherokee is not Cherokee but a garish performance of what tourists demand of the remnants of a fantasized Cherokee culture—is there to startle at every turn. That chicken, provoking laughter and suicides, however we want to interpret it, should probably be approached with great apprehension. As Herzog puts it, "If the devil existed, he would appear in the form of a chicken" (Herzog 2014f, 21). If the chicken riffs on, which is not to say represents, the maddening, dehumanizing individualism of capitalist social relations, what more can we turn to and take hold of against its menace? Herzog is fond of reminding his interlocutors of the magical element of the human condition, our ability to tell stories, stories that can reach out across centuries and world-systems and bring you to your knees, confronting you with the point of it all. "You are not alone anymore. The sense of not being alone anymore, that's very, very essential for me" (Beckman and Herzog 2007). So what life raft can we grasp against the hostility of the world? In the middle of its tragic cacophony of bells and whistles and dancing chickens, the film itself embeds an instinctive cry in response. See figures 9A and 9B.

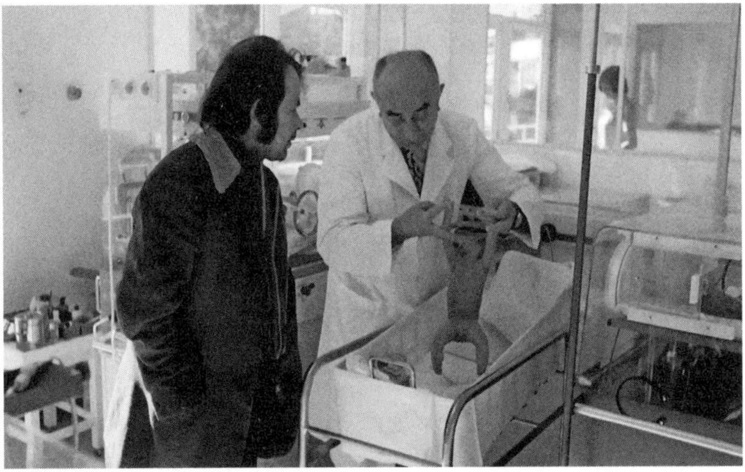

Figures 9A and 9B. The apish, prehensile grip of the newborn. Above, Herzog has said about *Stroszek*, "the humanity, the dignity, the mystery of what we are . . . needs to be in this film here" *Stroszek* (Herzog 1977). Below, Herzog (left) interviewed in his apartment by Erwin Keusch, with poster. *I Am My Films* (Weisenborn and Keusch 1978).

"I'm planning something geographical . . ."

> The stench followed me for a whole decade.
>
> —Werner Herzog, 2002

> We now know that Fitzcarrald and Herzog are like each other.
>
> —Evaristo Nugkuag, 1979

> But here it is standard expectation, and standard behavior, and somehow the—I don't know—the jungle sweats it out. It's not even obscene. It is . . . probably some fertility or whatever that's going on here in the jungle.
>
> —Werner Herzog, 1980

After coming within a whisker of being executed on charges of espionage, Carlos Fermín Fitzcarrald disappeared into the remote jungles of southeastern Peru. This was around 1878, the very dawn of a chaotic era remembered as the "rubber boom," three decades of almost unimaginable resource extraction from the Amazon River basin. The commodity price would subsequently and steadily climb to feed an international industrial market and then spike with the emergence of the great vulcanizing machines of Michelin and Goodyear. In their wake, gaudy fortunes in the precious sap were accumulated with such speed that entire South American cities were reinvented: titans of the industry established credit instruments in Belém; eight hundred miles upriver, the soggy town of Manaus—until then recognized only for a series of spectacular race wars—would transform as if by magical incantation into a bastion of European finery; another thousand miles west, ramshackle houses in tiny Iquitos would proliferate over its banks like mushrooms after a midnight thunderstorm as it went from a sleepy canoe dock to a rough-and-tumble frontier boomtown, a sort of Deadwood, or Potosí, on stilts. Fitzcarrald was at the lightly exploited edge of this main channel of rubber activity, fleeing Iquitos for the jungles hundreds of miles to the south. The son of an American sailor and a Peruvian aristocrat, and still only a teenager, he took his rudimentary maps, his polyglot heritage (Spanish, English, Quechua, likely Portuguese), his charm (he was something of a man about town), and his will into the Madre de Dios watershed, in those days a largely unexplored labyrinth of rivers, streams, and wetlands. "Largely unexplored," that is, in the industrial development sense. Below Cusco, the old Inca cosmopolis, and above Puerto Maldonado, an incipient riverbank settlement, the Madre de Dios complex of the late nineteenth century was well known by many people and teemed with a welter of human life that included more than a dozen indigenous groups of various linguistic profiles, small bands of European settlers, gritty traders, and ad hoc rubber tappers from a wide range of national and ethnic heritage (Peruvian, Brazilian, Bolivian, Spanish, Chinese).

The details of what happened to Fitzcarrald during the subsequent decade are not entirely clear, but we know that it involved the quiet accumulation of resources and power through shrewd alliance building, intercultural negotiation, marriage and arms trading.[85] In his 1942 account, the writer Ernesto Reyna tells of a fantastic origins story, reporting that during these missing years, settlers began to "speak of a 'white Indian' from the headwaters of the Ucayali, who appeared before the Campas as the Son of the Sun [*hijo del Sol*]" and that various tribes with whom he sojourned lauded his virtue and his example (1942, 21). Reyna cites a report of the Franciscan priest and government emissary Gabriel Sala that reads, "In the year 1888, the Campas were notified that an Amachengua had appeared . . . a reincarnation of the Inca Juan Santos Atahualpa. The tribes undertook a long march and met at the indicated site, where they found a 'white chuncho' [Indian] dressed in the customary way of the savages, but with greater sumptuousness, carrying in his hand a carbine of the latest model and bandoliers of cartridges like necklaces. He spoke the Campa language and told them that 'Father Sun had sent him with a message, that the errant tribes should live like civilized men, forming villages each with its own church. And that the man whom they were destined to obey in the world, as the representative of the Sun, was Carlos Fitzcarrald'" (21–22).[86]

Even if the outlines of these rather generic accounts are true—the rumors of a white Indian, the long march to hear his message, the linguistic fluency, the claim to a divine communiqué, *el hijo del Sol*—there is simply no way that this Ashéninka-speaking group took Fitzcarrald for a mythical savior; indeed Sala, Reyna's source, says as much explicitly, noting the open disdain that the Campas felt for this "false God . . . with or without whiskers" (1897, 141). In other words, they had seen his kind before. But what is certainly true is that Fitzcarrald demonstrated an impressive talent for negotiating indigenous antagonisms and ambitions and that he spent the 1880s parlaying that strength into a virtual stranglehold on rubber tapping and supply chains in the resource-rich forests of the upper Ucayali. He became filthy rich. His twenty-room mansion was the estate of a veritable *gamonal*—the Peruvian pejorative for new-money, semifeudal landowners whose social abuses were particularly notable—complete with a surrounding community of serfs, Chinese gardeners, and a warehouse full of imported delicacies.[87] Known for his affinity for European culture, he sent his children to study in Paris—truly an incredible trip from backwater Amazonia—and stocked his riverboats with the finest French wine (Varese 2004, 124–25). His riches went from filthy to astronomical when, in 1891, he tapped local indigenous knowledge to open up a new *varadero*, or portage, between two river tributaries, consolidating a monopoly over the region. To get the new route started, he had his slaves disassemble a steam-powered riverboat and haul it over the newly opened land passage. The massive hull took two months to transport. Now indisputably what Brown and Fernández (1991) call the "most powerful" (63) rubber baron of the Madre de Dios, and what Gray describes as the "richest . . . 'cauchero' (rubber baron) in the whole Ucayali region" (2004, 221), Fitzcarrald's life was cut short six years later while aboard a steamship that got tangled up in the rapids. He drowned, at least according to one of the legends, attempting to save the life of a business partner.[88] While I have found no evidence that he included opera among his passions for European culture, the meteoric trajectory of his life and the poetic justice of his tragic death certainly had something operatic about it.

Werner Herzog has a long-standing relationship with the opera, although not in any nostalgic sense: in an interview printed in the audience program for an opera that he himself staged, he remarks, "The opera? No, I never go. . . . In truth I feel much more comfortable on a soccer field" (Fancelli 1989). Alleged snobbishness aside, the form's grandeur, malleability, even interdisciplinarity, a theatrical world in which speech is song, clearly appeal to the director, and Herzog has become inextricably committed to the opera as both institution and discourse. From his earliest interviews, he cites Wagner and Verdi as sources of inspiration, and opera plays an important role in the soundtrack of many of his films. Beginning in 1986 with Busoni's *Doktor Faust* (a 1920s-era, unfinished masterpiece), which he staged and directed at the venerable Teatro Comunale di Bologna, Herzog has directed more than two dozen operas, to positive reviews, with especially prolific activity during the 1990s. His 1989 codirection of Verdi's rarely performed *Giovanna d'Arco* (1845) was also staged as an opera film for BBC television, a rather static exterior view of the production that recalls the long takes of his mid-1970s documentaries, especially the auctioneers in *How Much Wood Would a Woodchuck Chuck* (1976), although unfortunately with an effect more soporific than hypnotic (the film gives the sense that you really had to be there in person).[89] He would eventually declare an essential contradiction between opera and cinema, stating that the two are "as incompatible as cat and dog" (2009).[90] Nevertheless, he continues the relationship quite explicitly and years later went on to shoot a more intimate, interior view of opera in *Die Verwandlung der Welt in Musik: Bayreuth vor der Premiere* (*The Transformation of the World into Music*, 1996), a documentary that follows the preparations for the Bayreuther Festspiele annual summer music celebration of Richard Wagner's operas, for which Herzog had previously staged the influential *Lohengrin* (1850). In 2002, he prepared a short for the English National Opera, a remarkable hybrid of Puccini, modernist style, and ethnographic cinema: a four-minute recording of the genre's most beautiful duet, "O soave fanciulla" from *La bohème* (1895), over an abstracted wedding ceremony in tribal southern Ethiopia. While not opera per se, *Tod für fünf Stimmen* (*Death for Five Voices*, 1995), his imaginative documentary on Carlo Gesualdo—a Renaissance composer and pioneer of tonal theory—has an operatic feel in subject and ambiance.

But Herzog had never even attended an actual opera until he worked on one, and this opportunity came via his cinematic rendering of the life of Fitzcarrald.[91] And with his commitment to locations at once authentic, unusual, and often foreboding, it comes as little surprise that his first experience with opera would happen not in Bologna, Vienna, or Milan, but at the periphery of European culture: in South America, on the Amazon, at the celebrated, and notorious, Teatro Amazonas, the opera house of Manaus, Brazil. Herzog begins his loose rendering of Fitzcarrald's life there, now transformed into music and the more

Figure 10. Sketch (Henning von Gierke) from the program of Herzog's first opera direction, Busoni's *Doktor Faust* at the Teatro Comunale di Bologna, 1986. The *menhir* stones below the crucifix are a secret reference to *Fitzcarraldo*. Courtesy of the Archivio Storico del Museo della Musica, Bologna. Photograph: Natalie Lund.

operatic title of *Fitzcarraldo* (1982), the story of the rise and fall of the Irish immigrant's son, Brian Sweeney Fitzgerald, nom-de-guerre "Fitzcarraldo."

Fitzcarraldo is Herzog's best-known film. And while there is nothing in his oeuvre that measures up in terms of scale, we can probably speak of a broader operatic turn in Herzog's work spanning a number of his releases from the era. Evolving from his mid-1970s features, this turn is more of a mood than an actual point of reference, one that inhabits large pageants and small documentaries alike for the next two decades. During this period we can perceive an intensification of the discourse of struggle apparent from his earliest work: a range of films from this period will revolve around man's struggle against land and gravity, as protagonists push and pull objects and bodies up and over hills and mountains. But as with *Aguirre*, these travails are not limited to the film story. They govern the story of production as well. Alongside this newly intensified struggle within Herzog's work is the emergence of a certain commercial viability that—while Herzog approaches it somewhat gingerly, continuing to shoot obscure little documentaries alongside the big features—will underwrite the mere thinkability of a massive project like *Fitzcarraldo*. *Nosferatu: Phantom der Nacht* (*Nosferatu the Vampyre*, 1979), a remake of F. W. Murnau's classic *Nosferatu*, shot with an eye toward its international release and with a prominent cast—Isabelle Adjani, Bruno Ganz, and, of course, Kinski, as the vampire—most immediately establishes this new marketability.[92] But the better aesthetic point of reference, capturing the intensified mood of struggle and defiance of gravity, is one of his American films: *La Soufrière—Warten auf eine unausweichliche Katastrophe* (*La Soufrière*, 1977).

La Soufrière is a curious little film. A bit of a failure in more ways than one, its aesthetic and thematic garble somehow saves itself from itself by resonating with its own narrative of unmet expectations: you leave it somewhat baffled, but not having had a bad time. Its original German subtitle telegraphs this ambivalence, translating literally as "waiting for an inevitable catastrophe."[93] For about a year between the springs of 1976 and 1977, the Guadeloupian volcano, La Grande Soufrière, became increasingly unstable, culminating in a series of phreatic eruptions from July to January. Alarm spread, especially because it lay in the shadow of another nearby French overseas department, Martinique, whose own volcanic formation, Mount Pelée, had rumbled ominously and then exploded earlier in the century. Unevacuated, Martinique's entire port town of Saint-Pierre was swallowed in a flash of hot mud. Thirty thousand people perished, making the 1902 eruption the worst volcanic disaster of modern times. The tragedy was decades past, yet still fresh enough to inhabit living memory, and residents began to abandon the low country areas of Guadeloupe after the first explosions in July. By August, the evacuation was made official, and more than seventy thousand people, including the entire town of Basse Terre, were ordered to leave. An international news report made mention of a solitary peasant who refused to move. Herzog heard the story and immediately felt compelled to speak to this man, arranging plans for a shoot smack in the middle of an impending apocalypse, and, hastily agreeing in principal to a contract with a German television station, whose single term was that it would be executed if he were to "come back alive" (Herzog and Cronin 2002, 149). He arrived in Guadeloupe with two jeeps, two cameras, and a three-man crew of himself, his longtime cinematographer Jörg Schmidt-Reitwein, and another cameraman, Ed Lachman, a collaborator on *Stroszek*. The resulting work went on to win Best Short Film at the German Film Awards and holds a central place in the legend of Herzog.

A little jumpy in its narrative structure, the film tells a series of not-always-resonant stories. Much is made—and most of what is remembered by fans—of the fact of imminent danger to the filmmakers and their correlating bravery (or lunacy): sulfuric smoke billows ominously from the peak; the wind changes direction and we see Herzog hurry toward the camera, away from encroaching wisps of toxic gases; Ed Lachman forgets his glasses and there's no going back; the cameramen express their reservations; and so on. This vibe is compounded by shots of the city abandoned, its streets inhabited by mule and swine. Impending doom is made overwhelming by a three-minute interlude of black-and-white photographs, over which Herzog narrates the story of the 1902 Martinique disaster. The montage opens with an impressive photograph of explosions on the horizon and a sunken ship in the foreground as birds seek safety in flight; passes through images of the flattened city and a plate of charred-black spaghetti; and ends with a little story of the sole survivor, a thief held in solitary confinement who would parlay his burns and his miracle into a sideshow attraction for a traveling circus. The historical interlude is followed by interviews, largely rambling conversations with the witnesses to La Grande Soufrière, the men who refuse to move. Not one, it turns out, but three.

At the heart of the film, however, are none of these disparate narratives, each of which seems somehow inflated. Herzog's excursion, while providing an ecstatic record of the abandoned city, was a calculated risk, with much more weight on the calculated side. La Grande Soufrière is of a different geological phase than Martinique's Pelée, rumbling with greater frequency, but with no recent (that is, millennial) history of devastating magmatic eruptions. In spite of alarming reports in popular outlets no less weighty than the *New York Times*, Herzog's repeated claim to a scientific certainty and consensus around the imminence of a massive conflagration in 1976 is a significant exaggeration. Indeed, among geologists, the eruption is remembered mostly for the debate that surrounded it. One group of scientists led by the eminent volcanologist Haroun Tazieff declared, after the first phreatic explosion in July, that the volcano posed no threat to the population, a position that his team held throughout the emergency. This assessment was contradicted weeks later by Claude Allègre, the new director of the Institut de Physique du Globe de Paris, and with political pressure emanating all the way from the French presidency, cautious to avoid any blood on its hands, he recommended an evacuation of the population, which the local prefect executed soon thereafter.[94] The decision is still considered controversial.[95] As for the witness interviews, well, these too feel like waiting in vain. Prepared for peasant wisdom and deep thoughts about man's place in the cosmos, we instead get three eccentrics harried by demons, to put it broadly. One of the men, either intoxicated, sick, or just incredibly languorous, gives the bulk of his interview in short mumbles, lying down; another tries to get the crew to give him a ride ("I could leave here with my own two feet . . . but maybe you could give me a ride?"); there's lots of dialogue like this: "Tell me about the volcano, La Soufrière." "Yeah, the volcano, it's always up there above us" (this is Herzog's translation of the Guadeloupean French). "But the situation is very dangerous isn't it?" "Sure it is, of course it's dangerous, but I'm staying here, what difference does it make?": then cut to the next scene. It goes on like this for seven minutes. And as for the well-rendered Saint-Pierre montage, that's all accessible in history books.

So one can quickly sense that these dominant themes—risk, history, death, cheap fatalistic philosophy, all in play, are nevertheless not really what the film is about. The film is about the mountain, and it is here that we will find the film's strongest work. Herzog, as he has famously said many times, doesn't merely situate landscapes, he directs them, and *La Soufrière* is a signature attempt in this regard. The opening shots of the crater with billowing clouds of steam, the close-ups of "bottomless fissures" whose heat the viewer can practically feel, and the long tracking shots of the mountain horizon draped in volcanic smoke, these are the moments where the film most directly communicates the scope of its subject: the earth in rebellious upheaval. Everything around these shots, that is, everything human has something insouciant about it. The most uncanny images, juxtaposing the abandoned city with the looming volcano distant and ready to strike, are made strange to the point of silliness by their human trappings: stoplights direct animal traffic while the adagio from Rachmaninoff's Piano Concerto No. 2 plays—achingly beautiful and also saccharine enough to have been appropriated (just a year before the film) into Eric Carmen's hit "All By Myself," one of the cheesiest examples imaginable of the 1970s-era American power ballad—over which Herzog narrates, ominous in his deadpan tone, "the sea was full of dead snakes." It's hard not to laugh, and, as Herzog puts it, the audience is always right. The most momentous images of the volcano, the film's closing shots, are accompanied more bombastically with Siegfried's death march, from Wagner's *Twilight of the Gods*. But even that sublime counterpoint of sound and image is undermined by the narrator's off-key comment that the *real* story of *La Soufrière* is the "neglect and oblivion in which those black people live" (it isn't) and a subsequent confession that the whole thing "ended a little bit embarrassing" when La Grande Soufrière shrugged and went back to sleep. At the center of the film then, is not death, but the awesomeness of the mountain in relation to human life, ultimately, the *embarrassment* of our futile attempts to capture it (here, on film). Man dreams that he can challenge the volcano and invents stories (for example, about risking life, limb, and camera on an evacuated island) to that effect; and the volcano, indifferent, doesn't even bother to stare back, reducing our struggles to miniature spectacles. The importance of *La Soufrière* in Herzog's filmography is its crystallization of this truth, in both image and idea. The shots of mist, fog, the earth on fire, and mountain horizon become a canonical example in the grammar of Herzog's cinematography, recalling the opening images of *Aguirre*, and reappearing notably in films as diverse as *Heart of Glass*, *Fitzcarraldo*, *Lessons of Darkness*, *Grizzly Man*, and *The White Diamond* and recapitulated explicitly in recent Herzog releases such as the Netflix documentary *Into the Inferno* (2016) and the feature *Salt and Fire* (2016).

Within the more limited context of the operatic turn in Herzog's late-1970s work, the position of *La Soufrière* ushers in an extended cycle of films about mountains and man's pathos before them. And if *La Soufrière* stands as some kind of an arcane joke (Ames calls it a parody of "direct cinema" [2012b: 300]) about lucky disappointment—impossible to tell, Herzog is famously sincere and claims not to understand irony—it paves the way to the far more contemplative, and aesthetically engaging, *Gasherbrum* (*The Dark Glow of the Mountains*, 1985). With its unusual shots of Himalayan landscapes, extended dialogues between Herzog and the elite climber and explorer Reinhold Messner, and intriguing side characters such as Messner's sherpa, it succeeds in reaching a level of complicated introspection that *La Soufrière* never does. When Herzog's performative interviewing style unexpectedly reduces Messner to sobs, it yields one of the more affecting scenes in all of Herzog's films. Later, he would continue the theme of man against gravity with the largely forgotten feature film *Cerro Torre: Schrei aus Stein* (*Scream of Stone*, 1991), shot at the sheer obelisk of the otherworldly Torres del Paine at the tip of South America.[96]

But most immediately, *La Soufrière* precedes the mist, mountains, and ominous, pseudo-symphonic soundtrack of *Nosferatu* (1979). If the looming presence of human mortality and geology's indifference before it inhabits the discourse of *La Soufrière* and its cousins, in *Nosferatu* the problem is inverted, more interesting, and frankly more Herzogian: banished from death, the crisis of the vampire is his infinite solitude, his inability to enter into the human condition (in an indirect way placing the vampire in a family of characters like Stroszek and Aguirre). Shot on a modest budget, *Nosferatu* nevertheless attracted an impressive cast, circulated internationally as a big feature from its initial release, and was by far Herzog's most financially successful film to date. One of the director's very best, it is an ecstatic reimagining of the vampire classic, and critics have long celebrated its painterly quality. In terms of its cultural politics, Herzog has always positioned it as a kind of settling of accounts between his work and the German national cinema, as he puts it, an attempt to rescue its civilization from the barbarism of its ghastly midcentury decades. It is faithful to Murnau's 1922 expressionist masterpiece, sometimes reproducing shots and scenes to the letter, but also full of Herzog's basic iconography: the baroque overgrowth of man (a community of gypsies that swarms the protagonist on his travels) and animal (the ten thousand rats that bring the plague of vampirism), the stylized images of a flying bat, the opening pan of mummified children (in an expected cultural juxtaposition of a Herzog picture, the establishing shot is recorded in Guanajuato, Mexico), the mountain sublime of the quest to meet Kinski's Dracula. Aesthetically it has a strong foothold in the 1970s period pieces, visually related to *Kaspar Hauser* and *Heart of Glass* in its Alpine idyll, but here gone gothic, and providing both setting and cast for *Woyzeck*, which was shot in the weeks that immediately followed. But it's also something of a watershed in the director's trajectory, opening the way to larger ambitions of grand-opera scale and a kind of magic realism that will become a signature of Herzog's subsequent films. Moreover, the *Nosferatu* success capped the decade by consolidating Herzog's reputation as an *auteur* of the first order, one whose creativity seemed infinite, whose energy was unstoppable, and whose iron will could now pull off commercial projects. *Nosferatu*'s box-office success, along with the continued artistic appeal exhibited in films like *Woyzeck*—another hit at Cannes, where Eva Mattes won an acting award for her role as the unfaithful wife, and in which Kinski turned in possibly the finest performance of his career—put Herzog on the path to higher profile features. That is, the kind of work whose anticipation makes news long before the film is even released. It was through this kind of evolution of both ambition and possibilities that Herzog one day found himself on the Amazon with the most famous rock-and-roll star in the world. Let's return to watery Iquitos.

Fitzcarraldo certainly has its partisans. I would not argue, however, that it's one of Herzog's most aesthetically successful films. There's a staginess to the performances, common in Herzog who doesn't always demand a naturalistic style from his actors, but it works less well here than in other films. A number of the roles seem wrong or superfluous: Claudia Cardinale is unconvincing as a local madame, her chemistry with Kinski stilted, to put it diplomatically; the weird cameo by Grande Otelo is hard to watch; the important role of Huerequeque is played by an amateur (Huerequeque Enrique Bohorquez) trying really hard to act, and the same goes for the ship's captain (Paul Hittscher, an actual captain and restaurateur). The quality of the often-overrecorded dialogue is distracting. The story drags, even by the standards of Herzog's measured pace. And the ending doesn't line up with the tragic logic of the film, leaving neither a feeling of redemption nor denouement, it just sort of ends; counterintuitively for a two-and-a-half hour film, it feels a little rushed. Even the universally celebrated signature shot—the steamship being pulled up a small hill—seems more than a bit overrated. I'd put it nowhere near the top class of Herzog's catalog of extraordinary images; indeed, it's not even among the best five or so shots in the film. All that said, the impressive life of *Fitzcarraldo*—its conception, its production, its theme, politics, historical representation, and scandal—make it quite probably Herzog's most important work, winning him critical accolades and directorial distinction at Cannes. The long middle section, featuring Fitzcarraldo among the Indians and all the controversy that would ensue, is more than worth the price of admission. At the end of the day it's one of the signature films of the 1980s, Herzog's entry into the discourse of auteurist megaproject—Coppola's *Apocalypse Now* (1979), Cimino's *Heaven's Gate* (1980)—in its heyday at that time. And like his previous historical pieces, the intensity of its context of representation and the ambiguity of its politics leave it still standing as a fount of discussion and contemplation. As Walter Saxer, Herzog's production manager on set, put it in a recent interview, "These movies [*Fitzcarraldo* and *Aguirre*] are 33 years old, and they're still being talked about. Now films are made for hundreds of millions of dollars and after two weeks nobody talks about them" (Buder 2015). Its cascade of themes and objects, from opera to celebrity, from the history of recorded sound to the history cultural contact, from rubber to capitalism itself, make it, at some level, inexhaustible.

The film story begins with a perspiring Fitzcarraldo—Kinski here a more twitchy Aguirre, now almost explicitly bipolar and in a kind of frenetic mood—and his lover, a procuress named Molly, played by Cardinale, disembarking from a rickety canoe and rushing up toward the monumental Teatro Amazonas. Fitzcarraldo convinces a guard to usher them inside, claiming to have made the journey all the way from Iquitos.[97] For much of it, he reports, he had to row. A charitable audience will have to suspend disbelief: at one thousand miles of river, weather, disease, hostile Indians, and bandits, this is a highly unlikely trip. Fitzcarraldo and Molly in tow stumble into the opera house just in time to see the great Caruso—accompanied by a wonderfully transvestite Sarah Bernhardt—finishing the concluding song (a trio) from Verdi's

Ernani (1844). There's a well-framed shot, with Bernhardt's voice double in foreground and evincing as much emotion as the actress herself. Operatically, it's a little overwrought, even by the genre's standards: after beginning the scene by missing her cue, Bernhardt's Elvira ends it by breaking script and killing herself, alongside Ernani, and thereby, as Richard Leppert points out (2015, 61), mischievously upstages the great Caruso. Moreover, the kitsch of the scene—its decoration and costume, Bernhardt's amateurish lip-synching—calls attention to the indulgence of Italian grand opera: as much as the music, the spectacle is about the spectacularity of the spectacle, less the aching transcendence of Verdi's ethereal trio, and more about the celebrity of Caruso and Bernhardt, together in the tropics. Nevertheless, for Fitzcarraldo, the instant is overwhelming, sublime, epiphanic: he even convinces himself, with Molly's encouragement, that the stratospheric Caruso reaches out and locks eyes with him in stylized death throes.

Thus begins Fitzcarraldo's obsession, one that will require him to strike it rich. But, we learn quickly, it turns out that he's a bad capitalist. He's tried to set himself up in the ice trade, but with far less success than Aureliano Triste. And his plans to bring the light of culture into the darkness of jungle through a trans-Amazonian railway have also failed at the starting gate. We learn all this in the following scene when he makes an investment pitch, fidgeting—Molly helping him keep it together—before a member of the rubbered elite, who has for some reason called the meeting in the lobby of the opera house. It's a pretext: the scene gives the film the opportunity to speak directly, through the mouth of the would-be investor, about the imported opulence of the building. In other words, to point up the material culture accumulated through rubber wealth. While every shred of evidence indicates that the historical Fitzcarrald's drive was eminently capitalist—accumulation for the sake of accumulation—Herzog's Fitzcarraldo sees the accumulative impulse of the capitalist world-economy as a convenient means to a specific end: to bring opera to the jungle, to host the greatest stars of Europe in the middle of the Amazon. And not in a namby-pamby way like the fat cat creditors at the center of the system: Manaus, after all, was a city, and in 1897—the year of the Teatro's first performance season and also of the historical Fitzcarrald's death—its inhabitants could still dream dreams of permanence, of a never-ending boom that would consolidate a new world in the tropics. Fitzcarraldo dreams bigger than that: an opera house in the jungle, that is, *literally in the middle of the jungle*, inaccessible, lightly developed, wild-west, Iquitos.[98] That's how he gets into rubber. But ultimately, he's a romantic.

For any political reading of Herzog's film—that is, any reading intent on unearthing the possibilities and limits of its geopolitically material critique—its spatial, historical and aesthetic relation to opera cannot be overlooked. Indeed, as Herzog himself has stated in various ways, the ship-over-the-mountain image that motivates the film is straight out of "Italian grand opera" (in Blank's *Burden* [1982]). And, as Leppert (2015) works through systematically and states succinctly, "Opera is the film's form and content" (58). This relation is immediate. Before we even arrive inside, to the scene of *Ernani*, the opening montage of *Fitzcarraldo* runs directly from a panoramic extreme long shot of the jungle to the Teatro Amazonas. The juxtaposition—extravagant opera house, wild jungle—makes sense in ways that we might not expect. And it is also less ham-fisted than it might at first appear. The easy, and usual, critical move is to note some variant of a colonial discourse critique, revolving around civilization-and-barbarism metaphors.[99] The wild nature of pure life in the jungle over here, penetrated and tamed by the sophistication of an ordered European form over there. Or the attempt at this kind of pacification that will fail in the face of nature's inexorable force and, by implication, the wisdom of natural man, the way in which the jungle, in Herzog's expression, "always hits back."[100] The film is full of scenes that invite this reading: at one turn, Fitzcarraldo appears to tame indigenous war drums through the pacifying effects of Caruso recorded for the gramophone; in another, Fitzcarraldo plots to mobilize indigenous myth in the name of European domination; there is even a "first contact" scene, a rather lovely close-up in which white hand and brown hand meet in greeting; upon contact, the Indians fondle Fitzcarraldo's hair and suitcoat buttons with engaged curiosity. Fitzcarraldo and the other nonindigenous characters disparage the Indians with the epithet "bare-asses" (an inaccurate description, their asses are covered throughout), and Herzog himself, for example, in Blank's *Burden of Dreams*, transparently refers to "savage" Indians, straight, with no indication whatsoever of implied scare quotes. In short, as a matter of colonial discourse critique, to put it lightly, there's a lot to work with here. And yet: the blandly comforting binary of civilization and barbarism that this material suggests collapses into itself before the actual critical work of the film and its aesthetic impulse. Thematically and historically, *Fitzcarraldo* is not a film about the sublime trauma of discovery, contact, conquest. It is a film about capitalism; more precisely, about the capitalist irrational—a symptomatic intensification of what Jameson memorably called the political unconscious—and its governance of social life in the worlds of its leading edge of penetration, a chronotope of primitive accumulation. Worlds such as the rubber boom of fin-de-siècle South America.

Capitalist society as an overarching theme, with all its complexities and contradictions, emerges more clearly if we pay strict attention to the historical and contextual role of opera in the film and its critical reception. First is the question of opera itself, its status and history as an institution. It is tempting to unproblematically locate the opera within a hierarchy of formal high culture imposed on various forms of popular cultural expression, and of course there is much to that idea, it's where most critical interpretations of the film both begin and end. But as far as opera itself is concerned, this characterization is only half the story, and probably not even half: opera as a rich man's game has something anachronistic about it; that is, it runs counter to capitalism's historical trajectory toward mass culture. And, indeed, by the end of Fitzcarraldo's century, opera had long since descended from the courtly perch of its

Figure 11. Fitzcarraldo (Klaus Kinski) meets the fearsome Jívaros. *Fitzcarraldo* (Herzog 1982).

primitive expression and was at the very culmination of its popularization, even democratization. Its form and content cast an immediate and textured net across social contexts and classes, and it was even a site of contest between them. It was wildly popular, marked by high formality only in certain settings and generally a much earthier kind of song than we recognize today, which is largely reducible—in form if not in genre—to the repertoire of high-production grand opera.[101]

Fitzcarraldo suggests this history, both explicitly and implicitly. Take the opening scene of opera. *Ernani* was a midcentury smash hit, canonical among standard repertory fare by the time of Fitzcarraldo, its staying power such that it would go on to become, in 1903, the first opera recorded in its entirety. It is an adaptation of Victor Hugo's early play, *Hernani* (1830), itself launched as an insurgency of radical romanticism against the hierarchies of classicism. By this 1900 iteration in *Fitzcarraldo*, *Ernani*'s commercial trappings are fully realized, in Leppert's expression, as "music hall," a fact that Herzog's stage director, Walter Schroeter, wanted to highlight (Leppert 2015, 62).[102] Its taste is bad taste, an *arriviste*'s fantasy of wealth and power, the opera of an Atlantic City hotelier. In other words, it's not so much Verdi as it is Caruso. And Caruso sings beyond the form called opera, throwing the strength of his voice to its mechanical reproduction: commonly hailed as the first international superstar, this stardom rests not merely on the artistry of Caruso's talent, which historians and musicologists universally agree was formidable, but moreover on the fact that his voice was so extensively available, including, of course, in Latin America (Roselli 1990, 156). Caruso is a star, that is, a *popular* hero, because he is recorded, and thus brought into aristocratic homes, yes, but also all kinds of houses of ill repute. His recorded voice the herald of a form whose high expression comparatively few in the world would actually attend as event, Caruso becomes "the Great Caruso" via portable technology. In *Fitzcarraldo*, he'll take a fantastic star turn on stage, but his presence throughout the film is via shellac discs, with all their grit and pops, played on a lotus-horn gramophone, diegetically, as when Fitzcarraldo cries "Caruso!" and dashes off to blast a record as the ship crawls over the mountain. It is important, then, that Fitzcarraldo gives no indication of standing among the monied elite, of patronizing a box at a great opera house; he lives in a slum on stilts at the very edge of the capitalist world, and says explicitly to Molly that he likes it that way; that he dislikes men with money who go around acquiring whatever they please. And yet there he is with his gramophone, in his modest river shack, surrounded by half-naked children and a pig, captivated by Caruso's song.

But even placing to one side the fin-de-siècle recording explosion of Caruso and opera more broadly, for many decades the popular classes had been familiar with and interpellated by the form, if only indirectly and by degrees of separation. Foremost is the fact that what we recognize stereotypically as the staid, formal opera scene of today, of course throughout its history has numerous popular reinventions and collaborators. Zarzuela—emerging as an entertainment for kings, but spreading over time as a popular form of both urban and rural entertainment—roughly contemporaneous with Italian opera, owes much of its staying power (more than three centuries) throughout the Iberian world to its ability to accommodate, absorb and rearticulate operatic aesthetics for *el pueblo*. London perfected the ready-to-wear music stage called the operetta, while in the United States, generations of audiences in the nineteenth century were exposed to opera in the form of minstrel shows, racist variety performances whose actors and musicians in blackface regularly performed opera vignettes as reinvented romances and, more commonly, burlesque parodies, and whose traveling companies frequently called themselves "opera troupes."[103] Their critical thrust could cut in multiple directions, from the general degradation (and also appropriation) of African American folk cultures to lampoons of an elite, East Coast, operagoing bourgeoisie. Thus begins the canonization of familiar broadsides against the absurd self-importance of opera, and also the popular ambivalence before the form. On the one hand, it stands as easy target for social-class comeuppance, providing fodder for a range of jokers, whether blacked-up minstrels, the Marx Brothers (*A Night at the Opera*, 1935), Bugs Bunny (*What's Opera, Doc?*, 1957), or Woody Allen, when he was funny (*Love and Death*, 1975). On the other hand, out of the weird mix of minstrelsy, operetta, and vaudeville emerge the great American musical arts, giving opera a foothold in everything from the canon of jazz standards to modern musical theater, all the way down to the concept album and stadium rock concert (which, at their most performative—Bowie, The Who, R. Kelly, Prince, *The Rocky Horror Picture Show*—sometimes call themselves a "rock opera"). So even if *the people* don't go to the opera, the people know it through its digressions, and can perceive it as, at least, a kind of rich uncle, not of the people, but not completely divorced from them. During the 2016 US election season, the Donald Trump campaign included Puccini's aria "Nessun Dorma" in its rally soundtrack.

Moving back to the historical setting of *Fitzcarraldo*, however, one needn't necessarily leave the orbit of opera as such. That's because el pueblo, o povo, *did*, in fact, go to the opera. It should come as no surprise that Latin America—its very historical emergence owing to the invasion, plunder, and colonization by European powers, and its long-standing transculturation with European society—as a producer, consumer, and performer of opera has a history that runs coterminous with the history of the form (as Europeans first invaded the New World, opera did not yet exist). Already present in the early eighteenth century, with vice-regal performances from Lima to Mexico City, by the end of that century opera as an institution—with dedicated theaters, publics, and workers—had fully coalesced in the major cities of South America (Bereson 2002, 170). During the subsequent decades, Buenos Aires would become the continent's most vibrant opera scene, which by the late nineteenth century had a commercial base significant enough to support three overlapping performance seasons, a schedule unheard of in Europe (Roselli 1990, 169). Within this setting, it's important to remember opera's popular appeal, as Kotnik explains for opera in general, arguing that "distinctions between mass and high culture were never static, historically constant and clear, but discontinued, historically variable and, above all, often contested" (2013, 308), and that opera has for centuries been "multicultural . . . and transnational . . . venues where different people represented by different cultural backgrounds, class diversifications, ethnic identities, and national belongings gather" (305). Roselli (1990) makes documenting this kind of multicultural churn of human life at the opera an important part of his study of the institution in fin-de-siècle Buenos Aires, paying special attention to the complicated mix of ethnic identification and social class at the opera house, with an aristocratic Iberian-descended population occupying the boxes and an ethnically Italian proletariat and bourgeoisie in the cheap seats, or on stage (171). And this soft segregation played out not just within, but between, opera performance spaces, with the big state-sponsored opera house (after 1908, the majestic Teatro Colón) welcoming the elite and anybody else that could make it inside (the Colón seats more than four thousand), with the popular classes supporting all sorts of more or less improvised performance spaces around town, producing a kind of people's opera, one not immune to bourgeois slumming, and yielding entire transient neighborhoods populated by the not insignificant force of opera workers—opera ghettos, as it were (169; 175–76). Moreover, it's worth emphasizing that this opera proletariat was transatlantic in nature, migrating on confused routes from Dieppe to Brest to Buenos Aires, back to Bordeaux, then across again to Barranquilla, and so on (166), in a precise recitation of the center-periphery logic of the world-system—the routes don't move from Montevideo to Rio, you always pass back through the center of the system—*and also* its deconstruction. Not a passive recipient, Latin America is an active participant, necessary to the machine, providing both the sublime inspiration of artistic ideas and the brute fuel of revenues: the South American season would run opposite of the European one, anchoring a web of migrant labor in opera-singer work. Roselli cites the opera star Titta Ruffo "recall[ing] that for 18 years he never experienced a summer" (169). So even if fully bourgeois in its cultural *capital*, a mark of social distinction, at the turn of the century—as collectors today know, Caruso's recordings were more commonly purchased than played, an emblem of conspicuous consumption—it nevertheless comes as no surprise that opera as a cultural *practice* was something that everybody could recognize, whether from neighborhood performance or sound reproduction and would have the capacity to stir the spirit of *el pueblo*.[104] When the anarchist Pietro Gori, an Italian exile in Argentina, sought to capture and channel the energy of a body proletariat, he turned to opera, transforming the aria ("Va, pensiero") from Verdi's *Nabucco* (1841) into the "Inno del Primo Maggio" (1892) and eventually into the hearts of syndicalists in a transatlantic circuit from Tierra del Fuego to Marseille and back to Mexico. This not as any kind of elevation of the people, the hymn is their interpellation: he set their struggle to a tune that they knew.

So, on the one hand, opera's relation to the social world, and role in class consciousness, rests on shifting terrain. But, on the other hand, and at the same time, running parallel to the form's complicated cultural history is the social symbolism of opera, as *monument*, circa 1900.

In short, there is no way around the blunt fact that the opera *house* would be *the* expression of capitalism-fueled raw power in fin-de-siècle Manaus: among the various ruins, remains, and legends of rubber-boom excess, nothing compares to the Teatro Amazonas. The neo-Renaissance structure, made primarily of imported materials, is universally cited, almost always with a hint of "Can you believe this?" in literature both more and less critical of the culture of rubber-boom tycoons. Eduardo Galeano, in the celebrated *Venas abiertas de América Latina* (1971) calls it a "Baroque monument of sufficient bad taste and the greatest symbol of the vertiginous fortunes at the beginning of the century, where the tenor Caruso sang for the people on the night of its inauguration."[105] Caruso didn't, in actual history, sing there, but the legend is part of the mystique, an image that lends the city its renowned aura of magic-realist flair.[106]

But, like all magic realism, the magic always ultimately yields to the realist, and in this the rubber boom social forces at play are not in fact magic, not even operatic, but rigorously material, belching up a monument that is no more than a banal cultural expression of economic growth and regional identity.[107] In short, the Teatro is common. For example, another periphery of capitalism, the former Austro-Hungarian empire, saw a massive turn-of-the-century boom in opera houses, with the firm Fellner and Helmer alone designing more than forty music and theater houses—mostly for opera—between 1874 and 1911, from Vienna to Zagreb, from Brno to Rijeka (see Hoffman 1966; Sell 2014). South America participated in the trend, with the crown jewel, Buenos Aires's Teatro Colón (construction from 1889, opened 1908), still recognized more than a century later as one of the world's best. Expressions of bourgeois national pride, and brand new, it is really no surprise that these Latin American boom-economy opera houses would be, in the estimation of Roselli, the most technologically advanced (167–68).

The fact of this long history of Latin America's relation with the opera, not only its presence, but its active participation in a transatlantic circuit that would establish the modern form, raises an obvious question about the Teatro Amazonas: why all the fuss? Why the pro forma expressions of amazement in Manaus around a structure that wouldn't raise an eyebrow in Mantua? Historically, there is nothing especially fantastic in the idea that Manaus, with the impressive revenues of its industrial elite, would invest in an opera house. Already in 1813, Rio de Janeiro had opened a modern municipal theater that regularly hosted operas, the Real Teatro São João. By 1857, the state was financially committed to the institutional apparatus of not just hosting operas, but producing them, with the foundation of the Imperial Academia de Música e Opera Nacional. That institution and its corresponding company, the Empresa de Opera Lírica Nacional, nurtured the education of Antônio Carlos Gomes, who would eventually travel to Milan on a state fellowship and be received by the Milanese press as a "'savage' who could write opera" (Magaldi 2006, 211), resulting in the 1870 premier at La Scala of his *Il Guarany*. An Italian opera set to a Brazilian theme—adapted from José de Alencar's eponymous romantic novel—it would open months later in Rio to a hero's welcome. Returning full circle, a century down the road and a couple thousand miles north, the great Brazilian opera would inaugurate Plácido Domingo's direction of the Kennedy Center's 1996 opera season under the direction of, none other: Werner Herzog. So if the history of opera in Latin America, and more precisely, nineteenth-century Brazil, is so extensive and obvious, why the gravitational pull of its exoticism? The answer can be found in the very nature of cultural production on the periphery of capitalism and the misreadings that it imposes on us, misreadings directly relevant to rethinking *Fitzcarraldo* today.

Case in point: in a glossary entry that fails to situate the film in its context of representation, the encyclopedist Balderston opens the topic of opera in Latin America with a reference to Herzog, accusing him of "ridiculing" Latin American opera (in López, González, & Balderston 2000, 1076). Besides giving the first word on the real history of Latin American opera to the made-up story *Fitzcarraldo*, and misunderstanding both the setting of the film (not "Latin America," which as an idea never comes up, but the rubber-boom-era Amazonia) and its tone (utterly sincere, Herzog doesn't really do ridicule), the comment is also representative of a larger mistake: the fact that any perceived outlandishness of opera in *Fitzcarraldo* comes not from an artist's ridicule but from a completely different aesthetic impulse and social history. Well known to scholars of Latin American culture and history, it's the logic of the continent's most famous indigenous literary style, magic realism itself. If there seems to be something irresistible about the image of the aria in the jungle as the ultimate expression of decadence, whether in Herzog or in Nobel laureate Mario Vargas Llosa's 1966 work, *La casa verde*—"is it true . . . that operas came to Iquitos and that the rubber barons lit their cigars with cash money?" (2008, 203)—it doesn't stem from Herzog's or Vargas Llosa's (or Galeano's) desire to ridicule Latin America or its cultural practices, processes, and productions. It has to do with the Teatro Amazonas as the symbol of incalculable social and economic inequality: the counterpoint of obscene luxury and material poverty that amazed Herzog himself when he first visited Manaus. It has to do with the impossible aesthetics of a geohistorical confluence of forces at once underwritten by and resulting in bizarre behavior and unimaginable social crimes. Lest we miss it, Herzog surrounds the opera house with a plethora of references to the scale of the boom: as Fitzcarraldo approaches the Teatro, a horse is being hydrated—with champagne; a passing reference mentions that the rubber baron families send out their laundry—to Lisbon; one rubber baron has a personal chef—for his dog; we see an absurdly outsized fish in the pool of a rubber creditor being fed—with high-currency bills; and so on. All the while, racially marked servitude and poverty are glaringly present, whether in the amphibious Caliban children of Fitzcarraldo's neighborhood or in the trafficked children who staff Molly's brothel and whose flesh ultimately pays the costs of Fitzcarraldo's project.[108]

Confused about the object of critique, a deeply Eurocentric perspective can emerge almost reflexively and only perceive, or be offended by, the suggestion of cultural dislocation—as were certain Brazilian critics in 1870 when confronted with the idea of an Indian-costumed tenor singing in Italian the aria of *Il Guarany* (Magaldi 2006)—an exoticizing, even self-exoticizing, idea of Latin American opera.[109] But this reflex would seem to suggest either an ignorance of Latin America's prominent role in the history of opera or a misunderstanding of the long history of Latin American cultural producers' creative strategies for narrating and aestheticizing the intercultural traumas of the continent. Herzog seems to be ignorant of neither of these things. Scholars, critics, and consumers of Latin American cultural history often too quickly interpret aesthetic creativity as an effect of "tradition and modernity" or temporalities at cross purposes. What we could broadly call the magic realist tradition, however, is not about cultural difference (nonindigenous forms, misplaced, out of context), but instead about cultural sameness: the global expanse of resource extraction that churns up the opulence-misery dichotomy of capitalist societies, everywhere. A common dissonance that, for better and worse, includes everybody, as the Chileans put it, by reason or by force. What a careful materialist interpretation will catch here is the fact that any magic-realist exoticism (flying carpets, ships over mountains, cannibalism, opera) is only exotic in Roberto Schwarz's (1973) sense: that is, not exotic at all, but rather the productive artistic confrontation with a set of ideological parameters—liberalism and its attendant free-market democracy—that can't work ideologically, that can't correspond to appearances, that can't represent reality, not even falsely. That is, an ideological structure whose contradictions get especially vivid, and revealingly so, in the boom where, as Marx once wrote, they "go naked" (1853, 217).

The pyrotechnics of garish juxtaposition—the horse, the champagne; the jungle, the opera house—notwithstanding, as social historical fact the opera in rubber-boom Amazonia should be seen as common. It is only through this kind of banalization, by resisting the temptation to wonder at the Italian grand opera of it all, that we can begin to perceive the film as a potentially critical intervention in the history of modern civilization. Almost two decades before Manaus, opera companies weathered humidity and yellow fever to travel as far north as already teeming Belém, whose own opera house, the Theatro da Paz, opened at the mouth of the Amazon in 1878 just as the rubber market began to really heat up (see Roselli 1990, 161). On the other side of the jungle, Peru, too, has a long tradition of opera; indeed, recognized during its viceroyalty as host of the first opera composed and performed in South America, in Lima, 1701 (Stevenson 1973). So, while Kinski's colorful outburst atop the Iquitos church tower, where Fitzcarraldo bellows his claim for an opera house, is indeed hyperbolic, the project he announces is only a slightly more involved step away from, say, bringing in a cinema. This is what ambitious cities of the era did (and still do) (see Bereson 2002). But *Fitzcarraldo* adds a subtle twist: the aesthetic obsessions of the protagonist ultimately undermine the monumentalization of opera, distancing him from the expected trappings of a great patron of the arts. His project, then, is at once unexceptional—to bring a sign of national-capitalist success to a boomtown—and quietly radical: he really only engages opera as art and seems completely cavalier about the capitalist-nationalism part. As Leppert puts it, "they're interested in rubber for money; he wants rubber for opera" (2015, 62). It's worth recalling: Fitzcarraldo doesn't really *go* to the opera. He's a record geek. And his relation to the opera is one that is well known. His figure is that of the rabble critic, the clerical-class spectator in the cheap seats, hostile to arriviste socialization (again: he actively dislikes the wealthy patrons), dedicated to the aesthetic, a performer's terror. Not merely a chance to show off Kinski's unmatched talent for throwing a fit, this is the meaning of the scene in which Fitzcarraldo scandalizes a cocktail party where, unfortunately, he is seeking funders, with the words "Sir, the reality of your world is nothing more than a rotten caricature of great opera!" Marginal to the rubbered elite, Fitzcarraldo stands as the sign of opera's fundamental instability, its insurgent purity, its art, caught "between the pompous splendor of halls and the proverbial indecorum of audiences; between the highly formalized ritual of ruler's presence and the misbehavior of crowds . . . between the rigid conventions of the elites and the excessive folklores of the masses" (Kotnik 2013, 309). We might add: between tedious industrial capitalism and its popular transcendence.

In sum, I suggest that one must focus attention on the film's stabilizing motif in all its banality, this being not only opera per se, but also its physical institutionalization, *the opera house*, specifically the Teatro Amazonas, which, in its low angle representation of the opening shot, maintains a not uncoincidental visual resonance with the viewer's upward gaze at the ship traversing the mountain. First, the Teatro makes physical the specific accumulative intensity of the economic subsystem that created and sustained a mad rush in the tropics; the Teatro *is* the rubber boom and its primary symptom, rubber fever. Second, in its very etymology—a house of *opera*—the Teatro suggests the wealth-producing sustenance of capitalism in its most expansive and inclusive form, the kind of practices that we find in all resource-extraction boom economies. "Opera" denotes work, in its Romance verb form *operare* or *obrar*, to work, to labor, to exert effort—that is, after all, what the *operai*, the *obreros*, do—tied etymologically to the notion of *a work*, "opus," finished, the product of work. Even beyond and more succinctly: *Opera* is the plural of *opus* and, in fact, an opera is a compilation of several works in one. The nature of work that the capitalist world-economy (well mature by the time of the rubber boom) demands—that is, the transformation of all work into a commodity, labor, whether enslaved, free, or something in between—is first and foremost at stake in any of its subsystems. An opera is a work and it is through this metonymic relation that *Fitzcarraldo* constantly reminds us that at the heart of all booms—which is to say, the world-system in which we dwell—is the euphemistic disruption that capitalism yields through the demands that it exacts upon human community that we call work. And it is in the context of opera that both Fitzcarraldo and the audience learn the work of capitalism in its pure form, on the periphery, where it goes naked, as bare labor, unimpeded and unprotected, free, a pure market governed by the laws of the jungle. To understand this structure of relations is to understand the critical intervention of *Fitzcarraldo*, both its possibility and its limit.

As far as the modern history of resource-extraction booms go, the fin-de-siècle Amazonian rubber fever stands out for its complexity. In the context of the boom, the twin problems of finance capital and labor are harried by myriad logistical problems. First and foremost, the rubber of the boom was "wild rubber," its primary source—the latex-producing trees, *Hevea brasilienses* and *Castilloa elastica*—not farmed on plantations, but rather found sporadically in the Amazonian rain forest, some of the most forbidding terrain on the planet.[110] Thus, the masses of labor that go into plantation agriculture, or mining, become, in the rubber economy, something more akin to the accumulation of sea-mammal pelts, with small teams working remote zones, isolated for long stretches of time. The immediate product is sap, slow to extract and messy to transport, and even after its initial refinement, extremely heavy. So the labor requirements are at once massive—you need a lot of workers to turn a profit—and diffuse—they fan out over large areas of land. Add to that the fact that the labor pool itself is not readily at hand. The rain forest has a low population density and, in the nineteenth century, many of its indigenous inhabitants, while more or less directly incorporated into the capitalist world- economy (including, among other mechanisms, by way of human trafficking), were not engaged in formal capitalist relations of production and labor. All these obstacles taken together, it is no surprise that the biggest of the big-money rubber barons did not fit the made-for-the-movies image of the colonial plantation owner or *latifundista* with a relatively immediate physical relation to his slaves, serfs, or employees. Rather, they were financiers, residing in the cities—Belém, Manaus, Iquitos—and running the boom on a systematized process of *habilitación*, essentially a pyramid scheme or what economists call a "'dendritic' structure, consisting of a long chain of debtors and creditors" (Gray 2004, 222). But the most ambitious—Arana, Scharff, and Fitzcarrald himself—were hard men stalking the frontier of new production regions, recruiting so-called *caciques* who would mediate the supply of credit and provisions to rubber tappers, essentially none of whom could ever pay off their debt (223). A major expense for the barons, then, was enforcing debt bondage.[111] This could sometimes happen through political or material arrangements with this or that ethnically circumscribed group. But since caciques and tappers were paid in terms of rubber harvested, the lawless realms of the jungle and the unequal relations in firepower invited all kinds of human-rights disasters, most infamously *correrías*, "round-ups," literally the pursuit and enslavement (or extermination) of entire rain forest indigenous groups. A cottage industry of horrors revolving around debt enforcement and labor procurement thus echoed throughout the jungle.[112] It is accurately remembered, from Roger Casement's (1904) reports to Vargas Llosa's novel (2008), as an explicit exercise in a "crime without a name" that would later be called genocide.[113]

Then there is the geographical question. The mapping of the Amazon river basin is one of the great cartographic challenges in the formation of the modern world. Besides the virtual impenetrability of the jungle itself, there is the dizzying complex of rivers, tributaries, streams, and floodplains that cut through and frustrate any attempts to form rational grids of territory and property. An ambitious rubber baron might contract the rights to exploit this or that sector of jungle, but getting there, getting people to extract the rubber, getting both product and people out again (the latter usually an extraneous question; a significant percentage of rubber tappers never make it home), and finally getting the commodity to market, together amounted to a massive project. Making this problem operatic is in fact the basic aesthetic challenge of the film. Thus when a mission priest asks Fitzcarraldo about his business in the jungle, there is in fact nothing evasive about his seemingly indirect answer: "I'm planning something geographical," he mumbles, in an accurate recitation of the central puzzle for rubber extraction. Channeling a western tradition that runs from Kant, Humboldt, and Hegel all the way to Hartshorne, Fitzcarraldo in this simple phrase states the *precise* challenge of the rubber economy: mastering the relation between man and land. This is not an abstract proposition in the rubber trade, and again in this scene articulates directly to its aesthetic analogue in the film. In the next beat, upon learning that the priests cannot rid the Indians of the notion that the material world is an illusion behind which lies the reality of dreams, Fitzcarraldo mirrors the priests' failure by attempting to interpellate the other, not with faith, but with opera. "I'm also interested in these ideas," he says, somewhat misty, "I specialize in opera." But the historical-material world immediately sounds a rude alarm against the dream world, and the dialectic between the magic of opera and the corresponding nightmare of its condition of possibility will represent the harrowing balancing act attempted by the film.

The historical Fitzcarrald relied not on dreams, but on making concrete innovations in the basic practices of all areas of the rubber economy—finance, labor, logistics—and indeed, the scale of his fortune rested on "something geographical."[114] Among the major rubber barons, he was especially dedicated to a hands-on approach to his operations, that is, he wasn't sitting back in the city waiting for the interest payments to roll in. Of particular significance, he mobilized his indigenous sources to locate and develop the portage that has ever since borne his name, the Isthmus of Fitzcarrald. Linking tributaries of the Urubamba and Madre de Dios rivers, Fitzcarrald had hit upon a shortcut to both the Ucayali and the Madeira and thereby a fast track to the Amazon itself.[115] It was a discovery of logistics, not extraction, and points up the geographical nature of the great rubber fever. The forests around the Madre de Dios river complex were already in full development, roughly divided between three *caucheros*, the principal one being Fitzcarrald himself. (For narrative reasons, Herzog's film alters this point, presenting the portage as a route to untapped resources.) The shortcut radically reduced his production and supply costs and left his competition floundering in the jungle, dependent on Fitzcarrald's distribution chain, eventually forcing partnerships that consolidated his financial fortune, business reputation, and domination of the Madre de Dios (see Gray 2004, 223–24).

But, of course, even before the discovery of the isthmus, Fitzcarrald had long since placed himself in the position to leverage his already considerable fortune. Recall the missing years, the decade that young Fitzcarrald operated quietly in the jungle. In fact, these years were not quiet at all, at least not within the context of the intersecting community relations that defined indigenous life in the Manu-Mishagua region where he worked. By identifying a market and seizing it, Fitzcarrald hit upon a method through which he could secure the basic geographical relation—man and land, labor and territory—to exploit a still-nascent rubber industry and simultaneously outflank the financiers that would normally provide the start-up capital for such an operation. The articulating market product was guns, the customers were the Indians themselves, and the method of payment was laboring bodies. During these missing years, Fitzcarrald was busy deepening and mobilizing his knowledge of indigenous rivalries in order to set up a network of allies and a supply of labor nothing less than chilling in its efficiency. He traded guns for slaves. Cultivating alliances with one indigenous group, he would offer them quantities of high-demand Winchester rifles and ammunition in exchange for a supply of slaves, slaves that the Indians would procure by overpowering their rivals with their newly minted Winchesters. Fitzcarrald didn't stop there. He would then approach the tribe under attack and offer them rifles for self-defense, in exchange for more slaves from a third group. Completing the circle, he traded guns to the third tribe on the condition that they capture slaves from among the Indians that he had originally traded with (Varese 2004, 127; see also Huertas Castillo 2004, 51–53). Thus was Fitzcarrald able to sweep up entire communities into a condition of outright slavery and, in the same gesture, build a paramilitary force of Indians and settlers willing and able to maintain that system of bound labor (Brown and Fernández 1991, 63; compare Gow 2016).

He was not shy about mobilizing his army. Upon opening up the new route via the isthmus, Fitzcarrald was confronted with the task of clearing a section of the heretofore unpacified Manu river of its restive native inhabitants, the Mashco-Piro, famously resistant to integration into the rubber economy. After his threats to do great harm to the tribe—in the account of one Dominican missionary, Fitzcarrald himself promises violence "right down to the tiniest baby"—yielded unsatisfactory results, he unleashed his paramilitaries with such fury that dismembered corpses lined the riverbanks and, in the words of the same missionary, one "couldn't draw water from the river for all the bodies of Mashco and rubber workers because it was a war to the death."[116] Underwriting his European good taste and riverboats notable for their gourmet food, fine wine, and startlingly meticulous hygiene was an entire society engaged in relations of conquest, enslavement, robbery, murder—briefly, force—in which even the pleasure boaters invited for rides on his steamships participated by pillaging random villages in their cruises down the Madre de Dios (Varese 2004, 125). And this was a large-scale operation. Clearing the jungle space to make it safe for capitalism, it turns out, requires a cast of thousands, from large groups of men with guns to the eleven hundred indigenous slaves who hoisted his ship over the Isthmus of Fitzcarrald (Gray 2004, 221).

This is the historical context that Herzog will render operatic. The motivating image—the ship over the mountain—would, like any ambitious opera, also involve masses of men, the chorus of minor voices that sets the stage for the stars of the libretto. At once committed to stylization and authenticity, and largely disdainful of special effects, Herzog centers the film on the literal dragging of the ship between rivers, nineteenth-century style, with trees, rope, cables, pulleys, winches,

Figure 12. Fitzcarraldo's Jívaro workers struggle to pull the ship over the portage. *Fitzcarraldo* (Herzog 1982).

levers, and people. Lots of people. Lots and lots of indigenous extras. In other words, workers. In the jungle. With Herzog, and Kinski, and explosives. For many months. It was problematic.

A year or so later, in Munich, Herzog got kicked in the nuts. Shortly after *Fitzcarraldo*'s premier, he was walking down the street when a man rushed up to him, suddenly leapt in the air, and delivered a blow, karate-style, straight to the director's groin, denouncing him as a "pig" (Herzog and Cronin 2002, 169). The film was a critical success—it was celebrated with honors at Cannes, where Gabriel García Márquez, one of the festival's award judges, championed it as a kind of fraternal collaboration—but had churned up no small amount of rancor.[117] The bad feelings revolve around the making of the film which, in the popular imagination, has earned the project more attention than the film itself. The challenges, problems, and alleged crimes that surrounded the production are legion, mostly well known, extensively documented, and far too many to detail here. A truncated list would include war, bureaucrats, accidents, activists, dismemberment, skeptical engineers, two plane crashes, assault, drowning, mud, dynamite, dysentery, chainsaws, bugs, arson, Kinski, the jungle itself, machinery malfunction, conspiracy to commit murder, infidelity, ambush, piranhas, draught, lumbermen, priests, hygiene, domestic violence, debtors' prison, food shortage, falling limbs, falling trees, gun running, rebellion, prostitution, Jason Robards, arrows, an oil pipeline, drunken soldiers, harrowing rapids, field surgery, venomous snakes, armed vigilantes, resignations in protest, Mick Jagger, and a cameraman accidentally abandoned overnight on a boulder in the middle of a rising river. Most spectacular are the serious allegations of human-rights abuses involving Herzog's treatment of local contract workers and the occupation of indigenous lands that have dogged the director ever since. Major pressure was brought to bear against Herzog's production company by indigenous leaders, individual activists, and influential organizations—including Cultural Survival, Survival International, and Gesellschaft für bedrohte Völker, prominent nongovernmental organizations from the United States, the United Kingdom, and West Germany, respectively (and to this day, Survival International is a tenacious presence in Fitzcarrald's historical stomping grounds, the Madre de Dios). Legend has it that eventually

Amnesty International got involved, and while it may seem extraordinary that a film shoot rose so high on Amnesty's docket during, for example, the high times of US intervention in Central America, the fact that the tale has entered into the oral history of *Fitzcarraldo* bears witness to the media circus that had begun to swirl around the production.[118]

All this has made it impossible, quite possibly irresponsible, to interpret *Fitzcarraldo* as a film, or film story, limited to the confines of its own visual and narrative borders. More than a film, *Fitzcarraldo* is a kind of dossier, including at least the film itself; the novelistic screenplay; the historiography on Fitzcarrald; Blank's authorized documentary, *Burden of Dreams* (1982), and accompanying scrapbook; Herzog's published collection of diary entries, *Conquest of the Useless* (2009); Herzog's portrait of Kinski, *My Best Fiend* (1999); various statements by Herzog, most prominently his interview with Cronin and his DVD commentary (two versions on two separate *Fitzcarraldo* releases, and on the Criterion DVD of *Burden of Dreams*); and, of course, the reports, testimony, press clippings, scholarship, and ephemera regarding the allegations brought against the production. The totality of the scandal was put together by the filmmaker Nina Gladitz in a quasi-juridical indictment comprising a raft of documents, which has ever since been nicknamed *der Fall Herzog*, "the case of Herzog." Herzog himself eventually took the "witness stand" in a debate at a workshop in Bamberg.[119] *Fitzcarraldo*'s gravitational pull for political readings of Herzog's work thus proves irresistible. In this, scholars have followed the lead of the popular fascination with the film's production, and thus political readings of *Fitzcarraldo* tend to pander to scandal, focusing less on the film itself and more on mobilizing the film in the name of denouncing, or at best problematizing, Herzog's production activity. The force is strong: Carré's (2007) book on Herzog, for example, in a chapter called "Domination coloniale dans les films extra-européens," notes this fact and then proceeds to place the film to one side and speak almost exclusively about the polemics surrounding it. Koepnick interprets Herzog as reinforcing colonial logics of domination through his on-location film production (1993, 137, 158). Davidson speaks about the representational strategies, production practices, and marketing of *Fitzcarraldo* as an exercise in "neocolonialism" (1994, 80–82). Franco implicates Herzog as participating in a kind of "old-style capitalist enterprise" (1999, 188) that performs violence against the rain forest ecosystem and its inhabitants through what she calls "high-tech primitivism" (ibid.). Ascárate (2007) argues that *Fitzcarraldo* and artifacts both within it (e.g., the fictional map of Fitzcarraldo's territorial concession) and like it are grounded in a long genealogy of ethnographic imagery and represent a compensatory exercise, enacting textually a kind of colonial plunder that perhaps escaped Germany in comparison to other Western European powers. Leppert, while less tempted by the on-set hijinks than most, nevertheless reads the film in the standard key and calls Fitzcarraldo an "acoustic conquistador" imposing "technological authority" (2015, 63, 65) over the jungle. Not to mention the various activist reports that, from the earliest days of the shoot, have gone as far as to mobilize its politics of production as evidence of fascist sympathies on the part of the director. Even Ames, generally a sympathetic interpreter of Herzog's projects, seems to accept at face value the anticolonial critique of Herzog's films and activities (2012b: 148–49).[120]

This prevailing reading itself stands as a kind of monument in the literature on Herzog. And while some of the hyperbole we can confidently place to one side, there is nothing essentially incorrect about its generalizable conclusion: Herzog's film represents and enacts a range of uncomfortable details that relate it—with or without good intentions—to a long history of structural and active violence in the Amazon rain forest. But this conclusion, which can also be a premise, seems largely descriptive and doesn't get very far, analytically, toward complicating the film's possible discursive turns or critical interventions. It doesn't help us understand the perennial fascination with the film. And it doesn't help us explain its cultural impact and influence, which includes goofy little Vice-news-style documentaries like Pressman's *Reconquest of the Useless* (2015) and films with more serious ambitions that cite, criticize, and pay homage to it in creative ways, such as John Boorman's *The Emerald Forest* (1984), Icíar Bollaín's *También la lluvia* (2011), and Ciro Guerra's *El abrazo de la serpiente* (2016).

Three aspects of these critical limits stand out. First and most transparent is the self-evidence of this line of critique. If abuse, deception, coercion, or any kind of unethical practice occurred during the shoot and wider production, Herzog, of course, must be held to account. The overflow of those accusations, however, into the film itself has led to one-dimensional interpretations, where the primary objective seems to be the demonstration of Herzog's hypocrisy, his complicity with colonial discourse. As remarked earlier in the chapter, the common trajectory read onto the film interprets a kind of dandy conquistador penetrating the jungle in an imposition of modern technology over premodern man and jungle. But what actually unfolds in the story is much more complicated.

We could amass examples, but let's take one big one: the famous drums-versus-opera scene. Creeping upriver, the ship and its crew—namely Fitzcarraldo, the captain, the cook, and the engineer; the deckhands will soon abandon the operation—have yet to encounter the Indians. We know that they will not be the first nonindigenous people to meet the menacing Jívaro, and that the tribe is not unfamiliar with their civilization: we've heard stories of their violent encounters with soldiers and missionaries, and the Indians soon will float an inverted umbrella downstream to the ship, presumably the booty from that group of missionaries that disappeared some months earlier. In this context of suggested reconnaissance, reminiscent of *Aguirre*, the ship rounds a bend in the river and there suddenly explode call-and-response chanting and drums in the distance. This goes on for a while, dreamlike in the music's ability to track the ship over an unrealistic distance. The drums disappear for the umbrella scene, a cool effect, making things even more surreal. They reemerge momentarily, the chanting sounding more urgent than before. Fitzcarraldo decides to strike back: not with gunpowder, but with opera. "Now it's Caruso's turn," he declares, in the film's signature line. He cranks up the gramophone on the ship's upper deck.[121] There he stands, expectant and satisfied, as "Il Sogno" ("The Dream"), the aria from Massenet's *Manon* (1882), quite pretty, plays over a rhythm track of war drums. Leppert (2015) offers the standard reading: the Indians, beguiled, fall silent; Caruso wins the day; and the tribe is drawn out by the music, Caruso, the power of a higher form that "pulls them into visibility" (63).[122] But this isn't precisely what happens. First, the drum chant and the opera recording play over each other for an extended period, a counterpoint that Leppert hears as a "competition" (ibid.), but also interpenetrating and forming a kind of Caruso remix to pleasant effect. The Indians aren't struck in wondrous rapture at the Caruso recording. Instead their song simply ends, with no causal explanation (among other possibilities, the ship could have simply drifted out of earshot) and we are left with Caruso, only Fitzcarraldo listening intently, an enigmatic visage and a backdrop of mute, jade vegetation. The Jívaro's reception of Caruso, in other words, is opaque, left to our imagination. Placing to one side the inverisimilitude of the gramophone's capacity to silence the Indians—over the engine, the jungle, and the drums, it would simply be inaudible to them—the on-screen information suggests that it may in fact be Fitzcarraldo who is interpellated by the Indians (it is clear that they provoke him to act) and not the other way around. Not long after this scene, the Jívaro create a tree-trunk barrier forbidding the way for any pirouette escape, their canoes surrounding the ship, which they promptly board. Ambiguity ensues, a general mood that lends the film its mystery and its power. Are the Indians pacified, spellbound by Caruso's mellifluous tenor, or curious? Their body language upon meeting Fitzcarraldo seems to suggest the latter. Is it the song that has pulled them "into visibility," is this their inspiration to preserve—not massacre—Fitzcarraldo and his crew? It is not. As Huerequeque explains, their interest lies in the ship. The Indians don't relate to the recorded music of opera, not once, for the rest of the film. The steamboat, on the other hand, they will labor over, appropriate, and use. Are they in the thrall of a white god? Huerequeque answers directly: "They know that we are not gods," he says.[123] Most centrally, are they overwhelmed—conquered—by technology? Again, they don't seem to be. After all, it is their work and their initiative, as we will see, that makes possible and finishes the job that constitutes the story, a story at this point still hidden from the audience and still arcane to Fitzcarraldo himself.

The Jívaro, clearly, have devised a strategy and made a decision. Their motivations are certainly mysterious, a quality that is itself a cliché waiting (although perhaps a little obviously) for postcolonial deconstruction. But they are not, as Andrew Bush would have it, "silent" and certainly not "absent" (2012, 99); even if most spectators will not understand their unsubtitled dialogue, which is ample, it is *their* speech, perhaps more than Fitzcarraldo's, that drives the plot. And their activity is not, as Prager suggests, forgotten (2007, 42). Indeed, this activity is nothing less than the central sequence of the film. This common misinterpretation of the basic power dynamic at play in *Fitzcarraldo*—capitalist expansion confronted by its object of exploitation, which in turn *appropriates its tools* of would-be domination—produces all kinds of short-circuits when brought into contact with the material world of Herzog's production.

This leads to the second, and ultimately more serious, problem for the colonial discourse critique of the film, one almost entirely neglected in the scholarship: the way in which that critique too quickly and superficially renders—if at times only by metonymic suggestion—the relation between Herzog and his indigenous collaborators and employees as one of colonizer and colonized; more precisely, it reads this relation as one of victimizer and victims. This certainly isn't the case in the film. And it is far too patronizing a description of what went on outside the frame. A first step toward a critical reassessment of the *Fitzcarraldo* dossier must begin with the fact, well documented, that as much as Herzog is attempting to manipulate the local workers, these nonprofessional indigenous actors are strategically manipulating him and his film crew. In the words of Franco (1999), Blank's *Burden of Dreams* (among *many* other documents, including reading between the lines of Herzog's own comments) "shows the Indians to be anything but silent actors in the process" of production (188). Indigenous agency happens at the aesthetic level. Numerous actors break character, smiling when the scene's mood is grim, essentially winking to an unseen audience of millions anxious to see "authentic" Indians.[124] The indigenous cast was explicitly concerned about their representation, and it dominates entire scenes, including the most impressive ones. While Herzog, in his commentaries and documentaries, makes much of his claimed exploitation of indigenous rage (rage at Kinski, no less, a suspicious assertion), the blatant dramatic talent of the central indigenous character, the amateur actor David Pérez Espinosa, rivals that of Kinski. His presence is perfect, his lines convincing, his command of the screen the most consistent of the film. Even though Blank singled him out as impressive during the shoot, and even with his obvious status as the second lead in the film, his performance has nevertheless gone largely uncommented in analysis on *Fitzcarraldo*. This despite the fact that his work hijacks the film at key turns (Herzog claims to have never learned what the indigenous characters say) the way that the Indians of the script hijack Fitzcarraldo's project.

The real action, however, happened outside the frame, where, it's clear, various forms of activity emerged to put pressure on the production from a number of angles. Most famously, protests led by the formal Aguaruna governing body forced an entire relocation of the project and are at the root of the production's years-long delays. Herzog subsequently turned to a new labor supply, another group of workers mainly from Asháninka and Machiguenga communities, the former of whom he would have to recruit from a significant distance.[125] Herzog's work with these communities attracted the attention of the nongovernmental organization Survival International, which claimed that these new workers were less organized and thus more vulnerable to exploitation than the Aguarunas who had previously chased Herzog and his crew off their bend in the river. But they cite no evidence on this point, and, indeed, everything in the dossier suggests that this group, too, came organized, negotiating for wages and even legal assistance with land claims. More intimately, according to Herzog, they intervened in the production itself by offering to kill Kinski. While the anecdote smacks of legend—in Blank's diary, he reports incidents in which many in the production crew were threatened, perhaps teasingly, with murder (Gosling and Blank 1982, 45–46)—it is symbolically illuminating, indicating the fact that Herzog was dealing with an active community, not exploited hypnotics.[126] One can, of course, get into the nitty-gritty of the labor arrangements and will certainly find much to criticize: What were the Indian workers paid relative to the largely European crew? (On this imbalance, Herzog speaks openly.)[127] Was the access to resources in the workers' camp equal to that of the nonindigenous crew? Was the construction of a separate camp (detailed in *Burden of Dreams*, and reflected on in Herzog and Cronin [2002]) for the indigenous workers an act of bald segregation or, as Herzog would have it, cultural respect? Were the Asháninka and Machiguenga consulted on this point? Was the recruiting of prostitutes—according to Herzog, at the urging of a mission priest—a form of human trafficking? These are all important questions, provoking scandal at the time and continuing to generate comment today. But the common suggestion that the Indians are helpless victims of Herzog's abuses is wishful. That the Indian workers arrived as a dignified group, or groups, capable of, even motivated by, collective action is unassailable. In fact, it seems to be the Eurocentric observer who is most invested in their victimization, their difference, not as workers in an old-style capitalist enterprise but, in the words of Kinski, *Naturkinder* (cited by Herzog, in *My Best Fiend*). Blank's *Burden of Dreams* is exemplary here. Paying extensive attention to the everyday activities of the indigenous camp, which, in the garden-variety magic trick of ethnographic filmmaking, transforms the mundane into the exotic, the documentary skids off of its narrative rails about Herzog versus the jungle in order to dwell, in an admittedly voyeuristic way, on a loud argument between two indigenous women. Ostensibly included to show tempers wearing thin after a long stay in the production's migrant labor camp, and to offer some obscure lesson about the careless mixing of indigenous communities, the long shots of exaggerated strife nevertheless pander to all kinds of stereotypes about indigenous irrationality, violence, and unpredictability. Ultimately, the argument turns out to be over an accusation of infidelity; that is, the kind of argument that many have seen (that I have seen) in cosmopolitan workplaces full of PhDs. And, indeed, we can find far worse on the shoot itself. *Burden of Dreams* lingers over this banal moment of office politics, while, despite ready access to the footage, excluding the far more explosive and shocking recordings of Kinski throwing minutes-long fits of rage, urging Walter Saxer to "tongue my ass, man!" threatening physical violence ("somebody should punch him right in the face!"), and so on.[128] But then confirming indigenous meltdown in the face of outside intervention, and solemnly condemning that intervention, is a long-standing and expected trope in ethnographic cinema, the burden of the form.

The third major limitation of the prevailing critical discourse on *Fitzcarraldo* happens at a deeper, analytical level. Ultimately, the anticolonialist (whether old-style or neo-) critique of *Fitzcarraldo* misses the object against which the film intervenes. This is because *Fitzcarraldo*'s world, in fact, is not the colonial world of discovery, contact, conquest, and settlement, even in its ongoing coloniality-of-power mode. Rather, it is an intervention against the consolidation of a system, the capitalist world-economy, and its power of representation belies the fact that the time that it engages—the Amazonian rubber boom circa 1900—is the time of capitalism, the world in which we live. Far from walling off historical violence by banishing it to a distant past, the critical work of Herzog's film moves in the opposite direction: by making present this historical knot of capitalism's world-formation, it brings to our current modernity the nightmare of its contemporary past, suggesting that its very historical traction—literally, tires—of development is at play in its highest cultural forms: for example, opera. It's an exercise in the poetics of primitive accumulation (which, for Marx, is an infinitely repeated process of alienation fundamental to capitalism's historical unfolding). This perspective, I maintain, is the only one that can render *Fitzcarraldo* critically productive in a political sense, and its subtlety of representation accounts for its long-standing influence and fascination. Schwarz offers a clue about how this works, here riffing on Benjamin riffing on Baudelaire, when he concludes that *Les fleurs du mal* is "a poetry that has absolutely not aged—not because it was young when it was written but because the circumstances that it does not speak of, [and] against which the poet composed his voice and his character, are still in place and make *Les fleurs du mal* no less virulent and difficult today than the day they were born" (2001, 2–3).

The circumstances that it does not speak of, and, yet, against which the poet composed his voice. Most immediately, viewed in the light of this structural insight, the nature of the identity politics at play in *Fitzcarraldo*—European capitalism against indigenous resistance—are no longer capable of being thought about in the terms of a misty history of trauma, but rather now inextricably tangled up in the consolidation of the present, the capitalist world-economy. In other words, this Schwarzian perspective leads away from the shallow waters of the complicity critique that appears as a kind of mirage when the audience is confronted with the conversion of a scene of genocidal horror (the rubber boom) into a high-style opera. The fact that Fitzcarraldo—a slightly charismatic dreamer, mad, to be sure, but ultimately harmless, even a little fragile, and anyway defeated by the Indians—is *nothing* like the gun-running, slave-driving Fitzcarrald. And the parallel fact that Herzog would be accused of crimes strikingly resonant with those of the historical Fitzcarrald (as Ames 2012b puts it, "violations of native sovereignty, attempted bribery, slave labor, breach of contract, gun running, armed intimidation, and false arrest and imprisonment" [148]). These twin facts at once displace and recenter a world of boom economies that is very much our own, rendering it strange, surreal, operatic, and simultaneously material and immediate. As Thomas Elsaesser puts it, "Sometimes it seems that Herzog, for the sake of his films, makes himself into the instrument of this society, in order to simulate the conditions he set out to document"

(1986, 152). Taken together, all this confronts us with the *Griffith problem*, one very much in play and in debate in the filmmaking world today: denounce the project as racist and say nothing more about it, "cancel" it, as they say; or bracket the indulgence in colonial discourse and integrate it into an interpretation that reveals the film's achievements and also its own fissures, the critical possibilities that emerge in spite of itself.[129] Taken in the latter terms, Kinski's interpretation of an ambitious rubber baron does not have the effect of "humanizing" a historical individual worthy only of scorn, but rather in *heightening* our perception of the contradictions of a world-system premised on never-ending practices of primitive accumulation—"so-called," as Marx puts it.

There are many entries in the film's dossier for exploring this line of analysis, but of particular relevance is Herzog's constant and almost obsessive return to process aesthetics and what I call the *scene of fabrication*, cinematic representations of production and labor in the context of capitalism's savage mode. The detailed representation of productive labor—whether industrial or artisanal—is a stock moment that appears at some point in nearly all Herzog's films and, in his American work, it resonates with an entire tradition of Eurocentric confrontations with peripheries of capitalism, moments of horror rendered aesthetic when travelers and investors come face-to-face with the bare labor that stimulates the heartbeat of capitalist accumulation.[130] There is an encyclopedic history of narrative examples of this, but, in short: it seems that, when privileged travel meets the primitive practices of advanced capitalism another order of representation emerges, as if the quintessentially capitalist genre—Victorian-era travel writing, insofar as it was a genre whose realism was premised explicitly on the knowledge-power relation fundamental to capitalist penetration—short-circuits and breaks down before actual relations of capitalist production. In another literary paradigm, the long history of the Latin American *novela de la selva* would take as its very raison d'être the relation between horror and actual labor practices on the periphery.[131]

Something similar plays out in *Fitzcarraldo*, whose dossier has a literary foothold in both travel writing and the tradition of the jungle novel.[132] Much dismissed, the aching first hour of the film is crucial in this regard. It is here that the critical work of the film is established and grounded, without which the ship-over-the-mountain-and-down-the-rapids

Figure 13. The scene of fabrication, with stage. *Fitzcarraldo* (Herzog 1982).

narrative would stand as mere showmanship. During this hour we are introduced, in detailed fashion, to the workings of the rubber economy and Fitzcarraldo's somewhat bewildered attempt to negotiate them. The key scene is the scene of fabrication, when a massively successful rubber baron (José Lewgoy) takes Fitzcarraldo to visit an active rubber-tapping team. A two-minute sequence, Fitzcarraldo and the baron enter a clearing, the baron carried by porters. There they find a pair of men busy at work, extracting sap, heating it, and packaging it for transport. As Fitzcarraldo looks on in wonder, the baron holds forth on the specifications of rubber extraction and the size of his operation.

Two essential references collide in this scene. First, Herzog takes us through a kind of wormhole into the history of Latin American political cinema. Specifically here, he recapitulates a tradition that Salomé Aguilera Skvirsky (2017; 2020) calls "the process genre," films, often shorts, whose aesthetic logic rests on a detailed, step-by-step exposition of how things work.[133] Here the audience is introduced, rather meticulously, to the minutiae of rubber tapping. But it's an exposition with a difference. In this Herzog situates his film within a genealogy that inscribes the various avant-garde "new cinema" movements in Latin America, most momentously cinema novo, which began its life as a series of hyperrealist, stylized process films that celebrated folkloric production as a kind of science beyond, or against, capitalism (see Aguilera Skvirsky 2011).[134]

In other words, the process aesthetic in Latin America has been a way of engaging and challenging the normative representations of the basic human relation of production. Knowing this gives new resonance to the strikingly material plenitude of the mise-en-scène and the information it conveys. Most obviously, we witness raw rubber emerge before our eyes, from fresh-cut incision in the bark, its accumulation into a tin receptacle, and on to the first-stage refinement over a jungle fire pit. But then comes the second reference, the way in which this processual representation confronts us with a scene of fabrication dripping with power relations: the counterpoint between shirtless Indians and overdressed rubber baron, mediated, as it were, by the upstart Fitzcarraldo. Most bracing is the baron's pose—resting on a litter supported by indentured servants—and words in relation to the jittery, distracted actions of Fitzcarraldo, resolutely clad in his rumpled Panama suit. While the baron utters racist musings (denigrating the very language of his laborers) and calculations—"I have eight thousand five hundred men but am thinking of expanding to ten"—Fitzcarraldo quivers in near ecstasy over the materiality of the scene: the liquid latex, the hot kettles, the smoke, the impressive white turkey (a beautifully incongruent, Herzogian touch, which apparently left Kinski feeling "upstaged" [Gosling and Blank 1982, 50]), the bare, brown flesh. Koepnick (1993) argues that, while colonial relations of power ran rampant on set, in the film they are hidden from the audience (158) and Prager (2007) makes a similar point about the relation between work and opera (42; see also Leppert 2015, 71–72). These conclusions must come at the expense of this scene, in which all these relations are in fact presented to us directly. Confronted with the capitalist vertigo of accumulation for accumulation's sake, Fitzcarraldo responds with a kind of ludic answer—indeed, if one wants to go there, perhaps even a form of resistance. Madness, dreams: opera. None of the scene's staging of the relations between capitalist accumulation, work, and opera is hidden. In Blank's filming of the filming of the scene, we see nothing less than an operatic diva in Kinski, as he complains that the dialogue is simply "shit." Herzog is explicit in the touch of insanity he wants to inflict on the rubber project, instructing Lewgoy to get weirdly mystical as he speaks to the exploits of his baron's project. And finally, in case we are tempted to somehow perceive opera as the escape from, as opposed to the intensification of, the sweat of extraction, the entire scene is performed as if in a theater: the clearing, roughly the oblong half-circle shape of an opera house with the canopy above providing the decorative ceiling, from which our perspective looks at Kinski standing on a campsite platform, raised above the jungle floor as if on a stage. The dialogue, between Kinski's tenor and Lewgoy's baritone, with costumed Indians looking on, might as well be sung.

Here in the jungle—the aesthetic counterpoint to the built environment of the opera house, another kind of work—confronted with bare labor, Fitzcarraldo's adventure truly begins. "I have no interest in the rubber boom era," says Herzog over and again in the DVD commentary. And yet here we are with Schwarz, reminding us of those *essential* circumstances that the work of art *does not speak of*. With the scene of fabrication giving flesh to Fitzcarraldo's dreams of opera, our protagonist (with the *auteur*) goes on to trace the basic steps of accumulation in the rubber world: geographical discourse (he consults a map); *habilitación* (he secures a loan for supplies, from the spoils of sex work, no less); capital investment and technological mobilization (he appropriates a ship); and risk (he heads upriver). He will find himself bereft of the key element: force. That is, he has no force of labor to realize his project, and no force of arms to coerce this labor supply: no militia, no slaves, no debt peons. In a twist away from actual history that at the same time invites us to think history anew, Fitzcarraldo does not cajole, kill, and enslave a recalcitrant labor force; rather, he enters into a kind of misunderstood partnership with his indigenous laborers. And here the rubber-tapping scene becomes the overture to the memorable action of the film. Recapitulating and expanding the scene of fabrication, and tightening even further the relation between opera and work, Fitzcarraldo will now oversee his own scene of fabrication. This is the scene of fabrication that would make *Fitzcarraldo* famous, the precarious feat of engineering that will risk lives—in the film and in the world—to hoist the ship with pulleys and levers (and a backhoe), a special effect done the old-fashioned way, a host of laboring bodies that will transform the world into music, transform the work of the rubber boom into a feat not of violence but of aesthetics.[135] The project is over the top, impossible, sublime: the capitalist irrational rendered cinematic. If, in Herzog's own description, this is the film's moment of "grand opera," its relation to monumental work based on extreme labor conditions could not be made more blatant: while Fitzcarraldo hovers at the margins shouting, and the chief intervenes only to show off a block of ice, it is the everyday Indians who do all the pushing and pulling, straining against gravity, standing in harm's way (one is crushed when the ship slips). Fitzcarraldo's dream, the bit about the cow jumping over the moon, is the Indians' work. They are the hands that will construct the opera house, the infrastructure for Caruso's intervention (which happens here by way of a gramophone recording that fades into the extra-diegetic soundtrack). Even more, the passage represents the playful perversion of the class struggle at the heart of capitalist discourse by eroding its linear, productive terms of investment-force-production-accumulation. Without these terms, there can be no *actual* opera, no accumulation, no surplus value, no opera house.[136] And yet opera, the form, continues to animate the story, appropriated for extracapitalist ends like the Jívaro's appropriation of the ship itself.

The logic of the plot makes this deformation of the modern world's master narrative literal and direct. With the pyrotechnics of the ship-moving project still fresh in our minds, the nature of the endeavor is revealed to us. The Indians laboring on Fitzcarraldo's project, the audience knows, are never enslaved: they work of their own volition, something related to a curse over the land. Their project reveals itself when the story takes a final unexpected turn. The ship now safely docked on the other side of the portage, a celebration and pandemonium ensue, in which Fitzcarraldo finally goes native, face painted and dancing with the Indians. He passes out drunk in his ship's cabin, at which point, in the film's only shift away from Fitzcarraldo's perspective, the Jívaro stealthily cut the mooring lines, hop aboard, and send the boat downriver, through the deadly Pongo das Mortes. When the ship limps out of the rapids, battered and now useless, a pathetic drifting hull, we realize that in fact it was Fitzcarraldo who was working for the Indians. Their project, to shoot the rapids, triumphs, and this is the final twist that will render the story fully operatic: "La commedia è finita!" in the memorable last line from *Pagliacci* (1892), which not coincidentally appears in the film. La commedia è finita, and like Canio waking up to real life, Fitzcarraldo finds himself a performer in the Indians' great opera.[137]

How to interpret all this? More directly: What does it mean to reduce genocidal projects of primitive accumulation (like the rubber-boom

Figure 14. The Jívaro stop their work. *Fitzcarraldo* (Herzog 1982).

economy) to dreamscapes without a clear counterpolitics? Herzog calls *Fitzcarraldo* a meditation on the "weightlessness of dreams" and Fitzcarraldo a character that can help us to realize our own dreams (director's commentary, *Fitzcarraldo* DVD). Besides utterly banal, this strikes me as a blatant misunderstanding of the film. Not the unbearable lightness of dreams, *Fitzcarraldo*'s topic is the historical weight of open veins, Galeano's famous exclamation point on Latin America's twentieth-century consensus, from Mariátegui to Cardoso, that, in Dierdra Reber's words, "global power is asymmetrical, unevenly distributed between center and periphery, and fundamentally economic in nature" (2016, 269). The politics of art, from a materialist perspective, heightens and reimagines, but never renders invisible, this set of relations.

In other words, the difficulty here is that of all Herzog's major works. *Fitzcarraldo* confronts us not with an opportunity to dream, but with the problem of rethinking the foundational themes of our modern political imagination when they are rendered so radically unfamiliar, with seemingly clear lines of conflict blurred, buried under layers of mist and jungle and mud and opera. And work. The simultaneous subtlety and obviousness of the world-historical agency of the oppressed classes; the affective penetration of the nightmares of the world-system; the unyielding confrontation with what the director calls the "crisis of the image";

and the refusal to construct another world before our eyes, the unflinching estrangement born of staring into the dark corners of this one: this is the political imagination of Herzog, not a politics of pamphlets but somewhere between Rancière's *dissensus* and Bakhtin's *carnaval*, the ingredients that make sociocritical readings of his films so challenging and necessary. *Fitzcarraldo* does not denounce the world-system in all its injustice and cruelty. Rather, it inhabits that world, performs its contradictions, and leaves the work of praxis for the audience. As Schwarz, this time riffing on Lukacs, once said about another master of the margins, "let us only say that, contrary to what is generally thought, the material of the artist turns out not be shapeless: it is historically shaped and in some way registers the social process to which it owes its existence." And even when radically defamiliarized, rendered operatic, this subject matter "has always been world-historical. This the artists shape as well as they can, but it would not have been their subject, had they dealt with it directly" (1992, 31).

For the indigenous communities of the Amazon, the extraction of rubber is symbolic of a more deadly plague. In the last instance, the commodity and its cognates—lumber, gold, petroleum—are second-order objects of plunder. The real object of harvest is the Indians themselves, their homes swallowed by machines, their bodies dismembered by the vampirism that those machines require. Herzog unwittingly suggests this in Blank's *Burden of Dreams* (1982) when, in a denunciation of what he perceives as his unfair treatment by local Aguaruna communities, he complains of rumors that he had secret plans to "slaughter them and take the grease out of their bodies and cook the grease." In this portrait of Herzog, the director is merely the latest incarnation of a well-known local pestilence: the *pishtaco*, the white man vampire spirit that stalks the jungle, in search of Indian bodies to boil and refine, harvesting their fat to grease the machines of capitalist accumulation. Still very much alive today, the concept is centuries old and carries a number of disguises but features the constant motif of body parts plundered and exploited, often in service of lubrication.[138] It's not hard to understand Herzog's frustration. By his own account, and there is no reason to doubt his sincerity, he came in peace, for his own purposes, of course, and not just a little bit bumbling, but with the objective of making a film with indigenous collaboration that would present a dignified portrait of their world. As he put it himself in an explanatory op-ed in the Peruvian press at the time, which was also something of a plea, "My film project will not distort their identity and not touch their dignity. On the contrary, the spirit of the film will be on the side of the Aguarunas, and it will try to define their strong culture, as it used to be before John Travolta" [!] (*Survival International*, 1979a: 29). To hear Herzog tell it, he soon found himself confronting all sorts of agitators who conspired against his project with rumor and threat: journalists, anthropologists, an agronomist and an activist who wandered the area with a folder full of photographs of Nazi death camps, warning any Indians who would listen against the unreliable intentions of Germans. As for the Aguarunas, Herzog came to see himself as their politicians' symbol of legitimacy, the proof that they could effectively act, even if to do so they had to rely on propaganda and misrepresentation of his intentions. So, again, one can understand the disappointment.

And yet one can't overlook the cliché and arrogance of this position. Characterizing the active solidarity of oppressed groups as self-serving political opportunism, crying wolf against the machinations of outside agitators: these are the stock responses of the powerful to asymmetrical struggle everywhere, the universal reaction anytime anyone throws sand into the gears of the machines of extraction, development, profit. Whispers, rumors, nonparticipation, active suspicion, vandalism: the weapons of the weak, proven well justified in the rain forest, and sometimes momentarily effective, as a defense against the fanaticism of capitalist accumulation and the five centuries of horror that have accompanied it. And if the rumors were in fact founded on false denunciations, this likely only heightens their larger truth; we don't have to believe that Herzog was going to harvest the body fluids of Aguaruna children to understand that his project would have been, no matter how carefully executed, an invasive one. It involved digging a trench more than two kilometers in length and ten meters wide through delicate rain forest soils (*Survival International Review* 1982, 95), a fact plain for all to see in the movie itself. Resonating uncomfortably with centuries of land expropriation, the production required the construction of a camp the size of a small village, one that, according to the respected anthropologist Michael F. Brown, Herzog secured by contracting a local militia (Brown 1982, 20;

see also *Survival International Review* 1982, 95).[139] Most stridently, Herzog developed a general attitude of hostility to the proper negotiating body, the Consejo Aguaruna Huambisa, just formed in 1977 in the wake of national land-rights legislation (*Survival International Review* 1979a, 28).[140] In short, Herzog tarred with the same brush of bad faith both the journalist running around with pictures of Third Reich horrors and the one indigenous organization with legitimate claim to authority in the region. In a territory constantly under pressure by state-sponsored development schemes of "colonization," it comes as no surprise that the *consejo* would be skeptical.[141] (Indeed, the topic makes it into the movie itself: the lands that Fitzcarraldo buys have been declared by the state "baldío" [barren, fallow, unoccupied], a claim patently falsified by the presence of the Jívaro on them.) More juridical, and frankly much less hyperbolic than Herzog, council president Evaristo Nugkuag put it like this: "The problem is that the community cannot just hand over a bit of land to Herzog or anyone else, because by law and custom we're not able to do so. The land is small and is only for occupation by Aguarunas" (*Survival International Review* 1981, 95).[142] In light of immediate stress (there was both an international border conflict and active petroleum exploration in the region) and a long intercultural history that has never gone well for the Indians, it should have come as no surprise to Herzog that many Aguarunas would be less than thrilled with the idea of hosting the reenactment of a history of capitalist violence on their land, or that rumors would swirl, in the words of one of Brown's informants, about a secret plan to trick the Aguarunas into participating in a battle scene that would end in their literal deaths (Brown 1982, 21).[143] In *Burden of Dreams*, Herzog, now a thousand miles south of Aguaruna lands, gestures approvingly at his Machiguenga actors and laments their swift modernization: "I don't want to live in a world without lions, and these men are lions."

Exactly: like the lions that showed up at Herzog's doorstep at four in the morning, armed and prepared for war. Not long after the *pishtaco* rumors began to circulate, on December 1, 1979, Aguaruna villagers surrounded Herzog's compound, gently packed up the crew and their gear into motor-powered canoes, and burned the camp to ashes. Herzog's associates (the director himself was absent) fled downriver, literally waving a white flag (see *Burden of Dreams*). The following day, a group

Figure 15. The ship's track through the rain forest. *Burden of Dreams* (Blank 1982).

of Aguarunas who had missed out on the expulsion rebuilt part of the camp so that they too could participate in burning it to the ground. For many years, the village would recreate the event in a celebration of victory over intruders.[144]

This aborted beginning, transported to 1900, would have made a nice ending to the film. Indeed, *Fitzcarraldo* feels ready to end in similar fashion, after the daringly shot scene of the ship bouncing down the rapids, part of which was filmed with some of the actors, including Kinski, on board. The steamboat sputters into open water, visibly battered by the rocks, Fitzcarraldo aghast, the Indians smiling at their accomplishment. And *fin*. Or, if it were necessary to give Fitzcarraldo the last word, the subsequent scene would suffice: in a dockside office, reunited with the baron and holding a champagne toast with the Indians, in which he gives an opaque soliloquy on colonial wonder. Instead, for reasons unclear, the rubber baron buys back the wrecked ship, and Fitzcarraldo invests the tall stack of blood money to float in an opera company to the docks of Iquitos, where, dressed as New England pilgrims, they perform Bellini's

I Puritani on the river. Fitzcarraldo stands on the ship's deck, astride an empty silk chair—which earlier in the story he had promised to reserve for a pig—smoking a comically enormous cigar, Molly and the masses applaud from shore, the tone is triumphant. By far the least satisfying ending to the major Herzog films, it makes absolutely no sense, Herzog's explanations about following one's dreams fall flat, and the whole thing feels like a forced note of redemption, a desperately Hollywood ending. García Márquez captures the sentiment when he calls it a disappointingly "conformist conclusion in the style of Rossini, instead of the Wagnerian apocalypse that everybody hoped for, in order to feel complete after so many flights of the imagination" (reprinted in *El País*, 1982).

But there's an alternative ending, contained within the film itself. This ending comes right at the beginning. The film opens to distant thunder and fog over a panoramic long shot of the jungle canopy. An epigraph appears. It recites an indigenous myth in which it calls the jungle Cayahuari Yacu, or "the Land in which God did not finish his Creation." It's an act of ventriloquism, of course, there's no evidence that the Indians that act, or that are represented, in Herzog's film have such a myth. The line has been analyzed, correctly to be sure, in the key of Romanticism, with or without, in Franco's words, "the return of the culture hero" (Franco 1983, 187; compare Johnson 2016, 46). But in materialist terms, it can only represent the announcement of the violence of the context and the history that the film represents. The epigraphic Indians are already monotheistic Indians, their gods are God. The myth, in other words, explains not a primordial moment of extra-modern jungle life; the myth explains their contemporary moment, when the jungle can be fully imagined as part of a world. This overwhelming message from God, from across the ocean, is their subsumption into a world-system, their interpellation by the god called capitalism.[145] God, in this sense, is not the culture hero, certainly not the man of opera, not Fitzcarraldo. God, in fact, is nowhere on the scene. But his messenger is. This is the exterminating angel, the Destroyer, the plague of viruses and bandoliers, Fitzcarrald, the rubber baron. Herzog's Amazonian God is an angry god, and we can feel his spite as the epigraph continues, now accompanied by that weird, placeless choral music that we met at the beginning of *Aguirre*, here in a less ethereal, more Wagnerian (or is it Orffian?), tone: "Only with the Disappearance of Man, they believe, will he return, and his Work be completed."[146] Creation will be finished, and the real opera of the world, its eternal transformation into music, will be realized, at the moment when man is ushered off stage. For the living communities of the Amazon rain forest, the rubber baron has played a starring role in this task. While always praising the assumed wisdom of extramodern peoples, Herzog nevertheless likes to speak in rather developmentalist terms of human diversity, as in his short *Ten Thousand Years Older* (2002), whose title refers to the abrupt jump from "stone age" to "our world" when so-called uncontacted peoples come out of the woods.[147] What "contact" in this context means is the moment that these last wilderness tribes turn to engage in regular intercourse with capitalist modernity. This process is traditionally forced. The epochal invasion that began this unceasing historical turn in earnest was the rubber boom, its destructiveness so powerful that even today, an entire region of the Madre de Dios watershed is gripped by a conflict between the descendants of Fitzcarrald's slaves and those of the people that fled the baron's depredations.[148] The land of *Fitzcarraldo* is the visible meteor of impending apocalypse, the end of man: a land of conclusions, as the last free people drop out of human history, and with them the earth's lungs begin to collapse, as Fitzcarrald's river of rubber conduits is poisoned beyond recognition.[149] The rubber baron, God's messenger, sets us on this path, the beginning of the end of creation. The infinity of the physical world and man's pathetic insignificance within it—the sublime—is a big topic for Herzog, one that makes the happy ending of *Fitzcarraldo* feel like an act of denial. Rather than a Bellini and a cigar, the red thread of *Fitzcarraldo* is indeed Wagnerian in its terror, announcing a deep drive of self-destruction, and of pessimism before man's possibility as a species. In this it is the truest of portraits of the late-capitalist rain forest.

Black God, White Devil

> It was like tracking a wild, unsociable and rarely seen animal. If we wanted to catch him on film, we had to sit in the bushes for days at a time.
>
> —Werner Herzog, 1987

> Without slavery, no cotton; without cotton, no modern industry. It is slavery which has given value to the colonies; the colonies have created world trade; world trade is the necessary condition of large-scale machine industry. Thus before the traffic in Negroes began, the colonies supplied the Old World with only very few products and did not visibly change the face of the earth.
>
> —Karl Marx, 1846

> He dropped the chainsaw and thought about it for five seconds. Then he grabbed the saw again, pulled the cord, and cut off his own foot.
>
> —Werner Herzog, 1999

Cobra Verde (1987) can be understood as the third film in a loosely defined trilogy, Werner Herzog's dream-soaked contemplation of the formative moments of the capitalist world-economy. Gesturing back to *Aguirre, der Zorn Gottes* (1972) in temperament and pace, and coming closely on the heels of *Fitzcarraldo* (1982), *Cobra Verde* is the ugly duckling of the three, scantly known even among cinephiles, and having received the least and most uniformly negative response from scholarly criticism. Taken as a group, the three films interpenetrate each other in two elemental ways. First, each features a basic counterpoint. On one side stands the mercurial Klaus Kinski, as moody and often inscrutable protagonist, not even an antihero, more a subject patched together by Nietzschean desire and existential malaise. The memorable close-ups of Kinski's harried gaze ricochet off and harmonize with a basic aesthetic opponent, the landscape itself, which, as we've explored in Herzog's films, plays a starring—never supporting—role. And second, each film deals with a moment of watershed intensity in the history of modern world-formation. Discovery and conquest in *Aguirre*. Capitalist accumulation through resource extraction in *Fitzcarraldo*. The transatlantic slave trade in *Cobra Verde*. While more than half the film is set and shot in Africa, it is still very much a companion on Herzog's American nomadic.

Even though excessively amped up in a couple of signature scenes, Kinski is more consistently in his slow-burn mode here, and this combined with the uncanny mood of the film place it on an aesthetic plane alongside *Aguirre*. But in terms of story, *Cobra Verde* is essentially a variation on the theme of *Fitzcarraldo*. Interpreted through narrative structure, it can almost come off as a remake. The tale revolves around a historical personage, rather incredible in his exploits, whom Herzog manipulates and fictionalizes as his artistic needs dictate. A marginal figure on the periphery of the capitalist world-economy, we follow this protagonist through a number of scenes of extractive accumulation, including a parenthetical process-genre set piece in which an oligarch of industrial agriculture (a *latifundista* again played by José Lewgoy) walks us through the details of commodity production. From this generative moment the protagonist is launched on an insane mission that involves a long voyage on a boat, although in this case the trip itself is glossed. He commandeers a decrepit icon of capitalist violence—Fitzcarraldo's restored rubber-hauling steamship is here a reconstructed slave-trading fortress—and takes advantage of local knowledge and politics to his benefit. Again, an impressive force of indigenous actors makes possible the achievement of his goal. In the end, however, the natives prove too strong, and too clever, leaving our protagonist to founder in the surf. Far grimmer than *Fitzcarraldo*, he is nevertheless able to announce a kind of victory in the face of his destruction—stated, as before, via perfunctory soliloquy during a champagne toast—if not this time personal (Fitzcarraldo's declaration "because I have seen it" that ushers in his little opera on the river), then at least historical. There's even a memorable scene that involves pulling an impossibly large boat. This time the attempt fails of its own accord but, again, like the Indians aboard Fitzcarraldo's ship, a local witness lingers as a kind of specter alongside the debacle.

But even if the structural repetition at the level of storytelling may be a little tiresome in its obsession, *Cobra Verde* is very much its own film with enough originality to keep us on our toes, and, in spite of everything, one of Herzog's best. While we might recognize Aguirre's menacing gaze in Kinski's performance, the dominant visage is less nervous cunning than perfectly balanced simmering rage and resigned stoicism. Moreover, the gulf in historical worlds between the two films is significant. And while *Cobra Verde* is closer in time and place to the scene of *Fitzcarraldo* (less than a century separates their settings, and they both run through Brazil), the motivations and literal routes of the protagonists are quite distinct, even though both represent renditions of historical figures whose real contributions to world-formation are, simply put, ghastly: a rubber baron and a slave trader. Fitzcarraldo is an immigrant striver, with a clear objective, one who must swallow hard and engage in at least some vaguely humiliating interaction with the monied elite. Cobra Verde is a bandit. Firmly and consistently disdainful of the powerful, he simply glides along the circuits of capital accumulation, doing their bidding as a kind of challenge to their hegemony, cavalier in indulging his passions (theft, murder, rape). His only motivation is an obscure fantasy about someday seeing the land of snow.

Cobra Verde was a significantly ambitious production—Herzog called it his most exhausting, this even after *Fitzcarraldo*—and scandals echoing the earlier film pursued the director once again. First and foremost was Kinski, who, it seems at this point, was at the very end of his psychological faculties (he would die relatively young and suddenly, about five years after shooting). Witnesses attest to his troubled state; he succeeded in chasing the brilliant cinematographer Thomas Mauch, notwithstanding a two-decade-long creative partnership with Herzog, off the production in its first weeks, and Herzog referred to filming him in the terms of stalking a wild animal: "For sixty seconds it was possible to shoot a sequence and capture a moment, but we had to wait for days. . . . It's true that if you imprison a lion in a small cage, nothing of the lion remains, but giving Kinski more and more of a wide berth made the shooting increasingly difficult. I always had to creep up on him like a thief" (Herzog 2014a, 102). As with *Fitzcarraldo*, and in what now seems to be an obvious marketing strategy, a filmmaker, Steff Gruber, showed up to make a documentary of the production. *Location Africa* (1987) is not in the same league as Blank's work (and, in consonance with its object of representation, generated far less interest; today it is almost impossible to find), but, like *Burden of Dreams*, it also is relatively unvarnished and raises eyebrows at Herzog's methods. *Cobra Verde* is shot in Ghana and Colombia, and large groups of extras on both sides of the Atlantic broke out in small riots over contract disputes. The seven hundred or so Ghanian women recruited to play the fearsome warriors of Dahomey nearly ended up in a human trampling disaster. Half the Colombian crew, from the local film and arts community, was left off the credits.[150] More broadly, West Africa was in a highly politicized moment, with socialist movements on the decline, Benin (the historical setting of the film, although not where it was shot) in the last throes of Mathieu

Kérékou's Marxist-Leninist regime, memory politics exceedingly raw, and engaged African filmmakers seeking a language to avoid censors and tell their stories (Akomfrah 2014). Into the middle of all this parachutes the Great Herzog, a German filmmaker on location to restore a fortress of human traffic and build a movie-set village to stand in for Abomey, the royal seat of Dahomey. In short, to tell the West African story of slavery. From the perspective of a Brazilian slave driver. Played by Kinski. As usual, Herzog was asking for trouble.

For interpretive analyses that seek out the political dimensions of films and filmmaking, the slavery film genre is difficult to beat for polemics and scandal. *Uncle Tom's Cabin* (1927), *Gone with the Wind* (1939), *Burn!* (1969), *Addio Zio Tom* (1971), *Mandingo* (1975), *Roots* (1977), *Django Unchained* (2012), *12 Years a Slave* (2013), slavery films—especially (but not only) in the United States—are essential territory for the perennial debates about race and cinema. It is as enlightening as it is tragic that the movie that ushered in modern filmmaking, largely set during Reconstruction, has American slavery and its attendant racism as its raison d'être: *Birth of a Nation* (1915).

There are many reasons for this particular intersection of art and history. Slavery, as a topic, besides the baseline narrative of race relations and its attendant violence that it automatically invites, also invokes immediately the politics of memory, collaboration, and implication; the interplay between historical fact and contemporary accountability; erasure and monumentalization. Put all this on film and it becomes especially combustible. At its center we find the problem of *gaze*: who looks, who contemplates, who records, who organizes the images into story, who invites *us* to look, and to what end. In general, it has been white filmmakers—or a white filmmaking establishment, usually Hollywood or its satellites—telling a story that is always ultimately about a trauma whose central victim is people of African descent. In this, the slavery film has a foothold in ethnographic filmmaking.[151] It is right here, at the intersection of politics and aesthetics, inequality and cinematography, where Herzog's films would settle in during his post-*Fitzcarraldo* period.

Herzog's images of explicit slavery in America are relatively fleeting: a whipping post and plantation scene in *Cobra Verde*, and the indigenous porters along with the single African slave, Okello, of *Aguirre*;

we can suppose that at least some of the rubber workers of the scene of fabrication in *Fitzcarraldo* are also enslaved, but this is not made explicit. At the same time, his work in Africa is extensive. It stretches back to the impressionistic *Fata Morgana* (1971), and the continent is the site of some of his most straightforwardly ethnographic films. Two of them circulate around the time of *Cobra Verde*. First is the lyrical, and highly informative, *Wodaabe: Herdsmen of the Sun* (1989), a fascinating reflection on a culturally threatened nomadic group famous in anthropological circles for its liberal, animistic-inflected interpretation of Islam and for its courting rituals, which involve a complex pageant in which the men of the tribe vie for the title of *most beautiful*, while the women stand as judges. In one of his truly memorable shots, Herzog opens the film with a brief, deadpan description of the Wodaabe culture spoken over a heat-warped landscape of camel herd and desert and then cuts to the men straining and chanting, their voices edited out in favor of an ancient recording of *Ave Maria* sung by the last castrato of the Vatican. It's a profound moment, hypnotic, with a nod to the surreal that could compete with Buñuel, but with all the cynicism emptied out and replaced by pathos.[152] This story of a cult of beauty practiced among shepherds—highly idealized, to be sure—intercut with desert refugee camps and a history of border conflicts and shrinking territory ultimately makes for an affecting short film that raises a number of issues, from the politics of development to the politics of gender. A year later, Herzog released something like the opposite African treatment, *Echoes from a Somber Empire* (1990), a reflection on the world of the notorious dictator, Jean-Bédel Bokassa. A little choppy and meandering, the film's descriptions of cannibalism and a disturbing, long-held shot of a caged chimpanzee smoking a cigarette stick in the mind here. Accused of pandering to African exotica, Herzog would offer in his defense the idea that the portrait of Bokassa (and that we could extend to his treatment of the Wodaabe) isn't about the object of analysis—a tyrant, a tribe—but rather that it's about everybody, from the African peasant to the Eurocentric moviegoer (Herzog and Cronin 2002, 214, 218).[153] There is fire in the hearts of men and within it is contained the ultimate psychopathology of tyrants like Bokassa and the serene communal spirit of beauty witnessed among the Wodaabe. Resonating in the friendly authority of Herzog's slow, Teutonic prosody, this sounds

Figure 16. Wodaabe beauty pageant. *Wodaabe: Herdsmen of the Sun* (Herzog 1989).

philosophically impressive for a second, but of course it's the founding proposition of ethnological discourse: since Homer and Herodotus, it's never been about knowing the other; it's about estranging the self.[154] Indeed, returning to the topic at hand, it is only the rare slavery film that succeeds in obliging the spectator to see the age of transatlantic, chattel slavery as an obligation to rethink the world in which we live.

But, to forestall exploring Herzog's contribution to the slavery film genre one moment further, it's important to note that his films of this period would not only develop his ethnographic catalog. Herzog's work also took a decisively political turn during the two decades or so that followed *Fitzcarraldo*. In this, his constant rejection of the imputation of political themes or motivations to his work, or to his possible identification as a "political" filmmaker, starts to take on the feeling of a Freudian disavowal: the patient always also says yes. After the *explicitly* political battles over rights and representation that bedeviled *Fitzcarraldo*—a film set within a project of resource extraction whose production became embroiled in literal struggles over land—Herzog almost seems to invite the kind of controversy that had always crept around his films. Let's quickly review: With *Signs of Life* (1968) he begins his career as a German filmmaker taking up the setting of World War II for a film about German soldiers that makes no mention of National Socialism. He shoots a film cast exclusively by dwarfs and little people, evoking the exhibitionism of Tod Browning and that everybody understands as a parody of the world revolution of 1968. *Aguirre* invites allegorical readings related to the Third Reich and Vietnam, but with no clear position about either. He makes a film about labor and industry in which both camps are inscrutable, revolution is in the air, and with almost the entire cast acting under a spell of hypnosis. He follows that up with an indictment of the American dream. His interpretations of American capitalism seem at once mesmerizing and pointless (*How Much Wood . . .* 1976; *Huie's Sermon*, 1981; *God's Angry Man*, 1981). Starting with *Fitzcarraldo* (1982), scandalous interpretations and denunciations would pick up steam.

In his interviews, Herzog concedes having made only two directly political films, that is, "political" in the conventional sense, message films with a clear point and a certain didactic feel. One is an obscure little documentary from his early career, called *Handicapped Future* (1971), that he describes as a classroom film (Herzog and Cronin 2002, 73). (And while he doesn't himself speak of it in such terms, we might place the more sophisticated and less direct *Into the Abyss* [2011] in the same category, knowing Herzog's widely stated opposition to capital punishment.) The other is the moderately well known follow-up to *Fitzcarraldo*, a film about aboriginal land rights in Australia called *Where the Green Ants Dream* (1984). Sandwiched between opening and closing shots of metaphorical apocalypses (menacing recordings of Oklahoma tornadoes), an aboriginal boy listening to an Argentine soccer broadcast, and a landscape of mineral-extraction destruction, the film tells the story of a historical mining conflict that led to a major court case. While it features Herzog's penchant for striking images, here around juxtapositions between native cultures and machines of extraction and the eventual appropriation of those tools, much of the film is a pretty bland courtroom drama, a straightforward denunciation of the legacies of colonial domination. Herzog is sometimes critical about certain shots or turns in his own films—this comes up quite a bit in his comments on

Cobra Verde—but *Where the Green Ants Dream* is the singular example of a film for which he comes close to expressing dislike.[155] In its wake, the film would be denounced by aboriginal groups and participate in a debate about cultural appropriation, a controversy that relitigated and contributed to the growing clamor around *Fitzcarraldo* (Hurley 2007). Two decades later, Herzog will cap a long run of controversial films by finally confronting Germany's Nazi past, crafting a story called *Invincible* (2000) that takes up Jewish identity, community, mysticism, and the vicissitudes of race. An exciting prospect that cast Tim Roth as the villain and quintessentially Herzogian in that it centers on a circus strongman, but it turned out to be an aesthetically weak entry into the Herzog catalog and also a commercial flop.

During this period, war, the ultimate expression of politics as *polemos*, circulates through Herzog's work, and each project of the time ended up courting polemics of its own. After *Ballad of the Little Soldier* (1984), a film on child soldiers shot within the context of an active counterinsurgency in Nicaragua, something of a mess and full of historical errors, Herzog would be accused of acting as a CIA stooge.[156] For *Lessons of Darkness* (1992), a jaw-dropping treatment of burning Gulf War oil fields transformed into experimental science fiction, he was denounced for aestheticizing catastrophe and as an apologist for US military aggression.[157] But the most illustrative of his war films is *Little Dieter Needs to Fly* (1997), a little-known but highly regarded documentary. The film is a fascinating and moving biography of Dieter Dengler, a German immigrant to the United States who became a fighter pilot and was shot down over Laos in 1966. Taken prisoner, he eventually escaped and was rescued, against all odds, after nearly a month hiding in the jungle. It's a brilliant portrait, and a clinic for three techniques essential to Herzog's grammar of filmmaking. First is the rejection of any clear border between documentary and fictional filmmaking, with Herzog—as he had done since his 1971 film about the life of Fini Straubinger—scripting invented lines and entire scenes intercalated into Dengler's autobiographical discourse. Second is his idiosyncratic and powerful work of reenactment, which in Herzog's films is made more highly performative by being better described as repetition, and links the tight form-content relation of his documentaries to the discourse of struggle that inhabits so many of his feature films. Not a dramatization, and even resonating with the director's attraction to process aesthetics, Herzog restages Dengler's forced march through the jungle and aspects of his imprisonment by bringing him to remote mountain Thailand (near the Laos border) and placing the protagonist himself back into his own scenes of duress. It's a powerful move, and we feel the weight of history through the nervous body language of both Dengler and the villagers acting as his captors.[158]

A third structural element of Herzog's filmmaking, crucial for our discussion of *Cobra Verde*, comes through powerfully, and disquietingly, in *Little Dieter*. This is the nonpolitics of the politics of his films, the refusal, even stubborn refusal, to take or invite a position on histories whose reinvocations serve as flashpoints for dividing people into camps and that nourish critical perspectives on the human condition. Dengler's context was the 1960s US invasion and bombing of southeast Asia, a genocidal project that would end up costing well over a million lives on the peninsula. His participation in an aerial assault on Laos was part of a now-notorious secret mission, withheld from the American public, a relatively early sortie over what would become the most-bombed country in world history: more than two million tons of ordnance dropped on a small, underdeveloped country by the United States during a single decade. Herzog makes this sublime. Footage of napalm canisters floating, slow-motion, over peasant huts before they explode into hellfire—some of the most tragic shots in the history of film—are made horrifyingly beautiful accompanied by Tuvan throat singers.

Dengler was one of the rubble children of World War II whose village was shattered by bombs, and images of German towns in ruins—"like a dreamscape of the surreal," narrates Herzog—transition to warplanes outfitted on Pacific aircraft carriers, all accompanied by the wistful melodrama of Carlos Gardel, singing his signature "Volver." Early in the film, Dengler, a bombing survivor himself, comments, "But that there were people down there, who suffered, who died, only became clear to me much later, when I was their prisoner." Frames later, Herzog's narration elaborates, "But from the air, Vietnam didn't seem real at all. For Dengler it was like a grid on a map. . . . But even though it was all very real, everything down there seemed to be so alien and so abstract. It all looked strange, like a distant, barbaric dream." World War II dreamscapes; the distant, barbaric dream of Vietnam. People bomb. War is hell, in the vaguely fascistic expression that always seems to carry a subtext:

do your duty. Later, in an interview, Herzog would remark, "Though I feel that the war is always very much in the margins of the film, you have to remember that for Dieter it lasted only forty minutes. It was never his aim to go to war; he just wanted to fly, and the only chance as a German to do this was to emigrate to the United States" (Herzog and Cronin 2002, 267). The film ends up with a distinctly nationalist vibe—as Herzog puts it, "He had all the qualities that make America so wonderful: self-reliance and courage, a kind of frontier spirit" (ibid., 265)—that is yet at once uneasy.[159] The Americans, we know, bombed little Dieter's German villages. The Americans, we know, bombed Laos to a pulp. People bomb. Americans bomb. There's a provocation there. Herzog pointedly avoids any temptation to "denounce American aggression in the Vietnam war" (ibid., 267). And his story of an American hero is at the same time a meditation on political violence and real death. I have not come across any statement by Herzog of his position on the US-led military project in Vietnam. But everything in his artistic career gives a clear indication of where he stands on genocidal violence prosecuted by administrators of state propping up their actions on lies. What Herzog seems to be asking the audience is: do you need me to tell you that people shouldn't bomb? While this might be a mature position, an expression of respect for the ethical intelligence of the audience, when applied to scenes of genocide, it can represent a profound risk. This stance, Herzog's default posture in general, will play out to significant effect as he takes on the slavery film.

Swimming upstream against the main current of our capitalist modernity, Francisco Félix de Souza crossed the Atlantic from America to Africa in about 1800. He may have been fleeing persecution for political crimes, although about his origins we know next to nothing. His destiny, however, would be world-historical. Universally remembered—and described in various historical accounts—as mixed-race, or in the Brazilian racial nomenclature, *um mulato*, it is often proposed that he hailed from Salvador de Bahia, the son of a slave trader and a slave, and was possibly a manumitted slave himself.[160] Whatever the literal blend of his ethnic background, he was light-skinned enough to have his face blackened by indigo, legend has it, upon his sentencing for treason, because of a local taboo against killing whites.[161] Over the next three decades, de

Souza would seize the administrative functions of a decommissioned Portuguese fortress, be imprisoned by the king of Dahomey, and then pirouette to land on the right side of that king's ouster. He would leverage the subsequent political windfall and cultivate his considerable web of international associates into what was by the 1820s the largest slave-trading operation in the Bight of Benin. In this he stood at a joint point of the modern world. Brazilian traders were the most prolific during the three centuries of high traffic on the Atlantic, and also some of the very last, for Brazil, the final American country to outlaw slavery as such, was persistent in receiving slave ships long after the onset of the English navy's suppression of the trade.[162] Ouidah, economic capital of the so-called Slave Coast and de Souza's base of operations in Dahomey, was second only to Luanda as a port of exportation (Law 2004b). It drew on networks that ran throughout west-central Africa, and ultimately more than a million people in chains were sent from its factories to the New World. Its primary market, Bahia, was the trade's largest single point of import, and de Souza spent the better part of three decades as its major supplier, earning a reputation as a prominent arms merchant via the military cargo returning on off-loaded slave ships. Ouidah's population peaked in the early 1800s, precisely during de Souza's period of high activity, at about thirty thousand. The last slave ships didn't leave its shores until the 1860s. While business began to go downhill for de Souza by the 1840s, and he apparently died deep in debt (Araujo 2011, 89), it's still fair to say that, along with a couple of his partners and sometimes rivals, de Souza was essentially Ouidah's last titan of the trade.

Historical details make de Souza's life colorfully chilling and strange. Late to the trade, his commercial enterprise in human trafficking spent its entire existence outflanking British harassment. Mobilizing a series of quiet conspirators, labyrinthine wetlands, rivers, canoes, and bureaucracy—and in a Fitzcarraldian coincidence almost too incredible to be true, he gained advantage over his rivals by dredging lagoons and clearing a canal through a major sandbank (Law 2004a: 201)—de Souza would smuggle human cargo along the coast to secret redoubts from which the slaves were rushed to ships, which, once loaded, would sprint to the equator (Huntley 1850). The British navy had no slavery-deterrence jurisdiction over Portuguese nationals south of the equator until 1836, and on this administrative point, de Souza is characteristically cagey. He used his occupation of the Portuguese fort to claim Portuguese governorship, and thereby Portuguese nationality, despite the fact that he had never set foot within the borders of the old colonial power. Moreover, his usurpation of an official title over a military installation made Ouidah quasi-Portuguese territory, further entangling British intervention there. Having built up a legal bulwark against sanction, he went on to use his wealth to build local allies demographically. De Souza welcomed Agudas (also spelled Agoudas)—liberated slaves returning to Africa from Brazil, some of whom he himself had originally sold into bondage—en masse and became a kind of patron saint to their politically significant community in Ouidah.[163] His close alliance with the powerful king Gezo of Dahomey would leave the imprimatur of authority on his descendants, converting de Souza's nickname—"Chacha"—into an improvised title, bestowed on a single heir in a line of succession still carried on today.[164] For many among the political elite, he is revered as a kind of foundational figure of Benin, the independent republic from whose haunted past de Souza siphoned countless souls and drained the life from entire communities. It's no surprise that his legend is controversial. His ancestral home is now a prominent museum on the slavery tourism route and a shrine for the local population: the staff changes the linens of his untouched bed every morning and leaves a glass of rum on his ghost's nightstand; pilgrims set offerings before his tomb. His descendants populate Benin's administrative class, but with the nation still very much wrestling with the history of the slave trade, Ouidah is today divided between families that enslaved and those that were enslaved. Some of the latter refuse to speak to the descendants of de Souza.[165] He is said to have fathered more than eighty children.

Cobra Verde maintains some recognizable outlines of de Souza's improbable life story: the impoverished background, the middle passage in reverse, the adventitious command of the slave fortress, the guns-for-slaves commerce in the face of British suppression, and, most prominently, his participation in a coup against the royal seat at Abomey. De Souza was known to have marshaled a functional militia in the context of his commercial operation, but Herzog's version makes it all eight million times as spectacular by rendering it through long scenes of Kinski in frenzied command of an army of bare-breasted women warriors, the famous "Amazons of Dahomey."[166] But the film is not a biopic, and it invents both a backstory and a destiny for its protagonist that at once defy history and invite charges of heresy. Following the formula that he established with *Fitzcarraldo* (and, to a lesser degree, *Aguirre*), Herzog seizes on the outlines of a historical figure—the general form of a seductive and brutal protagonist of the consolidating capitalist world-economy, a weapons-trading paramilitary slave dealer and ultimately bureaucrat—only to depart from any attempt at narrative verisimilitude. And yet also as with *Fitzcarraldo*, it is the fealty to the spirit of the historical context of representation that gives flesh to the protagonist and that lends the film its critical restlessness. In *Cobra Verde*, Francisco Félix de Souza is rendered Francisco Manoel da Silva, in fact two-and-a-half steps removed from the historical referent by intervening texts. The fictional name is taken from Bruce Chatwin's rather weak experiment in magic realism, *The Viceroy of Ouidah* (1980), which serves as a very loose template for Herzog's story.[167] And the general trajectory of the narrative, especially its origins in the poverty-banditry relation, openly gestures to cinema novo and especially the great *sertão* trilogy of its high period.[168] By means of these intertexts, the character—de Souza, da Silva—will be transformed from the unimpressive, overweight ascetic of historical accounts, and moreover a major contributor to a history of human trafficking on a massive scale, into a classic Herzogian icon: the dreamy Sisyphus, an ineffable will striving toward the conquest of the useless, shot through with ennui, fire, menace, and an existential stoicism with which he confronts his destiny and turns epochal horror into art, the Brazilian bandit meets Paganini.[169] "Fate will bring you a lover, and one friend more" the oracle who opens the story tells da Silva. From then on he will be Cobra Verde, the barefoot bandit. He will encounter a hunchback dwarf who carries a mountain range on his shoulders, speaks poetry about the origins of snow, and warns the bandit against the sea. Fate does indeed bring him a lover, a Brazilian princess seduced in the *sertão* among chapel ruins. He stumbles into a job as an overseer, and promptly embarrasses all three of the plantation owner's legitimate daughters. In return, as a kind of pirate metaphysician, he succeeds in reigniting the stalled slave trade and rejuvenating the Pernambucan sugar industry. In the meantime he participates in a eucharist ceremony alongside a goat, forges a blood pact with a prince who claims to be the son of a lion, and is berated by a king while done up in blackface. By the end of the film, he is writing heartfelt letters in aching prose about the meaninglessness of his life. Certainly, Herzog's is the weirdest of the great slavery films. But as an opportunity to rethink our history and our world, what do we make of all this?

Cobra Verde's controversial representation of categories such as race, bound labor and capital accumulation stands as a significant critical challenge. The significance resonates in two broad areas. First, *Cobra Verde* can and should be interpreted as an intervention against the slavery film, as a cinematic subgenre. On the one hand, Herzog's film subverts the pieties of tenacity, patience, and eventual liberation that animate the stories and images of the genre's melodramatic tradition. Films such as *Uncle Tom's Cabin* (1927), *Amistad* (1997), *Django Unchained* (2012), *12 Years a Slave* (2013) and the epochal television series, *Roots* (1977) are representative of the form. But *Cobra Verde*, now on the other hand, also refuses the political didacticism and denunciatory revelation of genocidal violence that define the genre's structuralist accounts of slavery. Here we can think of *Burn!* (1969), *El otro Francisco* (1974), *Mandingo* (1975), *La última cena* (1976), *The Mission* (1986), and *Manderlay* (2005). Resisting these elemental narrative expectations and displacing the normative dictates of transcendence that define the genre, Herzog instead speaks another cinematic language altogether, one that confronts us with an immanent critique of our visualization of the capitalist world-economy. And this brings us to the second, and much broader, challenge of *Cobra Verde*, a challenge common to Herzog's films in general. If cinema is the great storytelling machine of our time, then, like in his other major political-historical films that grounded the previous sections—*Aguirre*, *Stroszek*, *Fitzcarraldo*—Herzog's representation of man's exploitation of man stands as an opportunity to rethink the possibilities for representing our world, not so much its past as its present. That is, Herzog puts into play the cultural-political foundations of modernity itself and the basic visual grammar through which we apprehend the ideological shape of the world-system. In this attempt, whether as success or failure, *Cobra Verde* is one of Herzog's most important films.

This stance on the film represents a critical departure. It's worth repeating that scholarly commentary on *Cobra Verde* has been somewhat unusual for a major Herzog feature, a point that stands out when one considers the controversial setting and content of the film: in terms of quantity, there is very little of it; and in terms of quality, it is pointedly unflattering. I'm quite certain that these two aspects of commentary on the film are interrelated. Something about *Cobra Verde*, the way that it upsets the basic expectations of the slavery film genre, renders it resistant to critical engagement. But I would make the case that we must engage. As Brad Prager notes by way of a page from a classic essay by Chinua Achebe, to represent Africa in any Western narrative form is to enter into an electric discursive history on race (2004, 6), and it is precisely *Cobra Verde*'s participation in illuminating (or obfuscating) this history that we must take seriously and handle with care. This is not exactly what's happened. Lucia Nagib complains about Herzog's failure to "lend any sense of realism to the film" (2012, 77) but does little work with the actual film to ground her assessment, missing *Cobra Verde*'s patent problematization of realism. Manuel Köppen argues that "Herzog is trying to show Africa's 'foreignness,' and to place his hero in the greatest possible contrast with his environment" (2012, 367), ignoring the fact that da Silva is *already* foreign in *all* contexts: the failure, the outcast, the bandit. And after a fascinating discussion on the role of Africa in Herzog's broader filmography, Manuela Ribeiro Sanches accuses Herzog of representing the Africans in *Cobra Verde* as the "lowest form of humanity" (2015, 99) without indicating how the film does so; and she understands da Silva as a classic instance of the European "gone native," despite the fact that he is nearly as downtrodden as the slaves, gives no indication of having adopted the Africans' cultural norms, and finally is not really a "European" in the first place, but rather a broken native of Brazil's *sertão*, the periphery of the periphery of the capitalist world. One blogger, freed from the niceties of scholarly discourse, sums things up when she describes the expression on the face of a scene-stealing nonprofessional actor as an abject denunciation of the entire project: "Film me some more," she imagines the actor seething, "stupid white devil director."[170]

As we can see from the tenor of these assessments, criticism of the film has rested more on assertion than analysis and revolves around not so much the aesthetics as the politics of its basic work of representation, more specifically, its representations of African culture, the history of the Atlantic slave trade, racism, and, most broadly, race. Prager, the widely published Herzog scholar, has taken the logic of this kind of critical discourse the furthest. In an essay-length critique of the film, he argues that, in *Cobra Verde*, "Herzog actively seeks to contest the claim that racism both motivated and was used as a justification for imperial expansion in the nineteenth century" (2004, 2–3), that he evades "important questions between racism and European imperialism" (3), and that "his film ultimately reproduces a variety of problems traditionally connected with Western European depictions of Africa" (ibid.). Failing to deal with the historical fact of slavery, Prager argues, Herzog instead offers up a vision of "the crisis and collapse of a single white man" (7) and, "in fixating on the travails of his main character, Herzog takes pains to set aside questions of race" (ibid.) to the point where he must "set aside numerous questions about his main character's own racism and about racism as a justification for imperial expansion" (ibid.). He concludes that da Silva's "race is treated as though it were transparent or immaterial in the same way Herzog asserts that the role of racism itself ought to be diminished in discussions of the causes of slavery" (16).

These are certainly fighting words. Unfortunately they can't withstand much empirical scrutiny. Prager, like other scholarly interpreters of *Cobra Verde*, conducts little analytical work with the film itself. And his central claim, that Herzog strives to diminish the history of racism, is not in fact based on any actual *assertion* (ibid.) by the director, and certainly not by the images or narrative logic of the film itself, which stages racist discourse—perhaps even indulging in it, a separate argument—in scene after scene. Rather, the critique seems to rest on a willful misinterpretation of a brief—also awkward and tortured—remark on the DVD commentary, in a stilted passage in the director's conversation with Norman Hill, the latter clearly not up to speed on the history of race and slavery. Here's the turn, the context for which is Hill quizzing Herzog and in which Hill seems to be in something of a state of upset disbelief about the idea that Africans actually sold "their own people" into slavery. You can feel that Herzog senses the delicacy of the issue, so I'll transcribe his response literally, with all the fits and starts intact: "Uh, yes, well, it's a well-established fact which is of course denied by many people who are against the slave trade. Of course everyone, every thinking person, is against it, but it's, has been a little bit wiped under the carpet that, uh, African kingdoms, and African potentates were very much involved in the slave trade as well. But of course, they would follow their, er, the demand. It's, it's an exchange of, uh, resources and demand, and a part of, uh, the slave trade between the New World and Africa, there was slavery of course over the ages, and massive slave trade between the Arab world and black Africa, and even within African nations a lot of slave trade. So, it's not such a one-sided affair as we normally are made to believe. But when I'm saying that of course, it, it, it is considered politically incorrect. But one cannot deny that there is, uh, a very well documented history of, uh, slave trade far outside and beyond the slave trade between, uh, North America or Brazil and Africa" (*Cobra Verde*, DVD commentary). There's a lot to potentially unpack here: it's not clear who the people of "denied by many people" are; the structural relations between slavery and commercial trade are crucial, fascinating, well known, and at the center of the film; Herzog seems to twice conflate forms of slavery that are essentially different, with the dividing line being the consolidation of the North Atlantic circuit in the context of the capitalist world-economy; and "not such a one-sided affair" (Prager reads this as Herzog *arguing* that slavery discourse has "unfairly vilified whites" [7]) seems poor phrasing for the call to consider more deeply the complexities of the relations between race and labor within the context of the transatlantic slave trade. Without apologizing for his inarticulate framing of the questions at issue here, I'll note that, in spite of being regularly taken for a deep thinker and source of insight on topics far beyond the world of filmmaking, Herzog is not a scholar of transatlantic history nor a philosopher of race relations. His best critical work happens in his films, on screen, not his often off-key interpretations of them. So to rely on what Herzog says about his self-styled critical position on dominant narratives of slavery and justice, rather than what the film does about it, seems to take the bait of the director's directing our interpretations of his films. But Prager knows Herzog's work as well as anybody, and so we should take his essay at its strongest point. The strength lies in its symptomatic value, the fact that his reading of *Cobra Verde* is generic and stands as the most evolved in a set of generalized statements about the film. Even while standing on shaky empirical ground, Prager's reading opens the way to a much more productive interpretation of *Cobra Verde*, one that pushes us to think about its work on and through the myriad problems of race and the modern world.

Indeed, the history of our multiculturalist present prepares the ground for Prager's critique, giving it a predictable quality. As to Africa, it's the always anticipated retort to Hegel. In a famous, and rather perfunctory, passage in Hegel's *The Philosophy of History* (1837) the Philosopher turns to Africa. His point of reference is precisely the kingdom of Dahomey, coincidentally (or not) the same object of representation at play in Herzog's film. Already by the early nineteenth century, Dahomey served a highly stable discursive function in Europe's imaginary world organization: the space of extreme savagery. In constructing this discourse, European explorers, diplomats, traders, historians, geographers, and abolitionists made much of any local custom that resonated exotic in the mind of the white man, especially if it involved literal or symbolic human blood. This interest of course was grounded in ideology and all the contradictions that it tolerates: Dahomey stood out for its complex civilizational structures, especially in the areas of government, military, and logistics and in its ability to repel European intervention, holding out against conquest until the French bombardment of 1892. Its purported "savagery" resided not in its totalitarianism—it was the Europeans who were feeding the fires of monstrous human traffic, the demand side of the mercantile symbiosis that Herzog stumbles over—but in its resistance.[171] So when Hegel (1837) needs a foil for the production and performance of otherness, ironically vis-à-vis a European culture famous for centuries of absolutism, racism, witch hunts and the perfection of the most ghastly forms of torture and execution, it's no surprise that Dahomey makes the scene. "In Dahomey, when the king dies, the bonds of society are loosed; in his palace begins indiscriminate havoc and disorganization. All the wives of the king (in Dahomey their number is exactly 3,333) are massacred, and through the whole town plunder and carnage run riot" (116). From this he goes on to conclude that "want of self-control distinguishes the character of the Negroes" and thus Africa is "capable of no development or culture" and that only slavery is "the occasion of the increase of human feeling among the Negroes" (ibid.). Hegel's banishment of Africa to the unconscious woodshed of history, indeed, to the miasma of nonhistory ("For it is no historical part of the World; it has no movement or development to exhibit" [117]), sets the table for postcolonial reversal. If for Hegel Africa must be represented as the dark mass of ahistorical savagery, and Europe must stand as the motor of progressive history, then the Eurocentric story of slavery can only reaffirm this conceptual model that underwrites a racist modernity: in short, it's not about the crimes of the European-derived world; it's about the barbarism of Africa. It thereby follows that in our post- (which is not to say anti-) Hegelian philosophy of history, the ethically correct position must flow in precisely the opposite direction, dialectically counter to the Philosopher. Herzog's aesthetic choices, then, necessarily yield immediate discomfort: he locates his story in slave trade Dahomey, sets against his protagonist a mad king (cartooning Hegel, in an intertitle, a "sinister and demented" king), and surrounds that king with trappings that include deranged pronouncements, a dozen totally subservient wives, a throne room paved with human skulls, and a ritual war snake.[172] But the problem of throwing Herzog in the same boat as Hegel and sinking it is that this well-worn critical position *against Hegel* obscures the fact that Herzog is offering up a slavery narrative on highly original terms, departing in suggestive ways from the expectations of the slavery film genre.

Prager's (2004) complaint about Herzog's failure to deal with "racism as a justification for imperial expansion" rests on the fact that *Cobra Verde* takes no opportunity to make any *explicit* comment on the history of race relations in the north Atlantic slavery circuit (16). The spectator's expectation of witnessing egregious acts of racist brutality—essentially, scenes of torture, both physical and psychological—runs strong in the slavery film genre, and the blood-boiling desire for denunciation and retribution rests at the center of all the genre's modern classics, from *Roots* to *12 Years a Slave*.[173] Herzog seems to push limits in resisting this norm. In *Cobra Verde*, the sugar industry's dependence on disposable human chattel is depicted in the tone of scientific instruction. The rape of domestic slaves is represented as a mutually beneficial seduction (twice).[174] Da Silva's exhortation to an escaped slave that he return to the whipping post—"don't run away . . . it'll only be worse for you"—is stated with spaghetti-western cool. As we've noted, *Cobra Verde* is matter-of-fact in its representation of the kingdom of Dahomey's active participation in the slave trade. And finally, Kinski, as the historical echo of the *mulato* slave driver de Souza, looks super white (it's Kinski, after all). The problem of marshaling this list, which could certainly be extended, as a set of counts in the charge of racism—or, at best,

Figure 17. Captives in a Ouidah slave factory. *Cobra Verde* (Herzog 1987).

failing to deal with racism—against Herzog is that its representational consistency is precisely the point of the film. In his DVD commentary, Herzog asserts that his goal was to capture a certain "climate of the thinking of that time"—that is, the "climate" of a capitalist world-economy resting on bound labor. This climate, then, would be structured on the reproduction of a set of assumptions that reigned in nineteenth-century Brazil, the motivational setting for da Silva's African sojourn, described so eloquently by Roberto Schwarz as a system of *favor*. This is a world in which each individual—excluding the slave, whose individuality in a social-legal sense is always already diffuse—had a stake in the functioning of a system that assumed, but had no need to name, the lacuna resting between its ideological and actual environments, a liberal worldview made material by a "basic productive relationship which was secured by force" (1992, 37). Herzog thus attempts to enter into the deep psychology of the black Atlantic without the anachronism of simplistic black-versus-white interpretations of the historical complexity of a slave-centered culture and political economy that coexisted with, indeed underwrote, the historical flowering of philosophies and declarations of the rights of man.[175] With Herzog we can easily argue that any clear statement on race and "against" slavery—within the context of the historical settings of the film, essentially nodes of intensity in the slavery machine—is beside the point: the *entire context of the film*, its very "climate," from the first shots of a notably blond bandit forced off his land by the unsustainability of capitalist agriculture to his upward trajectory enabled only by his rank exploitation of other human beings, *is a world that embraces freedom, but only insofar as it is premised on a hierarchical racial order*. In terms of reading race, the question becomes, Is a discourse operating nondidactically within this "climate" enough to enable productive historical critique? That is, why invite us into this climate at all?

One of the many examples of the ambiguously critical work of *Cobra Verde* happens at a moment of sexual violence generic to the slavery film, a scene of rape. The matter-of-factness in which the assault is carried off, in contrast with the brooding existentialism of its accompanying dialogue, make it unique to the genre. It's late in the story and da Silva's slave-trading operation is booming but also showing signs of stress, as the trade itself is portrayed to be in its death throes. Da Silva is hosting Pedro Vicente—a shipper and business rival—and the two men approach a slave factory's dungeon overcrowded with half-naked African women. Da Silva invites his guest to select a victim for the night, noting that he himself will sleep alone, as he is a little exhausted by the slave-trading lifestyle. A beautiful young woman is called up from the hole, a nonprofessional actor whose apprehension is so convincingly rendered as to be hard to watch. A conversation ensues between the slave traders. Da Silva explains that the women hope to become pregnant, for it will mean better living conditions and an escape, at least temporarily, from the middle passage. Finally, Vicente asks, "Who are these women?" Da Silva responds, in straight Camus: "Our future murderers." What does all this mean? We could certainly amass analytical turns and possibilities. Is the scene historically accurate in the details of its representation? Ruins and images of slave factories, and the long history of testimonies to systematic rape in the slave trade certainly suggest as much. Does the ominous spirit of the scene—"our future murderers"—raise questions about the history of slavery, its immediate and inextricable relation to racism, the nature of its commodification of women and men, its biopolitics, and the ways in which the universal human debasement essential to this "climate" has so deeply institutionalized race as a watchword of modern social relations?

The aesthetic problem is clear enough. The premise of *Cobra Verde* is that the mise-en-scène is overdetermined, made thinkable, by a racism so normalized that a grandiose statement denouncing it would be akin to breaking the fourth wall: the realism of its historical surrealism would collapse, be rendered immediately false, an essay film and propaganda piece, the Spielbergian cry of "I want free!," that is, the opposite of the ecstatic history that Herzog strives for. The sociocritical element is more difficult. For to enter into a climate of slavery is to produce a narrative logic in which racism works with a complexity that outflanks our simplistic anachronisms. Thus, in the world of *Cobra Verde*, the 1820s black Atlantic, the apparent surreal is the historical work of dreams, where Africans enslave "their own people" . . . perhaps a shock to some contemporary spectators and critics, but an interpretation that rests on the anachronistic notion of a common people that would be a historical absurdity.[176] A slave-driving *mulato* is blindingly white, just as he is remembered today by his descendants (Araujo 2011). And the trade itself falls apart not from any real anti-imperial resistance . . . but simply through the demise of its own systemic logic. Far from avoiding the basic questions of historical slavery (racism, imperialism, Eurocentrism, rebellion), *Cobra Verde* distills and intensifies them. And as the critical reaction to the film shows, this tendency can be difficult to perceive. Reinterpreting *Cobra Verde*, then, could be part of a larger critique of the slavery film genre writ large. To fully appreciate the critical possibilities and limits of *Cobra Verde*, we need to first reposition it in the context of its object of engagement. In this I'd make the case that *Cobra Verde*, ultimately, is not about slavery per se. But not in the way that Herzog himself says that it is not. That is, it's not about African culture, or the bandit, or his struggle and disappointment, a figure who just happens to traipse through a landscape of social relations premised on bound labor. Like Herzog's ambitious historical dramas before it, *Cobra Verde* is about the formation of a world. That world is our world, and it is underwritten and organized by a historical social system called capitalism. In this framing, the logic of *Cobra Verde*'s historical narrative is at once brutal and precise: you don't get capitalism without slavery. Herzog's "climate of slavery" is the melting pot of our world, of the capitalist world-economy.

This historical relation, of course, is an old idea. Marx took it as a working assumption and the harmony between capitalist development and slavery is a basic premise in the world-systems narrative of historical capitalism.[177] As a storytelling machine, the critical potential of the cinema is to illuminate this history, its logic and its fissures, as aesthetic representation and opportunity for both moral and analytical reflection. This is what slavery films do, or at least can do. This spirit infuses the films that take a more structuralist approach to slavery. In this, Herzog's is one of the most powerful, but also most subtle, in that it lacks the pointed didacticism that also marks this tradition. In order to open up the film, it is important to resist its decoys, beginning with da Silva himself. Critics have argued that *Cobra Verde* is essentially about da Silva—there isn't a single scene that doesn't involve his presence, either as image or reference—and Prager reads the story as "the crisis and collapse of a single white man" (7). But Kinski's da Silva is at once more and less than a single white man: no facile allegory of capitalism as social relation or form of accumulation, he is nevertheless the meteor of capitalism as historical system, its blunt instrument, a revolting protagonist and operatic figure who renders the political-economic project of slavery at once intimate and world-historical. Indeed, Robin Law, the contemporary historian who has written most extensively on de Souza (da Silva's historical model), emphasizes the fact that his powerful presence within the slave trade rested not so much on his local political alliances, but rather on his extensive and tightly articulated web of contacts and associates internationally, around the Atlantic slave circuit (Law 2004a, 196–97). In other words, what the contemplation of da Silva qua de Souza reveals to us is not so much Africa per se, but Africa as it bends back toward America and consolidates the formation of a transregional economic system. In order for these aspects of the film to materialize, two elements of the film's story are crucial: its itinerary and its end.

For thinking about *Cobra Verde* in world-historical terms, da Silva's narrative itinerary—which, as we've noted, resonates in significant ways with de Souza's biography—couldn't be more strikingly rendered. It is well known that historical capitalism, in its Eurocentric circuit (there are other circuits), propelled itself on the slope of the Atlantic, the expressway journey that dramatically expanded commodity chains (capitalism's lifeblood), bringing paramilitary merchant ships loaded with guns and other commodities to the Atlantic coast of Africa, slaves to the Americas, and raw goods back to Europe where they would off-load, reap profit, and start the cycle anew: in other words, the transatlantic trip from Liverpool back to Liverpool, or Lisbon to Lisbon, is all downhill. *Cobra Verde* is set along the cacophonous leg of this route that stretches between Africa and Brazil. But da Silva follows its logic is reverse, traveling against the "natural" flow of capital accumulation, and in doing so denaturalizes the stops on his itinerary as they unveil the intensities of the margins of the world economy. He begins at the frayed end of capitalist penetration, a dirt-poor white (or not; the ambiguity of race is part of the critical intervention here) rancher, one of the millions hurled forth from the bellows of accumulation into those marginal hinterlands where the earth begets monsters: barren lives, the spaces where the seed of capitalist civilization finds no purchase, and yet where the violence of the world-system exhibits its ferocity with greatest purity, its antagonists raging back against the machine in the form of environmental calamity, cadavers, Canudos, Corisco, Cobra Verde. Da Silva will return as one of these undead figures—mistakenly perceived as aping the spaghetti western when his literal ancestor is Antonio das Mortes—but what might be rendered as an antisystemic exercise in mysticism that ends up in a sprint to the sea instead reveals the bandit in all of his banality: a function of capitalist accumulation.

His literal banditry doesn't last long and is uneventful: about fifteen minutes of the film, most of it spent in conversation in a dark bar with his new friend, the dwarf who warns da Silva against crossing the ocean. Flanking the banditry episode, however, are two important way stations of extraction. First, having failed in the film's opening minutes as a pioneer of capitalist agriculture, da Silva turns to the mines, where he will labor in debt peonage. Not to be overlooked here is the film's first explicitly stylized reference to the relations between race and labor, as da Silva will be literally blackened, coated in a thick slime of dark mud as he toils for a slave's wages. There are a lot of ways to read the Salgadoesque image. Most critically, it is a gesture pointing to the race-making power of capitalist social relations. It's not that African subjects, as an ethnicity constructed as "black," must occupy the bottom of a hierarchy of accumulation. It's that the very work of this hierarchy produces certain geographically circumscribed subjects *as black*. Da Silva is blackened as he moves from small-time land proprietor to bound labor. He begins to shed the skin of this blackness with one of the few gestures of active rebellion in the film: he kills the boss, over a dispute about pay. From there he is on the run.

Barefoot, he soon lands on his feet, ushering in the second scene of his tour through racial capitalism. A wanted, but mysterious, man, he's passing through a town modeled on Recife (it's actually shot in Cartagena, Colombia), historically the *tristes tropiques* capital of the sugar-producing region of Pernambuco and a major importer of African slaves. There he comes across a *pelourinho*, or whipping post, surrounded by soldiers and a large crowd, as black slaves receive corporeal punishment; it's Herzog, so this stock moment of the slavery film is highly stylized, with a significant dose of choreography. One slave slips out of his shackles and dashes through the crowd, evading capture until he runs face to face into the bandit: da Silva quietly suggests that he return to the post—escape "will be much worse for you"—and he does, as if in a state of shock. Impressed, a local plantation owner raised up in a carriage says, "I could use a man like you" and hires him on the spot. Now as *capataz*, da Silva will harness the same color-coded relation of race that oppressed him in the mines. Overseeing a major sugar plantation, he is rewhitened, making even more suggestive the mixed-race status of his historical referent: while American audiences, governed by the hard segregationist logic of racial discourse in the United States, are accustomed to the white overseer—a role traditionally played in the tone of a kind of hickish sadism—in Latin American cinematic and literary narratives, it is common to represent the slave boss or overseer as *mestizo* or *mulato*, as in Tomás Gutiérrez Aléa's pedantic tour-de-force, *La última cena*. As he climbs the ladder of racialization, da Silva moves from the blackness of the mines through an explicit trajectory of whitening, recostumed in bright clean whites from the plantation laundry, and securing the sugar-refining process itself, from primitive deep brown to high-value crystal white. A mixed-race figure who can speak to the hearts of black slaves and simultaneously pass as white, asserting authority and yet entirely dependent on favor. But Herzog skips the requisite scenes of cane field and *senzala* abuse between overseer and slaves. Instead, he moves directly to the *casa grande* and the return of the repressed, revealing the black heart of the bandit and the face of the monster when da Silva breaks race and class lines and upsets the social contract by quickly, almost simultaneously, seducing and impregnating

Figure 18. Zuckerrohr pflanzer. Ich bin der bandit Cobra Verde. *Cobra Verde* (Herzog 1987).

all three of the plantation owner's legitimate children. Freaking out, the colonel confronts da Silva. The bandit removes his mask, coolly stares him down, and utters the line of the film: *Zuckerrohr pflanzer. Ich bin der bandit Cobra Verde*. But this rebellion, "I *am* the bandit," is ineffectual. The enemy is world-historical and eats bandits for breakfast by appropriating their productive energy.[178]

The sugar plantation transition yields two more stops on the itinerary, essential for da Silva's tour through the building blocks of historical capitalism. First, in a hallmark of Herzog's work that we considered at length in regard to *Fitzcarraldo*, the director returns to the basic aesthetics of what Aguilera Skvirsky (2020) calls the "process genre." Again we are introduced, in meticulous explication, to a process of industrial agriculture. This time, of course, it's sugar. More precisely, we are presented with an overview of the productive methods and capacity of nineteenth-century sugar production and its dependence on bound labor. The process narrative here is very much a recapitulation of the rubber-tapping scene in *Fitzcarraldo* and even features the same principal actors, José Lewgoy as titan of capitalist agriculture, Kinski as marginal upstart.[179] In the same way that we were presented sequential lingering shots of rubber tapping from the extraction of sap to refinement for transport, here we begin with slaves cutting cane in the field, the pressing of the cane juice, and then a step-by-step reduction—with instruction: "we heat the molasses to more than 120 degrees, well above the boiling point of water"—of the juice in simmering vats. But there are important differences. Overall, this redo offers a much more explicit set of references to labor, exploitation, and capital than the more lyrical scene of *Fitzcarraldo*—perhaps heavy-handed, but clearly necessary for the story, whose narratives of extraction have no opera house to hide behind. Whereas the rubber baron muses rather abstractly about increasing production and acquiring more workers, here the sugarcane planter speaks explicitly about geopolitical dynamics: he complains that the insatiable British appetite for sugar stands in hypocritical relation to their navy's suppression of the labor supply through maritime slavery policy. Whereas Fitzcarraldo is anxious to learn the details of the rubber trade, the secret bandit da Silva simply stands alongside the planter's discourse with a look somewhere between bored discomfort and abject disgust. And finally, against *Fitzcarraldo*'s rubber opera and in a gesture to all operations of extractive capitalism—including the "aesthetic extraction" of Herzog's own production processes, which in shooting *Fitzcarraldo* included a workman's severed foot—in *Cobra Verde* the scene of fabrication is interrupted by an explicit display of its human cost, the deep-history structural companion to what Jasbir Puar calls "the right to maim" (2015).[180] The planter is discussing his labor strain, the commodification of African bodies in the context of the numbers, requirements and disposability of his slave workforce. A scream interrupts his disquisition. A slave's arm has become entangled in the cane press. Da Silva, on his first day as *capataz*, and the planter look on, distant, while the victim writhes (incidentally, for this brief role Herzog recruited a man who had literally lost an arm in an agricultural accident). "Is there anything we can do?" asks da Silva. The plantation owner responds, "This kind of thing happens all the time. Somebody bring a machete!" The cane press continues its methodical churn and the amputation of the limb, the cut of race, yields no Makandal, but rather becomes the cut to the next scene, now the lavish manor house and the slaveowner's seduction of one of his domestic slaves, as he remarks, "I haven't yet fathered any children today." Thus, like *Fitzcarraldo* before it, but even more explicitly, *Cobra Verde* makes a point, early on, of confronting us with the beating heart of the film: the relations between production, reproduction, profit and accumulation, in the context of a monoculture resource boom, one that overdetermines social relations and historical processes, here rendered literally in a slave-powered industrial operation.

Having despoiled the planter's daughters and revealed his bandit identity, da Silva now finds himself in real trouble. Events will culminate in his departure for Africa, the final stop on his American itinerary, the point where the necessary threads for transatlantic world-formation weave together. The punishment for da Silva's crime is to be sent to Dahomey. The choice is less arbitrary than it might seem, for Dahomey was a feared destination of exile for political criminals during the late days of the slave trade age (Araujo 2011, 83). In the case of *Cobra Verde*, da Silva's deportation not only makes the story move but also provides structural integrity, because the punishment, while understood as a virtual death sentence, is, moreover, a hedge-betting business deal: the mad king of Dahomey is at war with his rivals and has cut off the supply of slave labor; da Silva will be sent to reignite the trade. Everybody assumes that he is unlikely to survive. But then again if he does succeed, so much the better, for business. Significantly, indeed crucially, this solution is hashed out in a secret meeting of distinguished gentlemen. (Not secret enough: in keeping with the omnipresence of the bandit, da Silva lurks in the shadows and overhears the plan; but he resigns himself to his fate; it's a little corny, straight out of a Hugo morality tale, but somehow it works.) The members of the cabal are nothing less than the protagonists of the capitalist world-economy, representing its component parts and advance guard: the plantation owner, a naval officer, and a governor; industry, military, and state. Far from the mere ideological apparatus of capitalism in its expansive mode, or, even worse, a hindrance to the laissez-faire mythology of capitalist development, state policy and military aggression reveal themselves as direct producers of capital. Conjoined to industrial need, they will be the tools for opening the spigot of fresh labor supply. And it is precisely this current that da Silva will ride to riches, the artery of capitalism itself, rendered transparent and stripped naked: da Silva—the bandit Cobra Verde—will run guns and, in exchange, he will send home laboring bodies. Guns, we know, were the lubricating currency of the slave trade, exchanged with a set of African kingdoms whose divisions were always exploited and exacerbated by the demands of the business. And indeed, guns will be at the center of da Silva's first contact with Abomey. Add to these already complicated relations between history and capital in play here: the military and commercial competition over high-seas routes; the commodity chains extending out from the sugar industry; and the political drama of paperwork and legal threat as nations jockeyed for advantage, not least of which involved, by the 1820s, the British project of articulating nascent West African cotton production to its own textile industry and thereby providing an important motivating factor to cut off America's African labor supply. Thus placed in the middle of this elusive story of a solitary "white" man, we find a truly disorienting tangle of forces animating Herzog on the periphery of capitalism: of resource extraction and circulation, of administrative initiatives and of political-economic articulations, throwing into the forefront of our imagination the world-making economy of the moral failure of slavery.

About half of *Cobra Verde* takes place in Africa, and there is more political intrigue here, also something of a trippy adventure drama and ill-conceived buddy narrative.[181] Structurally less interesting, and less important, than the American half, it's aesthetically staggering, and, unsurprisingly, the part of the film that has captured the attention of critics. (Herzog himself refers to it as the essential half of the film.) It represents a veritable catalog of some of the more impressive images staged in Herzog's oeuvre: da Silva's chaotic arrival on the beach accompanied by his appraisal that "Africa is quite a disappointment"; his leadership of the Amazons of Dahomey; the war snake and the barefoot kick; the flag messengers; the royal court; as usual, landscape; Kinski in blackface. But none of this moves in the direction, or toward the end, that the slavery film genre trains us to want. While there are some dungeons and shackles, the spectacular scenes of slavery-guided torture are largely absent. The normative racial logic is all mixed up in that, beyond the blond da Silva and a couple of associates, both slaves and slave drivers are black Africans. There is no real resistance to the system. At one point, a young singer seems to unleash an epithet at da Silva, although neither da Silva nor most of the audience can understand what she says (it's in Akan), and it never amounts to anything in the plot. Instead of a slave uprising against da Silva's violence, the narrative revolves around da Silva's role in a coup, not for justice but rather

Figure 19. King Gezo sends da Silva a group of slaves maimed by polio. *Cobra Verde* (Herzog 1987).

in the name of reconsolidating the slave trade. And the closest thing to systemic rejection borders on the surreal. It happens when the usurper king and erstwhile ally of da Silva—the historical referent here would be Gezo—sends him a load of slaves deformed and crippled by polio, thus defying the use-value demand inscribed in the commodification of laboring bodies. In other words, instead of bodies, the king's refutation is to send da Silva people.

Mostly, however, we watch the slow degeneration of da Silva, hot and humid, surrounded by beautifully rendered, uncanny images of Africa's fortress-dotted Slave Coast, as the historical system teeters on the edge of exhaustion. In the film's last dialogue, da Silva and Pedro Vicente contemplate their bankruptcy and uncertain future with the demise of the slave trade.[182] Champagne in hand, da Silva's rival raises his glass to slavery, "the greatest misunderstanding in the history of mankind." To which da Silva responds, "It was no misunderstanding. It was a crime. Slavery is an element of the human heart—to our ruin!"

This, of course, comes off as sort of a letdown as the final word against slavery. Dehistoricizing, to be sure, it's a slow target for claims against the film as a set-piece for the deracialization of slavery. For instance, Prager wants to read it as a case for extenuating the crimes of Europe, the universalization of slavery such that the genocide of the middle passage becomes a question of spreading the blame (2004, 7). And while we can patch the line to Herzog's DVD comments on the enduring tradition of slavery in Africa, preceding and following transatlantic chattel slavery, that particular interpretation seems to run counter to the general attitude of Herzog's larger work, the fact that he has never exhibited any particular allegiance to Eurocentric culture and enlightenment, and whose historical outlook is a muddy blend of mysticism, doubt, and recurring trauma, probably best described as Benjaminian. Whatever the case, it's a difficult issue, with Herzog's rather self-important descriptions of the taboo-breaking qualities of his own film itself grating against the age-old questions of privilege, gaze and the Eurocentric tradition.[183] In fact, while Herzog was profiting from the Ghanaian government's hospitality to his project, that same state was actively suppressing the voices of its own local filmmakers, many of whom were more interested in the erased legacies of socialist struggle than the well-known history of slave-trade collaboration. As the filmmaker John Akomfrah puts it, "here is this country (Ghana) that came into being because of this party and this figure [Kwame Nkrumah, an international socialist and pan-Africanist who led Ghana to independence and was overthrown in the late 1960s by a coup that has been widely attributed to US interference]—it wouldn't have existed without them—and yet when we [a group of exiled filmmakers] arrived there, the space of statement had been so *crippled by amnesia* that people believed that to not talk about it [the coup] was a good thing, and I couldn't see how not talking about it did any good to anyone, especially since we [the national film industry] were actively encouraging this guy, Werner Herzog, to come to Ghana to make the film based on real events. But as, literally, fiction" (2014, my emphasis). So when Herzog reconverts the centuries-long project of resisting slavery to a weary exhale and an "element of the human heart," well, it can be hard to take.

Disappointment like this, however, misinterprets the end of the film. We've dwelled upon the ways in which Herzog defies the conventions of the slavery film genre, and here it is important to indicate another pointed heresy. In *Cobra Verde*, there is no figure of the "good white man."[184] Commentators dwell on the film's obsessive focus on da Silva, and some go as far as to call his figure a sympathetic object of spectator identification (e.g., Prager 2004, 7), but such an understanding of the film seems tendentious. While there can be no doubt that he struggles, da Silva's striving is without purpose. He is unredeeming and unredeemed. His guiding philosophy is minimally expressed and unimpressive, his motivations opaque. Unlike Aguirre and Fitzcarraldo, there is no flicker of internal conflict, beyond a few overwrought expressions of melancholia. He's simply a sign, an empty one, gliding through slavery's diabolical ports of call. In short, to correctly understand the film, we need to see past, in fact reject, the notion of da Silva (who is also de Souza) as the wise man here. No antihero oracle, he's a cog in the machine. And as a cog, a manager of the fatally boring and terrible assembly line of slavery, he is capable of speaking truth only in that spirit. The crucial line is thus not any banality about "the human heart"; the crucial line comes just before. Upon learning of the demise of the slave trade, da Silva mutters, with Hegel or, for that matter, Alfonso Reyes, "Finally something's happened." The mind-numbing tedium of slavery is finished; history can begin again, repetition with a difference, a new yet familiar set of struggles. It's an intense scene, lingeringly shot, with Kinski's weathered ennui and distracted irritation in perfect resonance with what Saidiya Hartman calls the "nonevent of emancipation" (1997, 116, 139): embedded in the human heart, that is, the capitalist world-economy, the legacies of slavery, first and foremost its racialized logic, will continue to underwrite patterns of production and social relations. But in order to effectively complicate da Silva's remark, we need to begin by placing it in the context of the following scene, the final scene of Herzog's storied collaboration with Kinski, the best of the film, and one of the most evocative of the director's entire career.

We are on a long beach, there is no sound but the crashing waves. A young man is there, African, and badly deformed by polio. If we are paying close attention, we recognize him as one of the "cripples" imposed on da Silva by the king of Abomey. He walks on all fours, his arms and legs seem reversed in their ambulatory function. Suddenly da Silva is there too, and he is clearly startled by the man on the beach. He flees, looking back over his shoulder in apparent fear as the human crab creeps along his footsteps, inexorable. Da Silva arrives at a massive seafaring canoe. The wide-angle shots look like a Dalí. He struggles, Fitzcarraldian, against gravity and wet sand, to pull it into the Atlantic. To escape the menace of Africa, to embark for America, the pressure

Figures 20A and 20B. On the beach. *Cobra Verde* (Herzog 1987).

valve of the Old World's disappointments. (The historical de Souza, too, tried and failed to return to America.) The canoe won't budge an inch. The young man draws close. It's nearly three minutes and still the only sound is the waves. Da Silva collapses into the surf. One of Herzog's new-age choruses begins to hum. Da Silva agonizes and drowns.

We cut to the animalization of man as the figure looks on, face obscured in shadow, without threat, in profile. We cut to an ocean horizon, epilogue ("the slaves will sell their masters and grow wings"), and *fin*. Herzog says that he regrets this scene for its indiscretion, its voyeuristic gaze at the maimed body (*Cobra Verde*, DVD commentary). Perhaps. But indiscrete or not, it is an image that haunts us. Bracing in its aesthetic, and, yes, moving in its film-history context—essentially the death of the Herzog-Kinski collaboration—but its power lies elsewhere. Its affective penetration of our consciousness resides in its dialectical rigor. For it is here, finally, that the dictates of the slavery film are once and for all obeyed. But they are obeyed in their proudest sense, and in that, exploded. Da Silva wants to outrun his world, our world, his and our participation in its brutality, its pettiness and its sadness, its cowardice and its violence, but he cannot: the crimes of history form our reality and are lodged firmly in the human heart. The escape route toward America is nothing more than a well-traveled trail of tears. The capitalist world-economy establishes its foundation on the crippling of Africa, and this—the best that Herzog himself can muster in interpreting his own film—has long been understood as a functional truth of the world-system.[185] Jonathan Beller (2006) speaks of the power of capitalism to colonize and commodify our very dreams, hypothesizing a materiality of the imagination—"dream work turns out to be real work"—that must be mobilized in the name of antisystemic resistance. And here, on the beach, the image-as-resistance becomes at once nightmare and revelation: what appears as Africa's last gasp is also and at once that small voice of history, the continent's sending forth of people, not bodies, human subjects, human beings that simply no longer work in the system, that will not be incorporated into capitalism as use-value, as physical labor. As was once said about another region of the Global South, against the depredations of global capitalism, the continent responds *with life*. Like the cane press that consumes human limbs, the machinery of capitalist social relations maims our very imagination, our ability to see a challenge and question in the figure of the abject. This would seem to be the nature of da Silva's itinerary: not Herzog's perception of a persistent "dignity" (DVD commentary), but rather the total abjection before man's exploitation of man, the crime not of the human heart, but of human history, and the impossibility of escape. The question, for the artist, is how to represent this history of horror and how to participate in the vanquishing of its future. While the slavery-film genre has amply worked toward the denunciation of this history, it too blandly traffics in ideological trinkets of freedom and perseverance, in lessons that we all already know. With *Cobra Verde*, Herzog throws sand into the gears of this storytelling machine, stalls its basic logic, and confronts us with a hazy image churned up from the depths of the political unconscious. The nature of this project and this gesture will never yield answers ready-made for easy consumption, but its artistic result can perhaps serve as a small wonder in the construction of a new visual language for rethinking the most basic, and horrific, social relations that animate our capitalist, and postcapitalist, modernity.

Late Work

> It certainly will be an embarrassment for anyone: those who make the film, and those who watch the film. That can be prevented as long as I'm alive—when I'm dead eventually, I should try to give instructions clear enough that nobody should do it. You cannot prevent it. Some idiot will do it. But don't watch it.
>
> —Werner Herzog, on the future prospects of the biopic *Werner Herzog*, 2019

At what point do an artist's self-reflections cartwheel into the realm of self-parody? Werner Herzog, approaching sixty years of widely influential and often critically acclaimed cinematic production, more than sixty films to show for his prodigious work ethic, and a generosity of accessibility without peer, is certainly the kind of public figure well into his prime for this sort of turn. Indeed, it's impossible to be a living legend without developing the approximate aura of predictability. Always serious, and yet never too prickly about self-deprecation, Herzog has been toeing the line of crossing over from rebel to institution for a while now. His interviews are infinite, and his answers, with their expected performance—weighty Bavarian accent, deliberately paced speech, serious delivery of irreverent attitudes, absolute sincerity, and a friendly smile—have become rote. Memorable phrases cut through the repetition—film is the art of illiterates, it does not surprise me to be shot at, I am not an artist but a medieval craftsman of the guilds, the unknown soldier of the cinema, the truth of accountants, filmmaking comes from the thighs, never ask permission but be prepared to beg forgiveness, the audience is always right—and bubble up like lessons for life, regardless of their ability to withstand second thoughts. The maverick denunciations of the banalities of film school have yielded to a cottage industry of filmmaking pedagogy: a masterclass on the internet (in a series also occupied by Martin Scorsese, Spike Lee, and Ron Howard), the Rogue Film School, run out of his own production company (where up to sixty-five students can pay US$1,500 to spend a weekend learning about bare-knuckle boxing and the art of document forgery), and practical ten-day seminars (in which forty-eight young filmmakers work with Herzog on location in "savage Peruvian landscapes"; €5,000, transportation not included, no refunds).[186] The decades worth of broadsides against self-help, "herbal teas, discovering your Boundaries, and Inner Growth" (Rogue Film School website) have yielded a lifestyle guru whose proverbs on self-reliance, travel by foot, and just-do-it struggle against the elements (both natural and financial) are easily bundled into a ready-to-wear theory of practice. From the formative moments of crafting his persona, Herzog, who always resists and even denounces too much analytical probing into his work, has also never been shy about speaking to his own achievements and the struggles that accompanied them: he is, ultimately, the most self-referential of filmmakers. As he puts it himself, on the subject of the tremendous span of the styles and themes of his movies: while there is no unifying formula to his films, "say you turn on the television and see ten seconds of a film. You would immediately know that this must be one of my films" (Herzog and Cronin 2002, 68).

In his late work, however, the turn to self-reference in Herzog's films has evolved from the inevitable repetition of tricks and tendencies that show up in the movies of any prolific auteur into something that feels more like compulsion. A threshold marks this turn, one that, coincidentally, I essentially witnessed and that also marks my own introduction to Herzog's work. In 1999 I was a graduate student at the University of Minnesota when my dissertation director, the late René Jara, assigned *Aguirre, der Zorn Gottes* (1972) for his class on colonial discourse. My classmates and I were blown away by the evocativeness with which Herzog captured an imagined mood of the conquest, and I can still recall the joyful surprise of conquistadors opening their mouths and out comes German, provoking that kind of discursive-shifting whammy, a reaction something like what Foucault describes in his elemental encounter with

Borges. I was hooked. I tore through every Herzog film that I could get my hands on. At that same time, the Walker Art Center in Minneapolis hosted what was up to then probably the highest-profile retrospective of Herzog's films. The exhibit premiered *Mein liebster Feind* (*My Best Fiend*, 1999), and I still recall my friend, and now colleague, the Brazilianist cultural critic Malcolm McNee, telling me "You've gotta see this: at one point the Indians offer to kill Kinski!" Needless to say, I saw it. *My Best Fiend* is Herzog's affectionate documentary on his maddening and productive relationship with Klaus Kinski and is one of his strongest films. But enmeshed with the documentary's explicit topic is a feature-length reflection on the director's own legacy, his attitudes about filmmaking and the natural world, the centrality of the South American rain forest as both geographical space and moody metaphor for the unconscious mind, for his life's work. The film stands as a thinly disguised watershed in Herzog's long career, a summing up after which his work will (or might) enter a new phase. And he accompanied the film with a text: the insouciant index of his various musings on film, life, and truth, including his quotation of professional wrestler turned state governor Jesse "The Body" Ventura ("you can't legislate stupidity") in the so-called Minnesota Declaration (1999), delivered live before a museum audience.[187]

But the exercise in self-reference that is *My Best Fiend*, essentially an autobiographical work, rather than get these homecomings out of Herzog's system, seems to have unleashed a kind of desire to reaffirm monuments. His films since 2000 are full of repetitions not so much probing—that is, unlike his own strategy of performative reenactment in his documentaries—as championing, and in this, they can come off as slightly odd, a little too urgent. There are countless examples one could consider, some more charming than others. By far the funniest, and a wonderful rendering of Herzog's dry humor and intimacy with his audience, happens in *Grizzly Man* (2005). An almost perfect documentary (two interviews too long) and probably Herzog's most-loved film, it tells the story of Timothy Treadwell, a failed actor and eccentric who took up a quixotic project of defending Alaska's grizzly bear population by living among the bears and even mingling with them. He was eventually eaten. A good portion of the film is Herzog's cobbling together the hundreds of hours of video footage that Treadwell left behind, some of

Figure 21. "Now Treadwell crosses a line with the Park Service which we will not cross." Timothy Treadwell channels Kinski on set. *Grizzly Man* (Herzog 2005).

it outstanding nature cinematography, some of it breathtaking daredevilism, but most of it the self-reflections of a tortured soul. Herzog as narrator and interviewer (of Treadwell's associates) enters into dialogue with the ghost of Treadwell made incarnate through video recording, and the film becomes as much a platform for Herzog's ideology of filmmaking as for Treadwell's quest for the meaning of life. I had the pleasure of seeing *Grizzly Man* upon its release, in front of a full house, and when Treadwell—every bit as blond and fragile as Klaus Kinski—unloads a minutes-long barrage of epithets to the camera against an imaginary US Park Service foe, Herzog deadpans, "I have seen this madness before, on a film set." The audience erupted, altogether in on the inside joke. And Herzog, even with a degree of separation divided by sound, light, and an editing console, again emerges as the lion tamer, negotiating the magical, or toxic, mix between recorded images and the "incandescence," as he puts it, of the inner rage of the alpha star, midwifing it from chaos to art.

These repetitions, sometimes with a difference, go on and on. Both *Encounters at the End of the World* (2007)—a documentary on the scientists and maintenance workers at an Antarctic research station—and *Salt and Fire* (2016)—a fictional piece shot largely on a vast Bolivian salt flat—feature long takes of people lying pressed to the ground with ears to the ice (or salt), listening to the mysteries of the deep and thus repeating a signature shot on a frozen lake from an earlier documentary on religious practices in rural Russia, *Bells from the Deep* (1993). In *Into the Inferno* (2016), a Netflix documentary about volcanos and related topics, he takes the next logical step and has a paleontologist declare his love for the land by lying down to kiss the dirt. Each of these shots is staged. Herzog's love of forged or self-declamatory documents (see *Aguirre*) appears again at the center of *Queen of the Desert* (2015), both as a plot device (a forged government pass through Turkish occupied territory) and anecdote, in which one character tells of masquerading as a veterinarian with official papers in order to steal a valuable horse, a story right out of Herzog's own catalog of wild tales (also from *Aguirre*).[188] Landscape remains a central preoccupation, sometimes achieving the ecstatic quality of his best films (e.g., *The White Diamond*, 2004; *Salt and Fire*), other times descending into the postcard prop of a Hollywood movie that Herzog so deeply disdains (e.g., *Rescue Dawn*, 2006; *Queen of the Desert*). Whether more or less successful, landscape always plays a role, even in a film as tied to confined institutional spaces as the staggering BBC series *On Death Row* (2012—13), as in the long shot of the embarrassed landscapes of roadside Americana along the forty-mile route from Texas holding cell to execution chamber, suddenly a reverie in the eyes of the condemned man.[189] In an echo of the probing close-ups of Kinski's or Bruno Schleinstein's characters held long after they have finished speaking, the interview shots are always held well beyond the question being answered. *The Wild Blue Yonder* opens by referencing *Signs of Life* with a wide field of windmills, now modern, futuristic. Each film, almost without exception, features a random animal at some point.

Then there are the turns to explicit self-reference that are a little painful to watch. *Rescue Dawn*, of course, is an entire feature based on retelling a story that Herzog had already told, and told better, before. *Into the Inferno* (2016) has the distinction of indulging in this move twice, with a major character drawn directly from *Encounters* and a tedious discussion of Herzog's 1970s-era film, *La Soufrière* (1977). This kind of thing descends (ascends?) into near comedy—perhaps intentionally, for Herzog doesn't cut it—in the last episode of *On Death Row*. At several points during his interview with Douglas Feldman, we learn that the prisoner had a history of extensive travel, including to the Andean region, and he recounts a story of having fled soldiers during the early 1980s border conflict between Ecuador and Peru. Herzog excitedly explains that they must have been only miles apart, as he was shooting *Fitzcarraldo* (1982), and construes the famous act of indigenous protest that burned down his film set as part of that same war (it was not). He recounts to Feldman their common travels to Antarctica and twin experiences with little monkeys in the rain forest, which Herzog gathered by the dozens for a famous film shoot. In each case, Feldman, a sociopath convicted of a wild murder spree on motorcycle, expresses nothing but uninterested shrugs of "Huh." Conquistador of the useless, indeed. The moments of Herzog's excitement to share his work in a discussion of capital crimes—and the film's montage from condemned man to publicity stills from Herzog's old films—is incongruous, to say the least. Most disappointing for some Herzog fans (including this one) is the sacrilege of recycling Sonny Terry's "Old Lost John," the theme music to Bruno's unforgettable denouement in *Stroszek* (1977), to accompany an amateur break dancer, badly back-spinning before an absurd Nicholas Cage in *Bad Lieutenant: Port of Call New Orleans* (2009).

If the quality of this late work is less steady than Herzog's sublime two decades that span *Signs of Life* (1968) and *Cobra Verde* (1987), this is perhaps not saying much: few directors can measure up to that kind of consistency during any creative period. And Herzog certainly hasn't slowed down or run out of ideas: since *My Best Fiend*, he has directed no fewer than twenty-four films, in genres as diverse as fictional features, documentaries, experimental hybrid form (such as *The Wild Blue Yonder* [2005], a science-fiction idyll that harks back to *Fata Morgana* [1971]), an extended public-service announcement (*From One Second to the Next*, produced by AT&T in 2013, against the dangers of texting while driving), and essentially an involved editing job (*Happy People: A Year in the Taiga*, 2010); he has done extensive production, pedagogical, and lecturing work; he has acted in several films of various prominence; and he has lent his signature narrative voice to projects including a Miyazaki animated feature, an episode of *The Boondocks* in which he plays a documentarian named Werner Herzog, a short in which the protagonist is a plastic bag, a Ken Burns documentary in which he reads the voice of a German white supremacist, and Erik Nelson's bizarre dinosaur snuff film, *Dinotasia* (2012).[190] He is impossible to keep up with: as this book goes to press, three new Herzog films are just hitting the theaters: his conversations with Mikhail Gorbachev, a documentary on Bruce Chatwin, and a feature on family-for-hire in Japan. Among his late work, some of the recent documentaries are particularly strong, including *Cave of Forgotten Dreams* (2010), a three-dimensional exploration of the delicate Chauvet cave paintings in the French Ardèche that was received as a revelation (which, in some senses, it literally was), or *The White Diamond*, an inventive portrait of an ecologist intent on studying the jungle canopy of Guyana from the perspective of a small homemade blimp. In expected Herzogian form, both films become moving reflections on the human condition.

The features, on the other hand, have lost their luster. With Herzog, even in a dud there is always an amazing moment or two, and none of the films fall into the category of "not worth watching." But the magic is gone, and most have received critical ambivalence, or it seems in some cases, exaggeration. While all this is certainly in part the common phenomenon of the ebb and flow of a long career, some of Herzog's mojo seems to be sapped in proportion to Hollywood involvement, investment, and expectation. Taken as a whole, the quality of his features occupies an inverse dynamic between mainstream star power and actual storytelling. While in his prime, he would contract the occasional international art film star such as Isabel Adjani, Bruno Ganz, or Claudia Cardinale, the flirtations with megastars like Jack Nicholson (almost Fitzcarraldo) and David Bowie (almost Cobra Verde) never panned out, blessed be the gods of the cinema. Since Tim Roth's appearance as the antagonist in *Invincible* (2001), however, Herzog's lineup has been populated by impressive and well-known stars: Christian Bale, Steve Zahn, Nicolas Cage, Val Kilmer, Michael Shannon, Willem Dafoe, Chloë Sevigny, the brilliant character actors Grace Zabriskie and Brad Dourif, Nicole Kidman, Damian Lewis, James Franco, Veronica Ferres, and Gael García Bernal, to name some headliners.

The performances have been uncommonly weak. Bale and Cage seem to equate a Kinski-esque energy with lots of yelling, rushing, and manic expressions; Dafoe looks and sounds like he's reading his lines, lost on set; for some reason, in both of his major roles with Herzog (*My Son, My Son, What Have Ye Done?* [2009] and *Salt and Fire*), Shannon insists on not using any contractions in his speech, which would have been perfect for the hypnotics of *Heart of Glass* (1975) but which is simply distracting in these contexts; Kidman is as dignified and professional as always, but the role can't live up to her, and her appearance in a wet T-shirt is an unexpected touch from a filmmaker normally as chaste as Herzog; Ferres is almost unwatchable in a delivery cringingly stilted, and García Bernal drops in on the same film—*Salt and Fire*—by standing around impossibly short of stature next to Ferres, groping her breast on an airplane, telling a series of unfunny jokes, and then exiting the film abruptly and altogether, passing the baton to Shannon, and with a bad case of explosive diarrhea to boot; and we all have to suffer the indignity of watching Franco attempt to maintain a British accent for about twenty minutes before the gong sounds and he too waltzes out of his film on the early side (lovesick, he hurls himself down a waterfall, which, alas, we learn about only in a letter). Critically at the time, there was minor celebration of Bale in *Rescue Dawn* and Cage in *Bad Lieutenant*, the latter of which received some larger accolades as well (several prominent "best of the year" lists). But viewed against some of Herzog's earlier films, the praise seems forced, like an effect of the fact that Herzog had gone a good five years without a fictional film (and really more like twenty since his last feature of some impact, *Cobra Verde*). Cage careers around post-Katrina New Orleans with a badly feigned hunched back, maniacal laughter, and constant cocaine-fueled sneers; Kinski *became* his deformities, whispering, hissing, growling, operatic in his shouts, lost in the deep gaze of monkeys and men. The former is a child before the latter. Placed alongside the level of work that Herzog coaxed from Kinski, Bruno S., Josef Bierbichler, Eva Mattes, Bruno Ganz, David Pérez Espinosa, and even Norbert Grupe and Walter Steiner, the contemporary Hollywood performances simply don't measure up, objectively falsifying Herzog's regular boast that he gets the very best out of all actors that he has worked with. There's a freshness, an unidentifiable ecstasy, to the Herzog works of his classic period that is lost in the contemporary features; they already feel older than their 1970s ancestors. And yet Herzog can still blow us away. Almost universally panned as a spectacular flop, in *Salt and Fire* Shannon's weird presentation of the Trinità dei Monti convent and its anamorphic frescoes, coupled with the breathtaking shots of the vehicles traversing the salt flats of Bolivia, makes it all worth our ninety minutes of quiet suffering.

Still far from a properly political filmmaker, the politics of Herzog's work have become more explicit in this late period. A concern for the earth and the fate of mankind shows up with regularity, quite easily understandable as something like environmentalism. The through-line critique of capitalist modernity, extending from his earliest films, that at the same time does not wither before some irrational fear of that same historical process, maintains its force. It can be perceived explicitly in films such as *The White Diamond* and *Lo and Behold: Reveries of the Connected World* (2016), the latter a hodgepodge documentary that takes up what feels like everything: cyber-bullying, radio-static illnesses, Elon Musk, the relations between robotics and love, the internet and its relation to water, a history of email. Most prominently, his absorbing documentaries of capital punishment—the feature-length *Into the Abyss* (2011) and the series *On Death Row* (2012–13)—both extend from his openly stated opposition to the death penalty. For political interpretations of Herzog's films, aspects of his work have become stronger and weaker in their critical possibilities. Two films stand out in this regard.

Queen of the Desert is, in its formula, standard Herzog fare. More biopic than his earlier work on historical figures, its story revolves around a remarkable, and problematic, individual, in this case the British orientalist, spy, administrator, and activist for imperialism Gertrude Bell. Bell was part of that generation of Victorian diplomat-scholars, crossing paths with figures no less prominent than T. E. Lawrence ("of Arabia") and Winston Churchill, and who worked to manage the transition between two doomed empires in the wake of World War I, the Ottoman and the British. When compared with the world-historical footnotes that Herzog successfully recenters in Lope de Aguirre, Carlos Fermín Fitzcarrald, and Francisco Félix de Souza, Bell is something of a giant. An unimaginably wealthy aristocrat, she stands out for a number of reasons: as a principal negotiator between the British Empire and the tribal leaders of the Levant and Arabian Peninsula, her memory is still very much alive in the region to this day; as a writer, scholar, and traveler, she produced a trove of letters and memoirs that provide a telling snapshot of the age, and she wrote a landmark of orientalist diplomatic writing, her *Review of the Civil Administration of Mesopotamia* (1920);

and, as a woman, even as a certain type of Victorian "lady traveler" that was not uncommon, she accomplished all this while having to fend off the most virulent misogyny from interlocutors both local and global. In a line appearing in the film, the diplomat Mark Sykes once dismissed her as a "silly chattering windbag of conceited, gushing flat-chested, man-woman, globe-trotting, rump-wagging, blethering ass" (in Stewart 2007). And yet it was this same "blethering ass" whose recommended borders would be installed, in perpetuity and in infamy, as Sykes himself applied her redrawn map of the Levant, including the formation of modern Iraq and Syria through the momentous Sykes-Picot Agreement. In short, it was Bell and her colleagues who helped set the world afire by installing authoritarian leaders over poorly thought borders that ran roughshod over historic nomadic routes and traditional royal and religious houses and alliances. This kind of historical ambivalence—a force of will (and Bell was certainly that) at the heart of world-historical violence—is Herzog's calling card, but here he turns it into Disney. Herzog's Bell is a straight-up protagonist, showing pluck in doing the right thing, getting tangled into and out of a couple of excruciatingly bland love affairs, standing up to desert kings and imperial bureaucrats alike. Why? For El Dorado? For the American Dream? For Caruso? For a desire to see the snow? No, just because she loves the Arab people so deeply, because when the mother of her butler hails him, she says, "Faruk, the one whom I trust to bury me when I die." It really is this maudlin. Of course, the real Bell, a creature of her time, made Kipling proud in her commitment to the white man's burden and had deep misgivings about the native peoples of the Levant, referring to their culture as a long history incapable of yielding wisdom. Of her many recommendations for the prospects of future rule in the region, self-determination without imperial oversight was never one of them. But none of this comes out in Herzog's film, which ends with Bell blithely naming the future kings of Iraq and Jordan, as they gaze upon this queen of the desert with nothing but grateful admiration. The epilogue, without having developed any evidence for the claim, calls Bell the single fondly remembered imperial administrator of the British hegemony. It's not a surprise that Bell's name is one that peppers Edward Said's pioneering critique of the legacies of imperial culture, *Orientalism* (1978), but no whiff of these contradictions show up in the film. In the end, it stands as a kind of undoing of the difficult world-historical politics of *Aguirre*, *Fitzcarraldo*, and *Cobra Verde*.

If *Queen of the Desert* is Herzog at his worst, then *On Death Row* is quite possibly Herzog at his best. The film is actually a documentary series, produced for BBC television, Herzog's single foray into the genre. It's a spin-off from his highly regarded film *Into the Abyss*, and the form turns out to be well suited for the topic and its style of presentation, reaching a level of emotional intensity that ultimately eludes the feature film. While we might expect that eight nearly hour-long interviews of death row inmates would be a little much, it turns out to be mesmerizing television, best watched in binge form; at approximately six-and-a-half hours, it would work as a long-form arthouse piece, with intermission, although it seems that this hasn't been tried. The cinematography is spare, largely straight interview shots that focus solely on the interview subject, Errol Morris style, with occasional cutaways to landscapes or archival footage. Of course the condemned themselves are astounding in their lived experiences and their discourse around their crimes and trials—three of the eight admit wrongdoing—but the basic question of their guilt or innocence is largely irrelevant, a pretext for deeper explorations of the soul. Most enthralling is the effectiveness, compassion, and impeccably well-placed moments of ethical authority on the part of Herzog as interviewer. Indeed, Herzog's treatment of his interlocutors and his commitment to their dignity can indicate much about his cinematographic practice writ large, and we can sense the relations between the humans introduced to us here on death row and many of the memorably problematic characters that populate his films. Herzog's interviewing style is unique and seems to coax introspective insight uncommon in the crime-and-punishment genre. He's slow. He lets words sink in. His questions are often obvious, or sometimes completely unexpected. Almost awkward silences often traverse the space between the end of an answer and Herzog's next question or comment, fleeting moments where we glimpse the accused, or their accusers, or their loved ones, alone with themselves. Through all of this we get a portrait of the condemned rarely seen, at once less melodramatic and more emotionally profound than the Hollywood stylings of a film like *Dead Man Walking* (1995), which is coyly cited and displaced in *On Death Row*. It evokes the kind of lingering disquiet about the American experience usually achieved only in literary works like *Native Son* (1940) or *In Cold Blood* (1966). It ends up being Herzog's most conventionally political film, in the best sense.

Each episode begins, as in a traditional series, with a common opening shot—solemn music and titles over death row itself, with human cages to the left, at the far end of a passageway two phones (just like in the movies) and a room painted bright institutional green in which we can glimpse the end of a surgical platform, the camera glides slowly toward it and, to our right, a nondescript table set with various bibles (in English and Spanish), flowers, and tissue paper. Walking forward, the hand-held camera sweeps left and glances toward a cell, and then we slowly enter the execution chamber. Herzog offers the same narration for each episode (there is an unimportant alteration between seasons 1 and 2), briefly detailing the status of the death penalty in the United States, and then stating bluntly, and perhaps a little politely, "As a German, coming from a different historical background, and being a guest in the United States, I respectfully disagree with the practice of capital punishment." And that's that; the films launch into their respective death-row portraits.

For the next fifty minutes or so, Herzog mobilizes the same slow, earnest, empathetic, conversational style in interviews with the condemned and also with the people circulating around the margins of their crimes: accomplices, witnesses, collateral victims, law enforcement. The conversations with family members are, of course, deeply moving. But most impressive is the way in which Herzog's gravitas as an interviewer allows for insight into the politics of crime and punishment—indeed, the oldest political question—rarely accomplished by the outcome-driven discourse and gotcha traps of the *60 Minutes* or *Frontline* exposé. Such moments come most regularly in his conversations with prosecutors. Herzog is never unkind to his subjects, and here all maintain their dignity on camera. Indeed, it is not hard to be seduced by or even sympathetic to their law-enforcement position: the crimes they are discussing are the real-world embodiment of the unthinkable. Herzog's rare, polite, and strikingly efficient interventions are an effective counterpoint and suggest the darkness that lurks behind the commitment to exterminating human beings, whether as criminal or punisher. And he succeeds in doing so without any claims to innocence: perhaps some of the procedural elements raise troubling questions about the US criminal justice system, but none of his death-row subjects is even remotely convincing as falsely condemned. This subtle displacing, or even dismantling, of the ethics of the prosecutor's pose, the revelation that their work is ultimately about politics, makes *On Death Row* not only Herzog's most openly political film in its position taking, but also one that gets to the heart of his skills as a filmmaker and comes close to something like a statement of purpose on his cinematic practice. When judicial officials elaborate on the unusual sexual practices of Robert Fratta (convicted of contracting the killing of his wife), Herzog reminds them "but this is not a criminal offense." They concede. When state prosecutor Greg Davis explains his presentation of Darlie Routier (convicted of stabbing to death her two young children) to the jury as a heartless monster in seeking her execution by exhibiting video footage of her smilingly spraying silly string on her dead child's grave, Herzog openly disagrees with the manipulative tactic. Davis can only respond with a non sequitur about motherhood. When Michael Jimerson, the prosecuting attorney in the case of young Blaine Milam (convicted in the ritual murder of a toddler), ends a long soliloquy by stating that "*we* define who we are, and *we* are not capable of that sort of evil, and *we* are allowed to erase you from our existence, *we* are allowed to eliminate you from our race, our species, we have every *right* to do that as thinking, rational human beings. . . . [T]here's *nothing* wrong or inappropriate with us doing that," Herzog replies simply, "I respectfully disagree," to which the prosecutor, off guard, quickly says "Yes, sir." Over courtroom footage of the convicted murderer, Herzog continues, "I disagree. Erasing and eliminating a human being does not sound right." And finally, in what could stand as Herzog's subject in the most elemental sense—great intensity, great evil, and great humanity all tangled up together, *pura vida* as he likes to put it—comes his unflappable directness in conversation with Connie Spence, Harris County assistant district attorney and prosecutor of the case against Linda Carty, convicted of suffocating a young mother whose baby she was attempting to kidnap. Warning Herzog against the charm of Carty, Spence speaks to our (the filmmaker's, the audience's, society's) desire to humanize the perpetrator of ghastly crimes. She deliberately explains her position—she argues that we can hear Linda, but we can't hear her victim—and Herzog is patient in letting her finish her point, as she concludes about our childish desire to "think of people as being nice, and good," to, as she puts it, humanize them. A Herzogian pause. And then the director concludes, as the prosecutor's fixed smile turns to sand: "I have to make one remark. I do not humanize her. I do not make an attempt to humanize her. She is simply a human being. Period."

Notes

1. Indeed, "apocalypse" as a theme, while outside of the scope of this book, has attracted the attention of scholars writing about Herzog. See Singer (2012) and Chessman (1991).

2. The first monograph dedicated to Herzog's oeuvre is Paolo Siriani's *Il cinema di Werner Herzog* (1980), followed quickly by Emmanuel Carrère's *Werner Herzog* (1982). Recent books in English that take up wide aspects of Herzog's work include Prager (2007), Ames (2012b) and Johnson (2016). The most extensive multiauthor collection of scholarship on Herzog's work is *A Companion to Werner Herzog* (2012), edited by Prager. For an extensive bibliography of works on Herzog up through 2014, see Prager, "Werner Herzog" (web page), *Oxford Bibliographies: Cinema and Media Studies*, last updated September 25, 2018, DOI: 10.1093/OBO/9780199791286–014.

3. It is worth belaboring the point that this book's objective is not to place Herzog along a traditional spectrum of political-ideological position taking. On the one hand, he is famous (infamous) for trolling the left, through a number of statements, gestures, and films that will be discussed in the following pages. On the other hand, and at the same time, there is no contradiction between that history and the consistent critique of capitalist modernity that emerges from his art. While "the left" always has at least a toehold in Marx's foundational critique of capitalism, "the right" has long nurtured its own, conservative—if dialectically dubious—critique of capitalism. Kolozi's new book (2018) offers a sweeping review of this history, and Deneen's caricature of contemporary liberalism (2018) is another recent example of this position from the right. In short: to point up Herzog's critical positions on capitalist modernity is not a way of suggesting that he is a secret leftist; nor is it a way of excluding that possibility.

4. Prager (2007), for example, divides his book into sections on madness, landscapes, faith, war, and Africa. Ames (2012b), who focuses on documentary, opts for bodies, landscapes, journeys, Baroque visions, cultural politics, reenactments, and autobiography. Johnson (2016), who focuses on romanticism, divides her monograph into topical pairs: "Image and Knowledge," "Surface and Depth," "Beauty and Sublimity," "Man and Animal," and "Sound and Silence." The *Companion* is divided similarly.

5. "Spaghetti western" is the generic term often invoked to indicate western-genre films produced in Europe, most famously beginning in the mid-1960s

with Sergio Leone's collaborations with Clint Eastwood. Cinema novo is the Brazilian avant-garde, engaged filmmaking movement that spanned the 1960s.

6. Early versions of *Aguirre*, and I expect the original print, break the transition from script to expedition with a wide aerial shot of cloud-draped Andean peaks. The currently distributed DVD—which includes commentary by the director—that I am handling here eliminates this transitional shot. It's an agreeable cut.

7. For an extended invocation of the discourse on struggle in *Aguirre*, one only need listen to the director's commentary, in conversation with Norman Hill, on the DVD version. Herzog calls it a "very physical film" and makes much of privation, with stories of trading boots for breakfast and the like.

8. There is an impressive shot that makes this example literal: about minute 41, in the transitional scene immediately following the ascension of Don Fernando to the throne, the monk paces in front of some of the soldiers, and the background river currents perceptibly flow in two opposite directions.

9. See Emily Brady's *The Sublime in Modern Philosophy* (2013) for an excellent account of the various strands of debate around the sublime from the eighteenth century through today.

10. There are many interlocutors here, but by far the most frequently mentioned, by Herzog and his critical interpreters, are the painter Caspar David Friedrich, the poet and novelist Achim von Arnim, the poet—more idealist than romantic, but still—Friedrich Hölderlin, and the composer Richard Wagner. His self-proclaimed "illiteracy" aside, Herzog is an avid reader and studied literature, history, and theater as an undergraduate in Munich.

11. Beyond Prager's book, here is a basic anglophone bibliography on the sublime in Herzog: Brigitte Peucker (1984) offers an early, systematic analysis of the sublime in the context of its relation to German Romanticism; Alan Singer (1986) interprets Herzog in the light of the "ironic sublime" and productively destabilizes any temptations to universality by reading the sublime as an invitation to historical reflection; John Davidson (1993) advances a critique of both as historically underdeveloped; Matthew Gandy (1996) attempts to parse out various strands of the sublime, placing Herzog between Burke (for whom the sublime is "terrifying in its enormity, darkness or infinite extension" [4]) and Kant (for whom the sublime is "concerned with the mind's limit, a threshold of transcendent knowledge derived from our experience of nature which reminds us that our imaginative abilities are finite" [4]) and places both in tension with what he perceives as a larger preoccupation of Herzog, the existentialist premise that "the fundamental otherness of the world [nature] is inescapable" (8); Jacques de Villiers (2012) reads Herzog *against* the romantic sublime; Laurie Johnson's (2016) book provides a useful interpretation of the relations between the sublime, romanticism, and the idea of "inner landscapes" in Herzog. The well-known trajectory from some of the aesthetic and cultural programs of romanticism to the rise of national socialism and its own

aesthetic agenda has been brought to bear on Herzog, namely in light of his German identity. I haven't found this line of analysis, often revolving around the fact that Herzog likes to invoke mountains and fog, terribly convincing. For example, Dana Benelli (1986) makes the case that *Aguirre* cites Riefenstahl and implicitly deals with fascism, drawing our attention to the fact that, like *Aguirre*, Riefenstahl's *Triumph of the Will* (1935) opens with a shot high up in the clouds. Koepnick (1993, 144) and Villiers both cite this interpretation uncritically; Davidson (1993, 121) makes the same association. But in Riefenstahl's movie, descending from the clouds via airplane is a de facto national leader, the proclaimed *führer* who would lay waste to large swaths of central Europe and lead an active project of genocide; in Herzog, nobody descends from the clouds at all, and the eventual leader of this ragtag splinter battalion spends his screen time (and his life) essentially hacking into the jungle. More subtle, and less affirmative, than Benelli, Gandy (1996) makes a similar move, now via Kracauer, concluding that the "hidden dangers" of making a "privileged critical position" (13) of the aesthetic place Herzog uncomfortably close to the Nazis. Against this discourse, see Wahl (2012).

12. The expression is from Benjamin's dissertation on the *Trauerspiel*—"In ihnen allen ist die überwuchernde Metaphorik"—but the translation is John McCole's (1993, 143).

13. Eric Ames (2012b) cites Brian Hanrahan, who calls Herzog's "proliferation of yarns . . . a 'baroque phenomenon'" (106). Ames's chapter, "Baroque Visions," in his 2012 book-length study of Herzog's documentaries, is the most systematic treatment of Herzog's stated interest in the baroque. For Ames, the resonant point between Herzog and the baroque is not the rather narrow field of the "Bavarian baroque" and its "images of stucco angels and pilgrimage churches" (105). Instead, he rereads Herzog through the wider set of aesthetic tendencies of the baroque as outlined by Martin Jay (1993), Christine Buci-Glucksman (1994), and José Antonio Maravall (1975) and the transhistorical aesthetic mood of the "trans-Atlantic baroque" studied by Lois Parkinson Zamora (2006). In very broad strokes, a number of tendencies in Herzog's work articulate the baroque: the "ecstatic truth" and its recourse to faith over reason (see Ames), a certain Counter-Reformation tone that many have perceived as haunting his films, and, most clearly (as we will develop in the subsequent pages), the attraction to the melancholy of spectacular failure, for the baroque was, after all, an art of desperation in the face of systemic decline.

14. Unstoppable and unsustainable growth is a preoccupation of Herzog's that comes up in his interviews. In Herzog and Cronin (2002), speaking to the "danger" of "the lack of adequate imagery," he speaks of other "dangers that surround us" noting that "overcrowding of the planet is the greatest of all" (Herzog and Cronin 2002, 66).

15. Like many of Herzog's most memorable shots, there is a backstory here: "Whilst in Greece I walked around the mountains of Crete where I came across

a valley. I had to sit down because I was sure I had gone insane. Before me lay 10,000 windmills—it was like a field of flowers gone mad—turning and turning with these tiny squeaking noises. I sat down and pinched myself. 'I have either gone insane or have seen something very significant indeed.' Of course, it turned out that the windmills were for real, and this central image became a pivotal point of the film, a landscape in complete ecstasy and fantastic madness. I knew as I stood there that I would return one day to make a film" (Herzog and Cronin 2002, 39).

16. "When I returned to Lanzarote to start shooting *Even Dwarfs Started Small* I was full of bitterness . . . Somehow I had the feeling that if Goya and Hieronymus Bosch had the guts to do their gloomiest stuff, why shouldn't I?" (Herzog and Cronin 2002, 55).

17. It's hard to get a straight answer from Herzog on this point. In one brief turn with Cronin, he goes from saying that his critics "might have been right about" his "ridiculing the world revolution," to noting that the dwarfs' revolt is not in fact a defeat, "it is a really good, memorable day; you can see the joy in their faces." From "I told these agitators that the film had absolutely nothing to do with the 1968 movements" to "if they looked at the film twenty years down the line they might just see a more truthful representation of what happened in 1968 than in most other films" (55–56).

18. The substantial archive on Aguirre's fateful El Dorado expedition is based exclusively on several accounts produced by soldiers that survived the mutiny, the legal documents surrounding the case, and the historical reinterpretations of the journey by imperial *cronistas*. Aguirre's letters that form the center of this corpus include one signed original, the others stemming from transcriptions intercalated in various accounts of the rebellion. Historians have deemed three of them to be authentic examples of Aguirre's political discourse: the letter to Philip II (the most famous); the signed letter to the provincial administrator Francisco de Montesinos; and the letter to Pablo Collado, governor of the district of Tocuyo (today part of Venezuela). The dubious fourth letter is also to Collado. Historians today universally rely on the transcriptions of Jos (1927) for study of Aguirre's discourse, in some cases comparing his transcriptions with competing *relaciones* that deal with the Aguirre adventure. The most complete source of Aguirre-related material is Pastor and Callau's (2011) magnificent collection of documents—including analysis, bibliography, the letters, the seven *relaciones* or eyewitness accounts, the basic juridical material, a chronology, and a biographical sketch of all the major players in and around the rebellion—called *Lope de Aguirre y la rebelión de los marañones*. Páramo Bonilla (2009) also reproduces the letters, including the fourth letter. For comprehensive analysis of the historical Aguirre and the subsequent centuries-long discourse on Aguirre, nothing approaches Ingrid Galster's (2011) remarkable work. First published in German in 1996, the

eight-hundred-plus-page translation into Spanish, *Aguirre o La posteridad arbitraria*, is the version that I handle here.

19. The letter to Philip II was apparently sent, but no original has ever been found; it may not have made it out of America, and it seems doubtful that the king himself ever laid eyes on it.

20. These include *relaciones* from the navigator and loyalist Pedro de Monguía; the soldier Gonzalo de Zúñiga; the soldier Francisco Vázquez (the most thorough and famous account); the soldier Juan de Vargas Zapata, son of the first mate of the premutiny expedition; the captain Altamirano, a possible pseudonym; the Portuguese soldier Custodio Hernández, who will eventually deliver Aguirre's head to the authorities; and an anonymous account. See Pastor and Callau (2011).

21. See, for example, Pastor (1992) and Bost (1996, esp. 157–59).

22. I suspect that the Bolívar reference is apocryphal. The source always ultimately leads back to Otero Silva's (1982, 251–52) novelized version of the life of Aguirre.

23. Pío Baroja and Ramón María del Valle-Inclán were two of the major figures of the celebrated Generation of 98 in Spanish literature; each deals with Aguirre, Baroja in *Las inquietudes de Santi Andía* ([1911] 2010); and Valle-Inclán in *Tirano Banderas* ([1926] 1987), highly regarded in Latin America. Arturo Uslar Pietri was the great midcentury Venezuelan novelist and statesman, author of a liberal's reimagining of Aguirre in *El camino de El Dorado* (1947); Ramón Sender was a Spanish expatriate known for his political novels, the last of which is *La aventura equinocial de Lope de Aguirre* (1964); Abel Posse is a widely read Argentine novelist of the "boom" generation, author of the Aguirre narrative *Daimón* (1978). For comprehensive analysis of this corpus, see Galster (2011). Aguirre-as-inspiration penetrates a range of other disciplines: three theater plays, one published in nineteenth-century Venezuela (Briceño Picón [c. 1890] 1994), another posthumously in Colombia (Torres 1989), and the third from contemporary Peru (Vega Herrera 2000); a graphic novel trilogy (Hernández Cava et al. 1989–98); a Basque "dramatic narration" (Acosta Montoro 1967); a series of evocative vignettes by Basque historians (*Lope de Aguirre descuartizado*; Academia Errante 1963); an Argentine philosophical treatise on "the moral and ethical aspects of insurrection" comparing Aguirre and Che Guevara (Duhalde 1997); a Venezuelan collection of poems (Gerbasi 1978); a Venezuelan operetta with book (Pardo 1957) and score (Castellanos 1966); a Spanish ceramics exhibition (Oteiza 1972); and an Argentine psychological profile, including formal diagnosis: "personalidad anormal, psicópata anafectivo" (Lastres 1942).

24. I know of two other attempts to bring Aguirre's story to the screen. The most significant is Carlos Saura's *El Dorado* (1988), a somewhat plodding affair that never gained much critical traction. One can find references on-line to Andy Rakich's *Tears of God* (2007), apparently a student film, and something of

a homage-parody of Herzog's *Aguirre*, not widely available, but with a hilarious trailer available on YouTube.

25. See Ramos (1958) and Pastor and Callau (2011, 16–20).

26. Dated February 1, 1561, in the *relación* of Custodio Hernández, not everyone in the party signs this letter (Mampel Hernández 1981; see Pastor and Callau 2011, 348); most of the *relaciones* report an extended speech two months later by Aguirre, in which he more dramatically announces the expedition's secession from Spain. As Pastor and Callau explain (33), the various accounts diverge around the nature of Guzmán's appointment: some indicate it as merely leadership of the expedition upon Ursúa's assassination, others, more radically, as the figurehead of a secessionist principality in the Peruvian Amazon. A version of this scene will be central to Herzog's film.

27. The *relación* of Francisco Vásquez (Mampel Hernández 1981) is most systematic in detailing the steps of this plan.

28. Carvajal produced a *relación* on a different Amazonian expedition, called *Relación del nuevo descubrimiento del famoso río Grande que descubrió por muy gran ventura el capitán Francisco de Orellano* (1955). Herzog incorporates significant aspects of this Orellano expedition (including its relation to Gonzalo Pizarro) into *Aguirre*. See Fritze (1985). On the relations between *Aguirre* and the firsthand accounts of the Ursúa expedition, see Stone (2005).

29. The interview is from *The Colbert Report*, June 11, 2011; it's an entertaining bit.

30. For a long-form study that deals extensively with the notion of the "ecstatic truth" in Herzog, including philosophical genealogy, see Prager (2007); on the ecstatic truth in its relation to the baroque, see Ames (2012b).

31. In a 1973 interview with Noureddine Ghali (Herzog 2014f), originally published in *Jeune Cinéma*, Herzog states, "In *Even Dwarfs*, the dwarfs are not outside of society, they are society itself. . . . I think the hatred [toward the film] comes from having to recognize your own inner dwarf and realizing for the first time just how small we are. There's a rebellion in *Even Dwarfs*, but not a revolution. It's an insane, senseless revolt without end." (20).

32. See Bataillon (1963) and Pastor and Callau (2011, 16–20).

33. But even these portraits often descend into ambivalence. Vázquez, on whose life his denunciation of Aguirre depends, ends by asserting that actually Aguirre could be kind of a nice guy (in Pastor and Callau 2011, 277–8).

34. From the *relación* of Zúñiga (in Pastor and Callau 2011, 105–54).

35. Pastor and Callau (2011) reproduce the letter from Aguirre to Philip II (71–79). For the part about the renting of the fish, see page 76.

36. The anonymous *relación* provides an astonishing list of fifty-eight people, "those killed by the tyrant after the uprising," murdered by various methods: sword, garrote, spear, club, musket, knife, hanging, and dismemberment (in Pastor and Callau 2011, 337–39).

37. Pastor develops an extended analysis of Aguirre as baroque subject (1992, 194–204). Maravall (1976) is the classic source on Spanish baroque culture and its relation to the colonial Americas, which also sustains Pastor's account.

38. In the Zúñiga *relación*, Aguirre delivers a speech after the assassination of Ursúa, accompanied by a document (the one he will sign "por traidor"). In justifying the rebellion, he concludes, "I want to reveal to your majesties a secret that I have known very well; and it is that this Frenchman [Ursúa] wanted to bring us here long enough to disorient us, and then escape and leave us here lost" (in Pastor and Callau 2011, 348).

39. Most of the indigenous people playing enslaved Incas were recruited from the Cooperativa Agraria de Lauramarca and are listed in the closing credits as such, that is, en masse and not individually as actors; this includes the actor who plays Balthasar, who has a major speaking role in the film.

40. In a 1976 interview with Kraft Wetzel, Herzog states, "The decisive figure in *Aguirre* isn't Kinski but the dull-witted man [the actor is a street musician from Cusco known simply as Hombrecito] who plays the flute" (Herzog 2014d, 34). Herzog's obvious affection for the man doesn't do much to develop the notion of his centrality within the film, although the scenes in which he plays his flute—including a moody portrait with Kinski's Aguirre—are striking.

41. A fine point, but it is important to note that this is an *aesthetic* choice, and not necessarily in conflict with the *historical* representation of the Indians as self-evident political actors. In an influential postcolonial reading of *Aguirre*, Koepnick (1993) sets forth a debatable thesis worthy of further elaboration than I can muster here. In brief, he correctly perceives a certain continuity between jungle and Indians: "the native Indians never differentiate themselves from the forest, never achieve contour before the jungle's undefined anarchy" (140), but then in the same breath goes on to say that because of this they are "not perceived as members of an integrated political body" (ibid.) and thus "Aguirre's men have refused to recognize the Indians as possessing an organized culture" (141). This reads far too much into the film, in which I can't find any examples suggesting that a group of Spanish conquistadors in 1561 would be unable to perceive their indigenous opponents as capable of organized resistance (that is, culture and politics) when it is precisely this force that has been at the very center of imperial policy and paranoia for nearly a century. Indeed, injecting this kind of position into the film would immediately demolish its historicity into irrelevance.

42. This resonates harmoniously with the historical events of the expedition, as Pastor and Callau make clear: "But in the texts that narrate the Ursúa expedition, threats do not arrive from the outside but rather from within. The *relaciones* evoke an ambiance of general frustration and discontent, where rivalry and envy define the relations between the adventurers, and where any incident can provoke an explosion" (2011, 28).

43. The unusual name is in homage to John Okello, the 1960s protagonist of the Zanzibar Revolution, and whose hyperbolic proclamations fascinated Herzog, aspects of which found their way into Aguirre's soliloquies.

44. This is one of those shots where romantic sublime and baroque anxiety collide. It's also one of Herzog's favorites, as he explains in the DVD commentary: "This is for me one of the very mysterious shots in the film, the horse just staying there and disappearing . . . one of my favorite shots. That is something, some poetry that you can put into films that doesn't exist anywhere else. It doesn't exist in literature like this, or it doesn't exist in other media, you can do it on film and nowhere else, and that's why I love to do films."

45. This line riffs on Aguirre's letter to Philip II, when he accuses the king's auditors and judges of living by the refrain: "a tuerco o a derecho, nuestra casa hasta el techo" (hard to translate, but essentially the idea is that what they see, they possess; in Pastor and Callau 2011, 75).

46. The singular intertext here is the notorious *Requerimiento*, the 1512 juridical document formally invoked by Spanish armies of conquest in order to justify their plunder of indigenous lands and bodies. Madan (2013) deals with this history in the context of her powerful revisionist reading of Herzog as "double translator." For a general overview of the voluminous scholarship on the document, including an original interpretation of its formal and performative aspects very much in tune with Herzog's portrait of Aguirre, see Faudree (2015).

47. In one way or another, the big "colonial discourse" readings of *Aguirre*—Davidson (1993), Koepnick (1993), Madan (2013)—pay insufficient attention to the political-historical specificity of *Aguirre* and the fact that it does not represent the colonial project or even the conquest per se, but rather, paradoxically, an act of resistance against that project, its own internal contradiction.

48. Velasco Alvarado took power in the wake of a coup d'état in 1968. His "revolutionary" government allied itself with the Soviet Union and installed a number of progressive reforms, including nationalization of industries, agrarian reform, and, significantly here, it worked toward a plural notion of Peruvian culture through the officialization of the Quechua language. Facing open resistance from the military, Alvarado quietly stepped down in 1975.

49. This citation is from Páramo Bonilla (2009, 267) who unearths it from Galster (1996).

50. The New German Cinema is essentially shorthand for the generation of German filmmakers who rose up against the quietism and banalities of the treacly pastoral films of the post-Nazi era. It is often traced to the Kluge, Reitz, and Senft (1988) *Oberhausen Manifesto*, a declaration of the talents of young German filmmakers that concludes that "The old film is dead. We believe in the new one." For an art form that has traditionally punctuated its aesthetic transformations with manifestos—futurists, bolsheviks, constructivists, surrealists, auteurists, feminists, Rocha's *Estética da fome* (1965), Von Trier and Vinterberg's "Dogme" manifesto (1995), even Herzog's own "Minnesota Declaration" (1999),

not to mention the long history of "reactions" from papal decree to the Hayes Code—it's a curt and rather bland document. But it announces a principle that clearly resonated with an entire cohort and that Herzog regularly translates as the notion that Germany is a "cinema without fathers" that must look to its grandfathers (Lang, Murnau, Pabst) for dialogue and direction (e.g., Cott interview in *Rolling Stone*, Herzog and Cott 1976), a sentiment most immediately felt in the early 1960s vanguards such as Alexander Kluge (a signatory), Volker Schlöndorff, and the French expatriate duo of Jean-Marie Straub and Daniele Huillet. Its most internationally successful participants—Fassbinder, Wenders, Herzog himself—were a little young for the manifesto. With no unifying style, it's more of a mood than a movement, a child of the 1960s student agitation, although the masterpieces of the New German Cinema mostly emerge in the 1970s. See Thomas Elsaesser's *New German Cinema: A History* (1989) for the classic study on the era. Herzog's aggressive internationalism, his oft-expressed irritability with the notion of Germanness, and his stated sense of disinterest from the German public has long left him in an ambivalent position toward the category. Whether a fair assessment or not, he long felt "little but indifference" from his "compatriots" until the 1977 *Stroszek* (Herzog 2014c, 47).

51. The "secret mainstream" is Herzog's affectionate term for his fans, as recorded in an eloquent profile article of the same title by Tom Bissell (2006).

52. Often controversial—especially *Heart of Glass*—these films are generally considered significant works of the decade. *Kaspar Hauser* won the Grand Prix Spécial du Jury at Cannes in 1975. *Heart of Glass* divides critics, but it won a German Film Award for Jörg Schmidt-Reitwein's cinematography and is one of the more extraordinary films of the decade. *Nosferatu* is an homage to Murnau, an effective portrait of the vampire that is celebrated for its originality and its beauty, with Kinski winning the award of Best Actor from the National Society of Film Critics. *Woyzeck* landed Eva Mattes an acting award at the 1979 Cannes festival, and Herzog a nomination for the Palme d'Or.

53. Herzog's dismissal of his own, frankly quite moving and politically important, film is perhaps not surprising, in light of its instrumental nature (social critique and awareness raising). As one colleague put it to me, who, after all, wants their art to be "of use"? At the same time, we might ask what Herzog has to gain by throwing so much cold water on his own film. It's an open question.

54. Herzog's approach to documentary has attracted scholarly interest; most extensively, see the book-length study by Ames (2012b).

55. Somewhere between *Land of Silence and Darkness* and *Woodcarver Steiner* is a short called *No One Will Play with Me* (1976), a film about social exclusion inspired by a childhood story told by Walter Steiner.

56. John Davidson (2012) offers an intelligent, productive interpretation of these films, reading *Huie's Sermon* in the light of W. E. B. DuBois, and *God's Angry Man* through Melville. And although he's handling a rather unproblematized notion of *race*, he at the same time advances the subtlest analysis of

race in Herzog's films that I know of. He wraps the discussion up with some eloquent words about Herzog as an observer of US culture that summarizes the importance of these films: "Looking back today at the documentaries of this American period [Herzog's Reagan-Thatcher work], one sees how these early films engaged with the ghosts of religion, greed, and racism that have since reemerged to haunt the American political scene. If nothing else, there was an odd prescience in Herzog's un-Herzogian documentary practice some thirty years ago, that of a stranger looking at 'democracy in America' through a lens that illuminates where we were and were not heading with the language, situatedness, and material relations of our own hallucinatory self-constructions. The neutrality of his stranger's perspective helps us see that the doctrine of American self-interest should now be properly understood: not a sublime document, but one that is clear and unambiguous" (441).

57. Worth noting is that all three films were produced for West German television, and thus they share a high level of ethnographic distantiation from their subjects, a productive exoticization that played on German expectations about the eccentricities of US culture. A feature shared among the three is that they focus on cultural practices that one would never find in Germany.

58. For a helpful materialist reading of *Heart of Glass*, see Heringman (2012); while I disagree with its insistence on qualifying the productive context of the film as "proto-capitalist" (258), and "pre-industrial" (261) (while, like everywhere, feudalist trappings persist, eighteenth-century Bavaria is fully capitalist), the essay brings ample insight to the film. Rentschler (1986) and Singer (1986) stage a debate on the politics of *Heart of Glass* through the closing chapters of Tim Corrigan's collection of essays *The Films of Werner Herzog* (1986).

59. While Herzog would never be contained as a "genre director," he self-consciously produces intertexts with a number of genre histories throughout his career, marking out ample territory for analysis that has yet to be pursued. Indeed, his very next film after *Stroszek* will be a horror film, and moreover, his entry into the reigning subgenre of that genre, the vampire movie.

60. Chet Atkins's prominent role in the soundtrack is not accidental: a virtuoso guitarist and, moreover, author of the "Nashville sound," his prominence in the invention of American commercial country music makes him something of a patron saint to the soundtrack of white, rural, small-town America.

61. As Greg Grandin explains in his introduction to the 2011 edition of Williams's *The Contours of American History*, Turner's "frontier thesis" essentially withered in the face of Williams's critique; but, of course, it lives on through a host of ideological truths.

62. The film in question is *Bruno der Schwarze—Es blies ein Jäger wohl in sein Horn* (1970), directed by Lutz Eisholz. Schleinstein's nom-de-guerre of Bruno S. is interesting. On the one hand, according to Herzog, it is in deference to his wish to remain anonymous, which the director explains as a symptom of his mistrust for society and its institutions, which had abused him systematically

over the course of much of his life. On the other hand, the reduction of his name to a letter is a nod to those same institutions: in West Germany, delinquent children were indicated in court documents by an initialed surname, precisely to protect their identity. See Herzog and Cronin (2002), 116–20, and director's commentary on *Stroszek*.

63. For Herzog's recitation of these stories, see Herzog and Cronin (2002) and the *Stroszek* DVD director's commentary.

64. Both actors have an interesting back story, as Herzog explains on his DVD commentary. Wilhelm von Homburg, born Norbert Grupe, was a wrestler and boxer with some street-tough credibility, who went on to enjoy a variety of scary cameos in Hollywood. Burkhard Driest was a law student who was busted in a bank robbery, wrote a film script in jail, and then landed some film roles after his release.

65. Scholars have noticed this. Rentschler's insightful essay, "How American Is It?" (1984), lists an entire index of doubled repetitions in the film: Bruno's America is an intensified version of Berlin; both hoodlums and the banker will knock twice; the disenfranchised Turks of Berlin are mirrored by the marginalized Indians of the United States; while Berlin is vertical, America is equally vertiginous in its horizontality; the film opens with Bruno being asked his name by a bureaucrat and ends with him sitting in a chair on which is written "Is this really me?" As we'll see, there are countless additional instances.

66. Stephen Barber (2014), in *Performance Projections* (54–65), provides a fascinating contextualization of this scene by situating it in a German trajectory of semipublic performance, from *Berlin Alexanderplatz* (1931) to the late Cold War East German underground punk scene. Barber emphasizes the "vital obsolescence" (58) of these spaces in the face of neoliberal tenets of privatization and security, and a *New York Times* article (Kimmelman 2008) records the real-life Bruno Schleinstein singing in a bar, "Once upon a time there was a beautiful town . . . You could go everywhere, in all the courtyards and on all the streets. . . . After the wall fell, everything changed" (2008).

67. Besides May's perennial popularity, Germany was a major venue for fin-de-siècle traveling panoramas, anthropological exhibitions, and Wild West Shows, a cultural fetish that Herzog slyly taps into throughout *Stroszek*. On the history of these shows, see Ames (2009).

68. The looming presence of guns is notable in and around the film. The armed tractors are Herzog's invention, but in production terms, the shoot took place during the Thanksgiving holiday, deer hunting season, and this is incorporated into the film; Herzog claims that during unplanned and unauthorized filming at an idyllic pond, "the farmer who owned the land almost shot at us" (*Stroszek* DVD, director's commentary). Scott McKain, in his account of the shoot, doesn't mention this incident.

69. At the arrival of the mobile home, Herzog riffs on this topic—although in terms much more affirmative than Lévi-Strauss—in his DVD director's

commentary: "I was always fascinated by mobile homes of that size, moving cross-country. And much of American civilization is still very nomadic, in contrast to European, which is so settled, since centuries and centuries. . . . [For Bruno, Eva, and Herr Scheitz] [i]t's not something that is very low class, it's a big thing, a mobile home and you can move it anywhere, what a big thing that is. . . . For postwar Germans, that was almost a dream home."

70. The role of the cowboy hat in the film is worth its own little essay as a garish mark of an American cultural moment harking back to a frontier spirit of yore, and perhaps as a passing stab at the rather childish German cultural obsession with signs of the American frontier. Al, of course, wears a cowboy hat; Bruno's cellmate with the *Bonanza* poster wore a cowboy hat; in one scene, one of the Berlin thugs wears a fancy, fashion cowboy hat; the auctioneer will wear a cowboy hat; and Bruno himself, from the time he arrives in America, wears a cowboy hat. It's worth remembering that in US culture, the cowboy hat by the 1970s is something normally worn in specific regional settings (essentially the American west and southwest; *Stroszek* is a little before the miniboom in "western chic" that welled up around John Travolta's hilarious *Urban Cowboy*), and there often affiliated with a particular, usually rural, set of cultural practices. While it wouldn't be abnormal to see the occasional cowboy hat in rural Wisconsin even today, its ubiquitous presence in the film obviously calls attention to itself. I'm indebted to Deb Koleski for independent ethnographic work on this question.

71. McKain's story is fun and, like much of the cast of *Stroszek*, he is a "found object" of sorts: with a luscious radio voice and sincere Midwestern, folksy charm, he has gone on to become a successful author and speaker on questions of "distinction" within corporate merchandising. He gives an engaging account of what it was like to work with Herzog as a nonprofessional actor, available online in both written (2016) and spoken (2015) (highly recommended) form. Besides his scene-stealing cameos, McKain scouted shooting locations with Herzog every morning for about ten days; he was offered a role in *Fitzcarraldo*, but that fell through when the production was transformed from English to German with the illness of Jason Robards and his subsequent replacement by Kinski.

72. Enyutin (2011) calls the Berlin thugs "not just regular hooligans—they stage their actions making it aesthetically impressive performances. They are kind of artists of intimidation, harassment, torture and humiliation" (2011). The banker: "A new world authority, on the other hand, is personified by the clerk of money (the impeccably polite bank clerk)" (ibid.).

73. The significance of the courtyard ballad that Bruno sings in the Berlin half of the film is worth noting here, for it foreshadows the star-crossed romance with Eva. While the plot that it recites doesn't line up exactly, it certainly captures the spirit of Bruno's fall: a poor cobbler boy, a proletarian, tries to woo a beautiful girl, Sabine, but spends all his money on beer and eventually gets caught stealing silver spoons from his girlfriend's parents' home, leading to Sabine's disgrace.

In some publicity posters, *Stroszek* is subtitled as *A Ballad*; the French release was titled *La ballade de Bruno*.

74. Herzog's films are largely populated by men, with significant female protagonists countable on one hand. During his classic period (let's say, through the 1987 *Cobra Verde*), they are four: Fini Straubinger, the subject of *Land of Silence and Darkness*; the two great roles played by Eva Mattes, here Eva, and also Marie from *Woyzeck* (for which Mattes was celebrated with an award at Cannes), both of whom are sex workers who betray their romantic partners; and Isabelle Adjani's Lucy in *Nosferatu*. A sustained and thorough critique of gender in Herzog's work has yet to be written and would take me too far afield here. Karen Redrobe asks him about it in an illuminating interview from 2007 (published in print for the first time in this book). Here is part of his response, essentialist and provocative, indulging in and refusing self-reflection, all at once: "a woman would not dream about hoisting a ship over a mountain in the Amazonian jungle. Women do not have that kind of dream. It's a fever dream of men. And these fever dreams are very . . . very known to me, I feel familiar with it, I feel comfortable with it, and I do the stories that I do understand. So it's fairly simple and fairly complicated because I am not looking at myself and I don't want to analyze what I have done, so I'm kind of cautious. But your observation [that his films revolve around men] is right, undeniably. And, in a way, I believe that Ingmar Bergmann wouldn't be able to answer you why, in almost all his films, women are the leading, the central characters" (Herzog and Beckman 2007).

75. In his commentary on the DVD, Herzog notes that this is a proverb, "the last one is going to be eaten up by the dogs."

76. Davidson brings some fascinating historical contextualization to this "colonel" of the auction, and the often erased history between this relation and the US Civil War (2012, 426–49). Race (as "the color line") is central to Davidson's analysis and brings to attention the arresting interplay of auctioneering, plunder, repossession, transaction, real estate, and whiteness at play in Bruno's tragedy. The theme is worth further exploration.

77. See Hauze (2009), for an excellent study of sound in the film; she notes the same strategy of doubling that Rentschler (1984) calls attention to, here around the film's nondiegetic soundtrack. She also delves into Herzog's interest in tonally eccentric, or imperfect, music, which is abundant in *Stroszek*. Herzog slyly calls attention to this at a scene in Bruno's apartment in which Herr Scheitz, who turns out to be capable of kicking out a mean Beethoven sonata, criticizes his piano as having "a sluggish action and a dull tone." Bruno: "Yes, but it's better than no piano at all. If I didn't have it, who knows what would have become of me?"

78. Cherokee, today, is somehow the same and different from Herzog's 1976 shoot. While maintaining aspects of the tourist-trap aesthetic that attracted Herzog, the town has changed both culturally and economically. A casino, opened

a couple of decades after Herzog's work, has transformed the economy of the town; culturally, Cherokee is known for its work on preservation and transhistorical authenticity, much of that work revolving around the impressive Museum of the Cherokee Indian. The panoramic chairlift featured in the final scene of *Stroszek* still stands, at least it did during my last visit.

79. Herzog says that he knew that the dancing chicken would stay in the spectator's mind for a long time, and generations of spectators have agreed: Vincent Canby (1977), in his review, highlights it "among the dozens of images in the film that I'll remember for a very long time." Interpretations vary. Most read it as a mirror for Bruno himself, or for our generalized predicament as human beings (Prager 2007, 76), but Paul Sheehan (2008) calls it an "oblique condemnation of a system in which money can buy pain" (131), and Laurie Johnson (2016), in a compelling argument that revolves around Herzog's romantic approach to animals more broadly, interprets it at as simultaneously ineffable, possibly a "weird sign of hope" (167) and, ultimately, "triumphant" (173). Stephen Barber (2014) suggests the undeniable, twisted reflection of Bruno, who, within the films vertiginous doubling, we recall once himself performed in a sort of box (the courtyard) in exchange for the coins of ambivalent onlookers (59). Somewhat outlandishly, Friedemann Weidhauer (2003) interprets the scene as a warning to German filmmakers "if they leave the refuge of state-subsidized art in Germany" (206). In a violently negative review, John Simon (1977) interprets it as a crass indulgence in what he sees as Herzog's serial abuse of animals (72).

80. Curtis's suicide and its relation to *Stroszek* is a classic anecdote in the arcana on Herzog, made famous by shots that cite it in two biographical representations of Curtis, *24 Hour Party People* (Winterbottom 2002) and *Control* (Corbijn 2007). The affective dichotomy built into *Stroszek* is exemplified in a coincidence put together by BBC cultural reporter Jason Parkes: the BBC broadcast of *Stroszek* that anticipated Curtis's suicide would have been the same one watched somewhere else in England by David Lynch, who suggests that the film captivated him with a joyful spirit. Parkes went on to confront Herzog with this coincidence in an interview and reports that it "upset" the director. Herzog's response: "It is a very heavy question. There is no frivolity in answering this. I cannot really argue. It is as it is. I wish this singer was still alive and hadn't seen *Stroszek* at that moment. But deep at the bottom of my heart I do believe that *Stroszek* was not the reason that he killed himself" (interview from BBC 4's *Storyville* unavailable; this excerpt from a dialogue with Parkes on Julian Cope's blog "Head to Head," 2008). Incidentally, Elliot Smith, another moody rocker, cited *Stroszek* as a favorite and Bruno S. as a personal hero. Smith, too, committed suicide. See Schultz (2013, 270).

81. For a systematic analysis of "bullshit" and its distinction from garden-variety dishonesty, see Frankfurt (2005).

82. McKean, himself one of these can-do Midwesterners, offers testimony on the shoot that diminishes somewhat the "midwestern generosity" discourse

of Herzog, noting that it wasn't always easy or even possible to get permission to shoot at a number of locations. Outside of Bruno, Eva, Herr Scheitz, the hooligans, and the warden, most, maybe all, of the other characters are played by nonprofessionals. In the Wisconsin and North Carolina sites, these characters include Ed, Eli, Al, the farmers, the hunters, the banker, the truckers, the waitresses, the auctioneer, the townspeople, the barber, the Indian policemen, the oracle at the end, and others.

83. Herzog claims that Plainfield produced not only Gein, but several serial killers, although I was unable to verify his claim. The anecdote of how he came to Wisconsin is Herzogian: Learning of Errol Morris's fascination with the Gein case, Herzog hatched a dare in which the two young directors would rob the grave of Gein's mother in the dead of night, to verify whether Gein had disinterred her. Morris, according to Herzog, chickened out and never showed up. Herzog's car broke down in Nekoosa, where he met a mechanic who would end up starring in his film, as the not uncoincidentally named Ed (Clayton Szalpinksi).

84. And the critical impulse is explicit, as he positions *Stroszek* as an attempt to "define my position about this country and its culture" as a kind of artistic response: "*Stroszek* goes more vitally into what I'm concerned with, because in Western Europe, in particular, there is *such* a strong domination of American culture and American films! And *all* of us who are working in filmmaking have to deal with this sort of domination . . . and that's one of the major reasons why I made *Stroszek*" (with Ebert 1979, 11).

85. There is no thorough, objective biography on Fitzcarrald. Two short books by Váldez Lozano (1942; 1944) are the account of a former business associate, and Reyna's *Fitzcarrald. El rey del caucho* (1942) is written in the tone of patriotic nationalism, with extensive apology for the "leyenda negra" (144–9) surrounding Fitzcarrald, and often refers to the rubber baron simply as "el heroe"; both are useful, but both are ultimately hagiographic. A number of contemporary studies of the region and its indigenous inhabitants take up the history of Fitzcarrald and his world more and less extensively, with insight into the rubber trader's practices and strategies. Among the most enlightening are Varese (2004); Brown and Fernández (1991); Gray (1996); and Gow (2016).

86. Reyna goes on to cite the testimony of Sala, who explains that this set-up would have been communicated by a "ladino" (nonindigenous person) in the hire of Fitzcarrald, or sometimes simply Fitzcarrald himself (1942, 22).

87. For the most influential study on the figure of the *gamonal*, and the attendant *gamonalismo* as a cultural-economic problematic basic to Peruvian development, see Mariátegui (1928).

88. See Serier (2000, 7). The source of this legend is most likely Reyna (1942, 130–31). Gow surmises, without citing a source, that he was "possibly murdered" (2016, 126), a suggestion that comes up periodically in the literature. Fitzcarrald's profession was notoriously violent, and death by homicide was common.

89. According to a firsthand account by Agustín Fancelli (1989) in *El País*, Herzog was uncharacteristically tempestuous during the filming of the performance and abandoned the first night's shoot in frustration.

90. Interview in *The Telegraph* (Christiansen 2009).

91. Herzog elaborates on his personal history with the opera in the commentary section of the *Fitzcarraldo* DVD.

92. In his Chicago workshop with Roger Ebert (1979), Herzog speaks at length about the impact of *Nosferatu*'s commercial success on his career.

93. A quiet theme, but a palpable one in Herzog, this question of waiting for the inevitable that never comes: at some level it animates *Signs of Life*; we recall the petering out of Aguirre's adventure; Herzog calls his memoir on *Fitzcarraldo*, in wry reference to himself, *Conquest of the Useless* (Herzog 2009); looking ahead, *Grizzly Man*'s Timothy Treadwell never succeeds in saving the bears.

94. The polemic played out in the French press for over a decade, producing recriminations, dismissals, televised debates, shouting matches, an interview with *Penthouse Magazine* that would yield a formal judicial sanction (against Tazieff) for libel, and ultimately its own short film, Éric Bauducel's highly entertaining *Tazieff Allègre: La guerre des volcans* (2015), produced for the France 5 television series, *Duels*.

95. The scientific debate is intensified by a political one, in short, the boy-who-cried-wolf problem that besets all emergency management systems: when you evacuate seventy thousand people, relocating many for weeks or months to the difficult conditions of refugee shelters, and then nothing happens, the predictive capacity of seismologists is thrown into question and its legitimacy among the population diminished. For a very thorough review of the polemic, with ample documentation, reprinted primary sources, and bibliography (including praise for Herzog's film), see François Beauducel (2006); for a brief summary, in English, see the condensed outline of events around the eruption in Beauducel and Besson (2008). Beauducel was the scientific director of the Observatoire Volcanologique et Sismologique de Guadaloupe from 2001 to 2007.

96. Responding to a question by Benny María Lund at the Institut Lumière in Lyon in 2014, Herzog would confide that the one moment of true fear that he has felt in his filmmaking career was shooting atop the Cerro Torre when an unexpected storm kicked up.

97. It's worth noting that the role of the guard is a quick cameo by Milton Nascimiento, a significant figure of the *Tropicália* movement, the transformative Brazilian music scene that accompanied cinema novo.

98. Iquitos is the most important city of the Peruvian Amazon and often noted as the largest city in the world inaccessible by land routes (only air and water). Long a crossroads of various indigenous groups, in the colonial era it was a Jesuit hub for a constellation of *reducciones*, concentration camps in which the viceregal state forced indigenous people to settle and convert. It boomed with rubber at the end of the nineteenth century. Today it supports about half

a million people. Herzog would have already been familiar with the city from his work on *Aguirre*.

99. Dolkart (1985) begins this critical tradition on *Fitzcarraldo*, and he is followed by a host of prominent interpretations of the film, including Franco (1993), Koepnick (1993), Davidson (1994), Leppert (2007; 2015) and Ascárate (2007).

100. The documentary filmmaker Les Blank was present for a crucial stretch of the shooting of *Fitzcarraldo*. Despite being essentially "authorized," the resulting film, *Burden of Dreams* (1982)—released almost simultaneously with *Fitzcarraldo*—raises disconcerting questions about Herzog's project; to his credit, Herzog did not attempt to have unflattering representations suppressed (Herzog and Cronin 2002). It's a compelling film, capturing a number of famous Herzog quotations, including the "nature always hits back" comment. In an affectionate introduction to the Criterion DVD collection of Blank's films, Herzog praises the strength of *Burden of Dreams* and recalls that when he asked Blank to film a key moment in the shoot, which Herzog predicts will be "a real event," Blank drily responds, "Werner, I'm not here to shoot events" (from Blank, *Always for Pleasure*, 2014). In the same interview, Herzog explains that the auto-extraction of Ed's tooth in *Stroszek* (see the previous section) was shot in homage to Blank.

101. In an extensively documented review of the current research, Vlado Kotnik (2013) explains that "opera was gradually transformed from private court event of European princes and monarchs into the public ceremony of European cities. The cultural transformation of opera from the elitist entertainment of aristocracy and noble people into a popular socializational promenade of bourgeoisie and broader public, which started vividly in the second half of the eighteenth century and ended at the beginning of the twentieth century, has been for different social scenes widely shown" (306). Daniel Snowman's social history of opera, *The Gilded Stage* (2009), is a book-length demonstration of the political, social, and economic heterogeneity that swirls around opera. The pathbreaking interpretation of the relations between opera and colonial discourse is Edward Said's chapter on *Aïda* in *Culture and Imperialism* (1993).

102. Leppert's 2015 book is a wealth of information: on the historical references at play in the opening scene; on Schroeter's intentions in his stage-direction decisions and collaboration with Herzog; and for bibliography on the recording history of Caruso, which Leppert takes up extensively in a later chapter of his book.

103. For two good studies of the relations between minstrelsy and opera, see Mahar (1999) and Norris (2007).

104. Sharon Lockhart plays with this theme, in *Teatro Amazonas* (1999) no less, a film in which she invites the residents of a local slum to attend a performance of abstract minimalism at the famous theater.

105. Galeano's *Venas abiertas* is, like the Teatro, itself a monumental work surrounded by decades of anecdotes and legends. A leftist social history of resource

extraction in Latin America that today has been disavowed by its own author, it still carries significant symbolic weight. It showed up in political culture most recently in 2009, when Venezuelan president Hugo Chávez presented the book as a gift to US president Barack Obama.

106. One can't resist mentioning the historical continuity of these grandiose gestures that continue to haunt Manaus: today, alongside its opera house stands a world-class World Cup–inspired soccer stadium. Its forty-four thousand unusable seats—O Nacional, the local football club of Manaus, is not in fact a national draw—are today rented out at cut-rate prices for weddings, bar mitzvahs, anything.

107. See Ruth Bereson's *The Operatic State* (2002) for a book-length analysis of the relations between opera, national identity, and statecraft.

108. We don't get a back story on Molly, but in every possible way—complexion, stature, body language, dress—she stands apart from her workers. Since the language in the film is unrealistic (overdubbed into German, English, etc.), there are no cues there either. But it seems that she is an immigrant, or immigrant's daughter, like her man Fitzcarraldo (as "Molly" she is, like Fitzcarraldo-Fitzgerald, marked as Irish), and this works well with the history of the boom, when immigrant-run brothels were considered especially desirable and were often famously profitable. In short, that sex-work money would be invested in a rubber-exploration venture isn't entirely unbelievable in a historical sense. See Orum (2001).

109. Leppert (2015), too, seems to indulge in this line of analysis in his interpretation of the film's final scene, when a local opera company performs Bellini's *I Puritani*, associating the "mestizo musicians" (70; 288) with the apish artifice of camp and, without explanation, stating that "The Puritan costumes worn by brown-skinned people [the leads and many in the chorus are not brown-skinned] is perhaps visually jarring to our eyes [it isn't, really], but no such discomfort is evident among the singers or orchestra" (70). He closes the comment by relating all this to opera's will to "hybridization" (ibid.).

110. For a review of the species of trees targeted during the boom and the forms of rubber harvest that they required, see Jean-Baptiste Serier's *Les barons du caoutchouc* (2000).

111. From the foundational *La vorágine* (Rivera 1924), a novel that revolves around debt bondage, to the harrowing scenes in *El abrazo de la serpiente* (2015) (incidentally, something of an homage to *Fitzcarraldo*), Latin American storytellers have a long history of taking up this theme directly, struggling to find an aesthetic language for a historical crime that makes rubber-economy aesthetics a close cousin to the long history of slavery literature and film.

112. Forms of labor in the rubber industry were diverse and racialized. Varese's pioneering work on the region describes how mestizos were generally placed into a system of debt peonage through the practice known as *enganche*, and tribal Indians were simply enslaved (2004, 126). But this is a thumb-nail sketch, and

there were all kinds of arrangements, "better" and worse, between the frontier rubber barons and the largely indigenous communities that provided the labor supply. Gow (2016), relying on ethnographic research among the descendants of Fitzcarrald's workers, offers the most revisionist account in this sense.

113. The indigenous groups most directly exploited by the boom commonly experienced reductions in population of up to 90 percent. Casement was a high-level British consulary official who produced important testimonies on postabolition slavery in the Congo and, most relevant here, the Putumayo region, the Amazonian borderlands between Peru and Colombia. The 1910 *Casement Report* that would ensue from his investigation in the rubber-harvesting industry is a landmark in the history of human rights discourse. Mario Vargas Llosa published a powerful novelization of Casement's life, *El sueño del celta*.

114. In this turn to the geographical, Herzog is rigorously in step with the South American context of his story. On the centrality of geographical discourse in the narrative history of the continent, see Madan's brilliant *Lines of Geography in Latin American Narrative* (2017).

115. Brown and Fernández (1991) and Gray (2004) describe this history in detail.

116. These testimonial reports are gathered by Huertas Castillo (2004, 51–52). Valdez, a firsthand participant in the project, confirms the violence in his biography of Fitzcarrald. Huertas Castillo's study is also notable for the emphasis that it places on indigenous resistance against the incursions, including armed resistance, which often forced the invaders to abandon rubber-rich regions of the forest (ibid.). As Gow (2016) notes, almost all Fitzcarrald's business associates died by violence at the hands of their workers.

117. After the festival, García Márquez wrote in *El Espectador*: "The special prize of the jury seemed to me most appropriate for *Fitzcarraldo*, not because it was the best or the worst, but rather because it has that mysterious, undefinable, and devastating quality that permits us to identify immediately an authentic work of art: inspiration. . . . Many spectators believed they were seeing in the delirium of *Fitzcarraldo* something of a quiet plunder of the contemporary novels of Latin America. . . . [So] when Werner Herzog phoned me the next day to tell me, in his typical friendliness, that he would like to collaborate on something, I couldn't resist my bad manners in answering him: 'Don't worry about it, Herzog: we already have'" (García Márquez 2015).

118. While most of the chaotic incidents surrounding the production of the film are easy to confirm through witnesses, press reports, or even film footage, the involvement of Amnesty International always feels a little mysterious. Scholars uniformly take the intervention at face value, with statements along the lines that Herzog was "cleared" (Ames 2012a, 394) or even "officially cleared" (Prager 2004, 3) by Amnesty, but without citing a source, and despite the fact that Amnesty's normal role is to investigate and advocate, and that it would be highly unusual for the organization to "clear." *Der Spiegel*, in an October 1979

report called "Ein Gringo im Urwald," first announced in passing Amnesty's alleged interest (again, no sources) on the conflicts surrounding the production; later Blank's cameraman Michael Goodwin (1982) would report in *American Film* that Amnesty contacted Herzog to request that he use his name to help free some wrongly accused protesters who had taken action against his project. *Index on Censorship* (1980, 71) also makes reference to Amnesty's interest in the case, although more negatively against Herzog. ("Herzog alleges that Aguaruna Indians destroyed his camp, but other reports imply that the Indians were merely demonstrating against his filming in their area," ibid.) And again, where Amnesty "reports" this information, "last December" is still an open question. But the more tenacious—Ames would say "performative"—source seems to be Herzog himself. In a 1982 interview with Bion Steinborn and Rüdiger von Naso, he states that after a series of sensational press reports "Amnesty International began questioning me" and that the organization "did its research and determined that . . . nobody who was jailed had any relation to me whatsoever" (in Herzog 2014b, 78). (This is in conflict with the above reports: according to Goodwin, the point of contacting Herzog was precisely that the jailed activists had been protesting his film.) But by the 2002 Cronin interviews, the story has changed slightly: "Upon my request, Amnesty International looked into the reports of human rights abuses and I think they unofficially spread word that I was not causing any problems" (184). Both the beginning and end of this statement seem far-fetched. For what it's worth, I could find no sign of either Herzog or the production in any of Amnesty's hundreds-page, exhaustive and detailed annual reports for the years in question. Survival International, for its part, publishes a series of reports on *Fitzcarraldo* between 1979 and 1982, in which no mention is made of any Amnesty-directed investigation.

119. I've never gotten my hands on the Gladitz work, but Carré (2007, 82) and Ames (2012a, 2012b) both discuss it at length. On the debate, see Rost (1986), who makes much of its polemics; I've also seen it interpreted as more of a conversation, in which *Fitzcarraldo* was only one topic among many.

120. There are less excoriating readings on Herzog's production practices and their relations to colonial discourse and various strains of authoritarianism. Wahl (2012) defends Herzog against opponents, and Carré (2007; esp. on the *Fitzcarraldo* affair, 81–87), while a little imprecise geographically (she confuses Ecuador and Paraguay), offers what is probably the most nuanced interpretation of the polemics. Both advance aggressive criticism against Herzog's nemesis Gladitz. Ames's book, *Ferocious Reality* (2012b: 289–98), provides a thorough bibliography on the European debate surrounding Herzog and *Fitzcarraldo*.

121. Worth noting: this is the repetition of a previous gesture. At the aforementioned party of the rubber elite, seeking investors Fitzcarraldo pulls out the gramophone and blasts Caruso, in an attempt to convince his audience. Nobody really pays attention, a host comes to ask him to knock it off, and he freaks out. This is where he delivers the "caricature of great opera" line, and civilization-

and-barbarism is somewhat complicated by the two scenes when understood as echoes of each other.

122. Leppert (2015) also offers the most insightful interpretation of the scene's soundtrack, shedding light on the meaning of Massenet's song at this point in the film (63–64).

123. See Carré (2007, 121–25) for extensive consideration of the "white god" myth, which comes up at a pivotal moment in the film; it's worth noting that it also vanishes from the story at that same point.

124. See Kent Jones (2012) for an eloquent and suggestive essay on breaking character and its potential displacement of the hegemony of the *auteur*.

125. The various indigenous subjects in the *Fitzcarraldo* saga—the film, the production, the historical context—represent the ethnic diversity of the Amazon river basin, and their transposition and reduction to "Indians" are indicative of the homogenizing way in which indigeneity is produced in western discourse, with little regard to interchanging language, custom, dress, and geographical context (something like dressing up a Swedish farmer as a Tyrolese shepherd and having him speak Spanish; to Herzog's credit, he's relatively consistent with this kind of stylization across ethnicities, for example, the Germanic Aguirre, the Irish Fitzcarraldo). While I have not come across this critique in specific regard to *Fitzcarraldo*, Herzog was denounced for similar ethnic transposition in *Where the Green Ants Dream* (see Hurley 2007). The Jívaroan people portrayed in the film are an indigenous group from far northern Peru, widely exoticized as historically militant and trafficking in shrunken heads (a reference in the film). The Aguaruna communities that Herzog attempted to work with in the aborted first attempt at the film share some linguistic commonality with the Jívaroan people, but the relation between the two groups is uncertain. Their appearance, traditional dress, and language are different from those of the actors in *Fitzcarraldo*. Herzog shot the jungle sequences of the film around a Machiguenga village, called Camisea, many of whose residents acted in the film; the numbers were filled out by recruiting from a community that Herzog refers to as Campas, although this is a nebulous term encompassing a range of indigenous groups, including the Machiguenga themselves, who are sometimes called Campa-Nomatsiguenga. The "Campas" in the film would most likely call themselves Asháninka and they share a language with their Machiguenga coworkers. Paradoxically, the Indians that Herzog ended up working with would have been more immediately in the footprint of Fitzcarrald's rubber activity around the isthmus than the Jívaros of the story and Aguarunas from his original site. Most famously, however, Fitzcarrald's depredations involved groups of a different linguistic profile, which are indicated through a range of names, including Yine, Piro, and Mascho-Piro.

126. Herzog mentions the incident in a couple of forums, but the most famous is a turn, at once darkly humorous and bizarre, in *My Best Fiend* (1999). It's a decade and a half later, Herzog has returned to the Amazon to record

this reflection, and he sits alongside two of the unnamed indigenous actors, recognizable from *Fitzcarraldo*. Speaking in German with no indication that these men—mute, here positioned as props—can understand what he is talking about, he refers to "these two here" and goes on to tell tales about the Indians' reactions to Kinski's antics and suddenly confides that they offered to murder him. He even goes as far as to implicate David Pérez Espinosa in a conspiracy to commit homicide, indicating that he was the one who made the offer: "The proposal to do away with Kinski came from this chief," he says. ("This chief" is a strange characterization of Pérez Espinosa, a lead actor in the film.) He adds, "I at once regretted that I held the Indians back from their purpose." Pérez Espinosa appears in *My Best Fiend* only through film clips. Blank's version tells of an intoxicated Pérez Espinosa who denounced the production in general, without singling out Kinski, reporting that he "came to pay his respects, but not without boiling out all the complaints Indians have ever had against white men. We followed him back to his camp, where he railed some more" (Gosling and Blank 1982, 45). Later, along with "all the inhabitants of the Indian camp," Pérez Espinosa "pointed at us and screamed 'Kill them! Kill them!'" (46).

127. I haven't been able to confirm the wages of the largely European crew, but Blank's diary speaks about the wages of the Indian workers: three US dollars per day. In several forums, Herzog cites this as twice the going wage for lumber work in the region. Blank reports that Pérez Espinosa, with a lead role in the film, was paid US$3.50 per day.

128. From Blank's diary (Gosling and Blank 1982), on the fight in the indigenous camp: "Each side had spokespeople who kept the argument going for thirty minutes while we were there photographing away and feeling very voyeuristic—something of a documentarian's dream: beautiful women so caught up in their drama that they didn't mind the cameras. The light was nice" (63). On Kinski's fit: "Klaus felt neglected and screamed and cursed for five to ten minutes. The Indians were amazed. We filmed but didn't feel it would be fair to use it" (55). Seriously. Footage of Kinski raving was eventually released in *My Best Fiend*, years after the actor's death.

129. Worth noting: Herzog universally cites Griffith as the greatest of American filmmakers.

130. I've explored this phenomenon in another context, simultaneously distant and resonant with Herzog's work on *Fitzcarraldo*: González and Lund, "Mining the Tropics" (2012).

131. Ericka Beckman's chapter on the rubber boom in *Capital Fictions* (2012) is an exemplary analysis on this point.

132. I've mentioned previously the obvious relations between Herzog's Latin American films and the literary writing from that continent. His relation to travel writing is even more explicit. Herzog himself has written in the genre, including his celebrated *Of Walking in Ice* (1978), a lyrical and highly original book-length travel account, and his published diaries (Herzog 2009) on *Fitzcarraldo*, called

Conquest of the Useless, participate in the genre as well. His friendship with and admiration for the travel writer Bruce Chatwin, who inspired the basic story for *Cobra Verde* (1987) and aspects of *Where the Green Ants Dream* (1984), are well known and the subject of his soon-to-be-released film *Nomad: In the Footsteps of Bruce Chatwin* (2019).

133. Process films, in Aguilera Skvirsky's analysis, take us to the very origin of the form. If film, for both Bazin and Herzog, emerges from the country fair, it simultaneously emerges from the factory floor. Some early filmmakers immediately hit upon the utilitarian nature of exposition of the technology, recording and demonstrating how things work, step by step, a genre easily converted into the dystopian surreal (*Metropolis*) and high comedy (*Modern Times*); other early filmmakers just as immediately saw the chance to charge money for moving images of curiosities, freaks, and sex acts. Between YouTube and RedTube, not much has changed.

134. Aguilera Skvirsky (2011) traces this aesthetic turn to the watershed example of Linduarte Noronha's *Aruanda* (1960), widely recognized as the film that ushered in the cinema novo movement. She goes on to analyze the importance of process aesthetics in Latin American film from unknown documentarians to the titans of politically engaged cinema, such as Fernando Birri and Glauber Rocha, that made the region so appealing to filmmakers like Herzog, who cites their influence with regularity.

135. The film features two other, less momentous but not irrelevant, scenes of fabrication: Fitzcarraldo in the ice factory, with laborers; and the restoration of the ship, complete with molten steelwork.

136. Coincidentally, right about the same time as *Fitzcarraldo*, Herzog's elder peer from the New German Cinema days, Alexander Kluge, released a postmodernist study of the materiality of opera called *The Power of the Emotion* (1983). Caryl Flinn argues that in tracing opera's totalizing emotional thrust as the illusion of an industrial mode of production, Kluge unmasks large-scale "tragic" opera (Verdi, Wagner, Puccini) as a practice that "processes valuable raw material into consumable goods" (2004, 140), "disguises the material aspect of its production" (141), and ultimately stands as an "institution grounded in ruination, an extension of the machinery of war, industry, and capital" (144).

137. Significantly, *Pagliacci* makes its appearance early in the film, precisely when Fitzcarraldo wakes up, surrounded by local children, for whom he plays the record; after everything, this is where he will now wake up again, in failure, back at the beginning.

138. The *pishtaco* is usually traced to the Spanish conquest of the Andean world: Anderson (2016) associates the origins of the legend with none other than Lope de Aguirre; Weismantel (2001) with the colonial project more broadly, noting its historical representation as "a knife-wielding priest searching for human fat with which to forge his church bells" (3). Gose (1994) goes deeper and argues that the figure emerges from pre-Columbian Andean history and the

phenomenon of human sacrifice. But in modern times, the legend is universally understood as an indigenous response to the violence of extraction that accompanies the grand themes of capitalist modernity (accumulation, nationalization, modernization, development, and so on) and that, while the "pishtacos are not always white" (Weismantel 2001, 7) in every story, it is almost always associated with whiteness to a greater or lesser degree. Scheper-Hughes (1996) famously compares the *pishtaco* to similar myths globally throughout peripheral zones of intense capitalist penetration. Regarding the case of Herzog, Weismantel's (6–16) compelling reading of the *pishtaco* figure by way of Freud's *unheimlich* is helpful. It's not just that the *pishtaco* is a fearsome stranger. Strange indeed, the trouble is that he (the *pishtaco* is almost always masculine) is also familiar, intimate even. As I put it earlier in the chapter, in regard to Fitzcarrald, the Indians had *seen his kind before*. And this, of course, is a problem for Herzog.

139. This is a controversial point. There were a lot of men with guns in the area, including soldiers, especially in the context of a simmering border conflict with Ecuador. Herzog vehemently denies contracting soldiers, whether regular army or paramilitary. Gosling (Gosling and Blank 1982) gives the impression that the formal soldiers were not especially helpful to Herzog and his project. That Herzog provided arms as a form of barter payment with his indigenous workers around Camisea (the second location) is beyond dispute, colorfully documented in Blank's *Burden of Dreams* (1982).

140. The legitimacy of the council was eventually reaffirmed, specifically regarding their negotiations with Herzog, by Peruvian state agencies: the Ministry of the Interior; the Comisión de Promoción Cinematográfica; and the Dirección General de Reforma Agraria y Asentamiento Rural (*Survival International Review* 1979b: 31). Maureen Gosling, working with Les Blank on *Burden of Dreams*, was witness to a tense meeting between Herzog and the Council that immediately descended into a chaotic shouting match, although she reports that Herzog kept his cool. Her account through diary entries (Gosling and Blank 1982) is full of insight and is one of the key primary sources on the sequence of events in negotiations between Herzog and the Council. See also the regular updates in *Survival International Review* (1979–82) and Herzog's own description of his experiences in *Conquest of the Useless* (2009).

141. *Colonization* here refers to the state's recruitment of settlers to occupy and develop supposedly untilled or barren lands, lands often neither barren nor untilled. The practice has a long history throughout the Americas.

142. Herzog holds a particular antipathy toward Nugkuag, and in his explanatory op-ed to the Peruvian press he appears to insinuate, without presenting evidence or detail, that Nugkuag asked for a bribe, a characterization swiftly denounced by Survival International (see *Survival International Review* 1979a: 29). Perhaps it's just a coincidence, but in the film, one of the deckhands who turns out to be a drunken rabble-rouser and is expelled from the voyage has the name Evaristo.

143. As the great industrial-capitalist narrative art, it comes as no surprise that film has a long and cozy relation with histories of exploitation in every sense. The Indians, in Herzog's story, were not the first to express trepidation before possible violence. When contracted to work on *Stroszek* in the role of the banker, the nonprofessional actor Scott McKain suffered panicky suspicions that he was being lured into a snuff film (see McKain 2015, 2016).

144. Gosling (Gosling and Blank 1982, 19–20) is the source on the reenactment. Documentation on the chaotic series of events during the last half of 1979 is difficult to consolidate and full of errors. By far the most interesting source is the report by Shane Greene (2004), an anthropologist who has studied the roll of the eviction of Herzog's project in the consolidation of Aguaruna political identity. Eschewing international reports committed to sensationalizing the desired barbarism of indigenous political actors, Greene relies on the very local press—including on-the-scene coverage in the newspaper *Nor Oriente*, which dispatched community reporters as "war correspondents"—and testimonial memory from local residents on the indigenous protest. While it was widely believed that Nugkuag was behind the armed eviction, Greene's research reveals that he was nowhere near the scene and that the action was concocted autonomously by Aguaruna elders, thought explicitly as a war raid and placed within a larger historical consciousness of struggles with European invaders (Greene 2004, 183–88). For a description of the international media representation of the incident, see *Survival International Review* (1979b: 31–32).

145. In a further irony, in the film Huerequeque explains an origin story for the Jívaro, saying that they have left their homeland to wander the jungle for many years in search of a white god. This goofy legend is half right: the explosion of uncontacted tribes coming out of the woods in recent decades has to do with being chased out by "white gods"—extractive capitalism—not going in search of them.

146. The epigraphs are my translation, from the German.

147. Over an impressive 1981 video recording of a so-called first contact between government agency workers and an Amondawa group of the then largely uncontacted Uru-Eu-Uaw-Uaw tribes of Rondônia, Brazil, Herzog narrates, "Without the knowledge of metal, these people lived a stone age existence. . . . What they do not know, is that these minutes will propel them forward thousands of years. It will be a progress into the void" (*Ten Thousand Years Older*). For an alternative understanding of anthropological temporality, see Fabian (2014).

148. It's also a region that the living ghosts of *Fitzcarraldo* can't seem to outrun. In a bizarre series of coincidences, in 2012 Mick Jagger, who starred alongside Jason Robards in the aborted first attempt of the film, found his home picketed with signs reading "Remember Fitzcarraldo!" and the like. The zone that contains the Isthmus of Fitzcarrald is a protected biosphere and home to several uncontacted tribes, but the Isthmus itself was being targeted for petroleum development, with a block of exploration claims even named Fitzcarrald.

Peru's honorary tourist ambassador and international protector of the Madre de Dios Region was Jagger, and environmentalists staged a campaign to recruit his voice to their cause.

149. For a tragic account of the environmental catastrophe unfolding around the Madre de Dios today, and Fitzcarrald's legacy in the human conflicts in its remote corners, see Anderson (2016). Some striking images can be viewed in Ernesto Cabellos's *Hija de la laguna* (2015).

150. For an entertaining and extensive firsthand account of the film's location shoot in Colombia, see Romero Rey (2008). On the African shoot, see Gruber's *Location Africa* and an enlightening piece in *Interview* by Bruce Chatwin (1988), who sat in for several days during shooting.

151. Despite its status as a lightning rod for polemics, the slavery film genre is still in its infancy of scholarly analysis, with most treatments subsumed into larger questions of African-American cinema and visual culture. Some recent attempts to systematize scholarship on the slavery film genre include Martin and Wall (2013), Gordon (2015), and aspects of Wilderson (2010) and Guerrero (2012).

152. Against these kinds of images, Erica Carter asserts that Africa's function in Herzog's quest for the sublime is a stereotypically bourgeois space of terror (2012).

153. A third, highly ethnographic, film emerges from Herzog's portfolio during these years, although it is outside Africa: *Jag Mandir* (1991), a recording of a theater parade that took place in India. In keeping with Herzog's "ecstatic" ethnography, he invented the back story for the festival.

154. So, while Herzog may reject the ethnographic out of hand—"I never think in terms of strict ethnography: going out to some distant island with the explicit purpose of studying the natives there" (Herzog and Cronin 2002, 214)—his cinematic interests and work is fundamentally grounded in an ethnographic spirit: "I work with human beings because the way they function in different cultural groups interests me. If that makes me an anthropologist then so be it. . . . My goal is always to find out more about man himself, and film is my means" (ibid.). For the history of this attitude, see Lévi-Strauss ([1955] 2012 and [1956] 1977).

155. On *Where the Green Ants Dream*, Herzog says, "Well, the film is rather blatant about having something of a 'message.' It has such a self-righteous tone to it that I wish I had cut out of the film; it stinks to high heaven. The film is not that bad, it just has a climate to it that I cannot stand" (Herzog and Cronin 2002, 208).

156. The film came out during the high times of US intervention in Nicaragua, and was shot in an area of active conflict in that country's civil war. The indigenous-rights activist Roxanne Dunbar-Ortiz greeted audiences during the film's run in San Francisco with leaflets stating that "Herzog's romanticism about the Indians, actually a form of racism, has transformed one of the brilliant living film-makers

into an opportunistic lackey for the CIA" (Csicsery 1985, 7). Herzog responds that the film is beyond politics, about the tragedy of child soldiers, "in no way any kind of direct comment on American foreign policy," and that he was eventually "invited by the Sandinistas [the leftist political movement about whose actions the film is critical] to screen the film in Nicaragua" (Herzog and Cronin 2002, 192).

157. Herzog understands *Lessons* as an antiwar film, so, again, disavowing politics as he participates in an openly political genre (here, the antiwar film). He comments, "When *Lessons of Darkness* was shown at the Berlin Film Festival, with one voice nearly 2,000 people rose up in an angry roar against me. They accused me of 'aestheticizing' the horror and hated the film so much that when I walked down the aisle I was spat at. They said the film was dangerously authoritarian. . . . [But] This could be *any* war in *any* country. The criticisms of the film in Germany come down to this: if you do not make a black-and-white political statement you are on the side of the devils" (Herzog and Cronin 2002, 245–45).

158. The technique of reenactment through repetition is one that Herzog mobilizes frequently and to great effect; *Stroszek*, for example, derives much of its power by reproducing a number of scenes from Bruno S.'s life. But of course, the trick isn't Herzog's, it's an old one in cinema, spanning the decades from Audie Murphy in Jesse Hibbs's *To Hell and Back* (1955) to Lady Tabares in Víctor Gaviria's *La vendedora de rosas* (1998), all the way to the torturers and assassins in the Herzog-produced masterpiece of chilling massacre performance in Joshua Oppenheimer's *The Act of Killing* (2012).

159. There is some quiet ambivalence around the question of nationalist patriotism in both *Little Dieter* and Herzog's feature film remake of Dengler's story as *Rescue Dawn* (2006) (a wide-release Hollywood picture starring Christian Bale and Steve Zahn), although both are up front about their discourse of heroic survival, just as both indicate little countervailing ambivalence around the war itself. Jennifer Fay (2013) takes up these issues systematically, interpreting the two films alongside Dengler's autobiography and Herzog's approach to war more broadly.

160. Bahia seems to be de Souza's most likely place of origin, although some accounts suggest he came from Rio de Janeiro, or even Havana; see Law (2004a). While he is almost always described as some version of mixed race—*métis*, *mestizo*, *mulato*—the exact mix varies. The *son of a slave and slave driver* narrative is dominant, but others, including a family historian, describe him as "white, with Portuguese ancestors on his father's side but native Amazonian heritage from his mother" (Araujo 2011, 87).

161. The legend comes up among stories of de Souza's political rise, and a version of it will be staged in *Cobra Verde*. The scholarly source that discusses it is Hazoumé (1937, 28–30).

162. The selective enforcement and general effectiveness of the English suppression of the slave trade is still open to debate, but whatever its effect in

generating historical momentum toward abolition, its practical effect on the traffic of slaves was limited. A figure no less than Karl Marx (1972), writing in 1861 on the US Civil War, cites the US senator Stephen A. Douglas stating in 1859 that "During the last year more Negroes have been indented from Africa than ever before in any single year, even at the time when the slave trade was still legal" (69).

163. Adding to the web of complexity around the relations between race, community, and slavery, some manumitted slaves migrating to Ouidah would themselves become slave merchants (see Araujo 2011, 85).

164. The current chacha, Moise de Souza, is a construction engineer who assumed the title in 2017 (Sieff 2018).

165. See Araujo (2007, 2011) and Sieff (2018). The gentleman historian and conservative politician Hugh Thomas, Baron of Swynnerton (1997), cites a French traveler's account about Souza's outlandish fertility (695).

166. The women fighters of Dahomey were an actual historical phenomenon, made famous in part through the popularity of Richard Burton's travel accounts. Here's Robin Law's summary: "The most celebrated instance of 'Amazons' in Africa was undoubtedly the female army of the kingdom of Dahomey . . . recruited from among the King's wives. These were described in a series of European accounts during the eighteenth and (more especially) nineteenth centuries—perhaps most influentially, those of the British naval officer Frederick Forbes (1851) and of the British Consul (and pioneer anthropologist) Richard Burton (1864). Their renown in Europe was further enhanced by the first war between Dahomey and the French in 1890, in which female soldiers took some part, and which was followed by the exhibition of (probably spurious) specimens of Dahoman 'Amazons' in an ethnographic spectacle at the Jardin d'Acclimatation in Paris" (Law 1993, 245). Recent book-length studies on the fighters include Bay (1998), Edgerton (2000), and Alpern (2011).

167. Prager (2004) weaves in some of the important differences between novel and film in his essay on *Cobra Verde*.

168. The *sertão* is the semiarid backlands of northeastern Brazil, a historically momentous region of the country that holds an important place in the Brazilian imagination, not unlike the US western frontier, but with a much stronger resonance between social struggle and economic (in)justice than any discourse of nation building or proto-national history. This landscape and its struggles were mobilized to significant effect within the most famous works of the politically engaged cinema novo generation of experimental filmmakers: *Vidas secas* (1963) by Nelson Pereira dos Santos; *Deus e o diabo na terra do sol* (1964) by Glauber Rocha; and *Os Fuzis* (1964) by Ruy Guerra (who incidentally played the role of Ursúa in *Aguirre*), all revolve around the aesthetics of the *sertão*, as does the later *Antonio das Mortes* (1969), also by Rocha. *Cobra Verde*'s opening shot of the *sertanejo* peasant *cordel* fiddler who tells the story of the bandit

Cobra Verde immediately places us within this tradition. Nagib (2012) explores this relation at length.

169. The two or three contemporary images of de Souza that circulate strike a direct resemblance to Giuseppe Garibaldi, the Italian nationalist and South American insurgent, and are sometimes actually confused. The mistake would seem to have some basis, for in one of the best European accounts of meeting de Souza, Henry Huntley (1850) describes de Souza's preferred outfit in terms quite similar to aspects of Garibaldi's famous faux-gaucho look: "his apparel, unlike that of others present, is a loose dressing robe, with a small velvet cap on his head, from beneath which his long hair is flowing, hardly even yet turned grey, his linen underneath not carefully changed, and his large loose trousers trail over his slippers which he wears without stockings" (119–20). As the bandit in the early parts of the film, da Silva approximates this costume (although, once in Africa, he is consistently dressed in soldier's uniform). Huntley describes de Souza as a "sallow, corpulent heavy-featured man" (119) who seems to take little joy in the material luxury of his riches, which are amply displayed at table for himself and his entourage, "consisting of everything held to be a delicacy in these parts,—tea, coffee, claret [wine from Bordeaux], 'Guinness,' and 'Bass,' bread prepared in many different ways, fruit and preserves, all are spread in luxurious disorder for these dealers in human flesh" (118). He surmises that de Souza is likely one of the richest men in the world, but with little means for spending his fortune, given his outlaw status for the British authorities whose financial industry and merchant routes largely control West Africa's access to the world economy at that time.

170. The reviewer in question is the feminist fantasy writer Jessica Salmonson, and her review is posted on a defunct blog called weirdwildrealm.com where she goes by the name Paghat the Ratgirl. The scene involves a singing group of young women, listed in the credits as Zigi Cultural Troupe Ho Ziavi; the leader of the group has the prominent speaking role, although it is difficult to tell whether she is listed in the credits, because the actors are not lined up with their roles. The scene is patently creepy, made creepier by Herzog's explanation of it. The women, playing the role of a white priest's "nun's choir," quite young, sing happily in topless costume while Kinski's da Silva wanders among them, leering. Herzog says on the DVD commentary that the scene makes him uncomfortable and wishes he had cut Kinski from it. He goes on to say that its purpose—the singing is of very high quality, the song, a fable of slavery, beautiful, if chilling—was to bring some spirit of life and hope to the film, this being the responsibility of the singers. But while the singers' status as slaves is ambiguous, nonetheless there is a "performing for the master" element to all this that goes unremarked and seemingly unnoticed by Herzog; on the long history of this kind of leisure-time violence, see Hartman (1997).

171. The productive force of Dahomey for European-derived theories of humanity and civilization spans the decades. Besides the countless travelers'

tales that nourished Hegel—and also Chatwin, who drew, anachronistically, on J. A. Sketchly's *Dahomey as It Is* (1874) for his novel—as late as the 1960s Karl Polanyi churned up polemics with his final book on the relations between economy and state, *Dahomey and the Slave Trade* (1966). The contemporary Hollywood superhero hit, Coogler's *Black Panther* (2018), developed its "women warriors" theme on the inspiration of Dahomey. From the opposite political perspective, conservative revisionists like to bring up Dahomey as a way of minimizing white responsibility for the slave trade.

172. Another of Hegel's Dahomey set-pieces is reproduced, almost to the letter, in *Cobra Verde*: "Sometimes also a deputation is sent, which intimates to [the king], that the burden of government must have been very troublesome to him, and that he had better rest a little. The King then thanks his subjects, goes into his apartments, and has himself strangled by the women" (Hegel 1837, 115). In the same passage, he also has some lurid comments on the women warriors of Dahomey.

173. Steve McQueen's *12 Years a Slave* motivated a wide-ranging debate on what came to be called "torture porn," for its graphic representations of the racist brutality essential to slavery. Two of the more thoughtful considerations include Brody (2013) and Cobb (2014). In this spirit, Tarentino's *Django Unchained* (2012) can be understood as a kind of meta-performance of the degrading violence at play in the slavery film genre. Hartman's classic book-length study, *Scenes of Subjection* (1997), on the psychological, aesthetic, and social risks of a black body constructed as an object of abuse underwrites Jasmine Nichole Cobb's cogently stated truth about the slavery film genre and its overdetermined relation to historical accuracy and exhibition: "watching the reenactment of slavery for the screen might always already be a bizarre thing, in and of itself. Settling in to view violence, rape, child abuse, kidnapping, corporeal punishment, labor theft, wrecked families, and the wholesale objectification of human beings as an opportunity for education or entertainment might forever be a problematic enterprise where precision is inherently a question of motive" (2014, 344).

174. Ever since Ed Asner's Captain Davies wilted before his Christian convictions ("Oh . . . merciful heaven") and raped the unnamed character played by a trembling Rebecca Bess in the captain's quarters of the slave ship on *Roots*, reversing, or at least rearticulating, the dominant narrative of interracial rape in American culture that achieved its on-screen canonization as early as *Birth of a Nation* (1915), scenes of violation or their suggestion have been a generic mark of the slavery film genre.

175. Fanon's classic (1961) jump-starts this tradition. Among many more current sources on this relation between slavery and enlightenment, besides Schwarz and the work of Bernasconi and Lott (2000) generally, two of the most impressive treatments, both revolving around the Haitian revolution, include Michel-Rolph Trouillot (1995) and Susan Buck-Morss (2000).

176. The supply side of the transatlantic slave trade arose in part from intra-African rivalries that cut across political formations, languages, and ethnic groups; in short, between communities that predated a common consciousness of colonial oppression rooted in blackness or Africanness. Africans would have seen distinct and sometimes rival communities, but only Europeans saw "blacks."

177. Marx addresses slavery at points throughout his life's work, but the most systematic and expansive comments can be found in Volume 2 of the *Karl Marx Library, On America and the Civil War* (1972). For a good summary of the world-systems theory approach to slavery, see Immanuel Wallerstein's long review essay, "American Slavery and the Capitalist World-Economy" (1976).

178. In this sense, da Silva is a clear example of that age-old protagonist of capitalist world-formation, the military entrepreneur (Gallant 1999).

179. There's a productively palpable tension in the scenes between da Silva and the planter, one that corresponded to the mutual contempt between Kinski and Lewgoy on set (Romero Rey 2008).

180. Puar's (2015) powerful advance on Foucault's idea of biopolitical sovereignty revolves around the increasingly contemporary sovereignty not simply over life and death, but over the production of a living death through active policies of maiming. Clear examples include authoritarian states against racially differentiated populations, whether actively insurgent or not; for example, Israeli military and security forces against Palestinians, or US police forces against poor, and often black, citizens. But the sugar planter here exemplifies a long-standing right to maim within the de facto sovereignty exhibited over a circumscribed economic zone, the plantation, raising the question: Isn't Puar's right to maim a feature of the structure of domination in capitalism's historical traffic in violence?

181. Early in the African section, da Silva meets Taparica, played by the director and producer King Ampaw. Perceived to be deranged, he introduces himself as the drum major for the "free Yoruba, first regiment of the Black Militia" and the only survivor of the king of Dahomey's campaign of extermination. For reasons unclear, he befriends da Silva and hangs out around the margins of the rest of the film, even being imprisoned with his apparent patron; equally strange is the extended military salute that he directs toward da Silva at the end of the film.

182. Pedro Vicente is an interesting, undeveloped character, and an opportunity missed in Herzog's film. The historical reference comes from Chatwin's novel (1980), which speaks of a Pedro Vicente, but the historical source is from the 1850 account by Huntley, who tells a story of one Paolo Vicente, "the captain of a Brazilian slave ship" (122), who cheated de Souza out of a load of slaves. Huntley's story is a tale of de Souza's largesse, that he forgives Vicente and rescues him when his ship is stalled, stating that "I cannot believe you will deceive me again" (1850, 123). Chatwin's tale of "Pedro" Vicente is similar. Herzog renders it as one of Kinski's signature hisses of revenge ("Nobody deceives me twice!"). But the real opportunity missed is the chance to push the race-and-slavery confusion

even further. Herzog casts a white actor as Pedro Vicente, the spaghetti-western character player, Benito Stefanelli. We know nothing about the small-time Paulo Vicente and his ethnicity. But the real threat to de Souza was a slave merchant who did in fact enter into traitorous competition with him: a man named Joaquim Almeida (Strickrodt 2004, 221). And Almeida, like many of the late slave merchants of the Bight of Benin, was himself a manumitted black slave.

183. Herzog frames his film as a contribution to Africa's reckoning with the legacy of slavery. While I have not been able to find anything about the reception of the film in West Africa, it seems unlikely that it had a significant effect in pushing the local debate. But the film was certainly known, and its local political function was not irrelevant, for better or worse. The film was shot in Ghana. Herzog, in his DVD commentary, again transcribed here literally, states, "Yes, uh. I think Ghana, well uh, in Africa it was very much understood that this subject was somehow kept like almost like a taboo. But the time had been ripe to, to speak about it, to make films about it, about this atrocity. Strangely enough, Africa immediately would speak in open terms about colonialism, but the wound of this catastrophe of slavery is so deep, it's so deep implanted and so hurting that hardly anyone would speak in public about slavery in Africa. Of course, in the United States people would speak, or in the Caribbean they would speak, about slavery and they . . . or in Brazil. . . . A very, very strange, almost untouched subject in Africa itself" (*Cobra Verde*, DVD commentary). There may be something to this. Herzog shot *Cobra Verde* in the mid-1980s. The confluence of factors that drove a new conversation about West Africa's participation in the trade—UNESCO initiatives, a new regime in Benin, the various justice and antisystemic movements that coalesced around 1992—didn't really kick into high gear until the following decade.

184. Another staple of the slavery film genre, at some point the enslaved protagonists will find a white ally. The family of poor whites in Chomsky et al.'s *Roots*, Anthony Hopkins's John Quincy Adams in Spielberg's *Amistad*, Christoph Waltz's Dr. King Shultz, who seems more outraged by slavery than Jamie Foxx's Django in Tarentino's *Django Unchained*, Brad Pitt's cameo as Bass in McQueen's *12 Years a Slave*, Robert De Niro's Rodrigo Mendoza in Joffe's *The Mission*, Javier Bardem's Uxbal in González Iñarritu's *Biutiful*, even the challenging structuralist slavery films—Pontecorvo's *Burn!*, Gutiérrez Aléa's *La última cena*—feel compelled to make the turn, more ambivalently, toward an explicit opening for interracial reconciliation and potential white audience identification. Beyond the genre per se, Coogler's *Black Panther* asserts itself as a generously pan-African superhero film, one that places as the antagonist an angry American black nationalist descendant of Nat Turner and the young Malcolm X, and foists a white CIA agent as an ally on Black Panther and his crew. There is none of this in *Cobra Verde*.

185. In the DVD commentary on this scene, Herzog states, "This is somehow the disaster and the crippling of a whole continent for me."

186. Hosted by masterclass.com, Herzog's course offers six hours of video lessons on various aspects of filmmaking. The Rogue Film School (http://www.roguefilmschool.com) is an occasionally convened weekend seminar whose last meeting was in 2016. The long seminars are organized by Black Factory Cinema, a production and film consulting company in Barcelona. The first, from 2017, took place with Herzog in Cuba; the second, in May 2018, was in Puerto Maldonado, Peru. Herzog took over the project from its first instructor, his friend, the legendary Iranian director Abbas Kiarostami. These long seminars are highly productive and well regarded, with each student producing a short film, the best of which are screened at prominent festivals.

187. In what turned out to be a fortuitous pairing, the Walker Art Center followed the Herzog retrospective with another on the Cinema Novo generation of Brazilian filmmakers. The Walker has recently posted on YouTube Herzog's live reading of the Minnesota Declaration, subtitled "Truth and Fact in Documentary Cinema: Lessons of Darkness": https://www.youtube.com/watch?v=GkJiasC3cRI.

188. Herzog is fond of telling the tale of when he smuggled the dozens of monkeys necessary for the final shot of *Aguirre* through Peruvian customs by posing as a veterinarian. See, among other sources, his director's comments on the *Aguirre* DVD.

189. Herzog narrates: "Inspired by Hank Skinner [convicted of murdering his girlfriend and mentally disabled sons, who was taken to the death chamber only to receive an eleventh-hour reprieve], we took this trip for ourselves. The landscape bleak, forlorn. And yet everything out there, all of a sudden, looked magnificent. As if entering the Holy Land. Hank Skinner's Holy Land."

190. Herzog has found time for parallel endeavors as well: at least nine operas since 2000 and *Hearsay of the Soul* (2012), a video art installation commissioned by the Getty in Los Angeles.

Interview with Werner Herzog

Werner Herzog politely declined to be interviewed for this book, responding to the author's invitation as follows: "Thank you for your mail and your work about my films. However, I have shut down all deeper conversations about my films, because I have talked myself empty. Apart from that, knowing everything about a film, or a book, takes the mystery and wonder away from it. It has been very unhealthy in my case."

We reproduce here a previously unpublished conversation between Herzog and Karen Redrobe from 2007, at the Slought Foundation (University of Pennsylvania). The transcript of the conversation has been edited for content and reading efficiency.

KAREN REDROBE: So our task today is a simple one. We have to get to the heart of "ecstatic truth" in forty-five minutes. And my sense from your films is that this truth is not something that reveals itself directly, but something that you move in and around. So I wanted to start with a question, that was inspired by something in *Encounters at the End of the World* (2007).[1] You mentioned the possibility that after the demise of the human species, alien archeologists may come to Earth. And I want to ask you if those alien archeologists do come and all they find are the films of Werner Herzog, what is it that you hope that they will learn about the human species from your films?

WERNER HERZOG: I don't know but, and of course, alien archaeologists, aliens landing on our planet is a figment of our fantasies. It's something born out of *Star Wars* (1977).[2] Aliens will not reach us. They are just too far away, and we are too far away from the next star out there. It sounds quite close but Alpha Centauri is four and a half light years away and at the highest velocity that we have ever achieved, it would take you about seven or eight hundred thousand years to get there, so how do you do that? And you will not be able to reach even a small, tiny fraction of the speed of light. No matter what you try to tell me it, it will not persuade me. And you cannot accelerate a human being to let's say 10 percent of the speed of light. We would be crushed, immediately.

KR: But aliens can.

WH: Aliens would be crushed as well. They will not be able to achieve that end, as my real science fiction film, *The Wild Blue Yonder* (2005), shows, they're not these superhuman creatures that can destroy this planet in five seconds flat.[3] They all suck. They are just a failure. They've achieved nothing, and they're kind of deceived and kind of desperately lost on our planet. I think if alien astronauts, and again as a figment of our imagination, ever land, they would probably flee as quickly as they can.

KR: So from the statistics that you've just given us, and from your films, it's clear that you have an interest in flight and the flight of the imagination outside the Earth.

WH: Yes.

KR: And you seem to be drawn to characters who are compelled to fly, in spite of their human condition. And your camera seems to be compelled to fly too, and you use aerial shots a lot. So one question I would like to ask you is, what is it about these characters who yearn to fly that draws you repeatedly to this character? And what is it you think that aerial shots in particular can show us about the Earth? Because it seems that if we're looking for moments of ecstatic truth in your films, that ecstatic truth often comes from above.

WH: I'll try to sort it out and do one question after the other. Yes. Sure, I would love to be able to fly and I'm one of these people who has these dreams of being able to fly. And the motive of flight, of the need to fly, appears many times in my movies, *Little Dieter Needs to Fly* (1997), is sort of paradigmatic, a sort of type.[4] Yes, there is a man who needs to fly but yet like in ancient Greek drama. My assistant director, collaborator, and friend Herb Golder, who is a professor at Boston University for the classics, explains to me, "Werner you are doing a film exactly like the ancient Greek drama. You have a man and his dream and punishment for the dream and at the end some sort of redemption."[5] So, yes, there is a great wish in me to leave the confines of who I am. To be able to fly physically was my dream as a kid, and, yes, I grew up in the Bavarian mountains. And I literally grew up on skis and for us kids there was only one dream: we would fly, we would become ski jumpers. And my best friend wanted to become a German national champion. And I said, "No, that's not what I'm into. I want to become world champion of ski flying." And we were fiercely competing and my career as somebody flying and going into this complete solitude and ecstasy of being airborne without instrument, but just as a human being to fly. That ended unfortunately very, very abruptly, from one second to the next when my best friend had a near fatal accident on the ramp and we were all alone out there in training. And it was so horrifying that from that moment on I could never get close to a ramp anymore. It just ended. It is this dream, there is flight in my imagination, there's flight that is something beyond our physicality, something which is not in our bodies and in a way, *The Great Ecstasy of the Sculptor Steiner* (1974), the two-time ski flying world champion, became some sort of emblem of my own dreams.[6] Somebody who physically steps outside of me and materializes in someone else whom I love very dearly, because he flew. And he flew instead of me and of course I had to do a film on him. This motive returns quite often. And, in a way, you have distant relatives too, those who try to fly, ultimately it is a, how shall I say, defiance of gravity. And a film like *Fitzcarraldo* (1982) where I move a three-hundred-sixty-ton ship over a mountain, is the defiance of gravity, it has to do with a similar sort of dream, of leaving the physical body.

KR: One of the things I love about images of flight and leaving the earth is that it's not just pure transcendence, it's also about the effort that humans put into their urge and that need to defy gravity and at the same time the experience of falling, you called it tumbling, and that it's as much a part of your films as ecstatic flight.

WH: In a way, yes, of course, we are prone to crash and we are prone to come down. My wife who is afraid of planes when they bounce badly in turbulence, she once asked me, and she still holds it against me, she asked me "what's gonna happen, what's gonna happen?"[7] And I said, "well don't worry, in one way or another the plane will come down." Yes, it will come down. And that's the only answer you can give. It's not a very husbandly answer, I have to admit but . . .

KR: Oh, I think it is.

WH: But, of course, we do see, we do see the downfall. And the danger in the fear of falling, people have it in their dreams. Unfortunately I do not dream at night, so I have no experience of that. But in our case there are other forces and there is a sense of tragedy which is within all of us in a way. I believe it has to do with things that go on inside, deep inside of our hearts.

KR: Another thing that I wanted to ask you about is your frequent comments about our impoverished imaginations and our lack of images. In one of your interviews, you particularly lambast television as a medium. You say that our grandchildren will blame us for not throwing hand grenades into the television stations because of our exposure to advertisements by them. And you talk about it as the biggest danger, along with different kinds of war. And yet you have also worked in television.

WH: No, I have not, really, worked in television. But sometimes television has shown my stuff. But I'm always aiming for theaters.

KR: That's probably what I wanted to ask you. What do you see as the difference—partly I want to ask you to say more about television. And then I would like to talk about the difference between television and cinema.

WH: Yes. You asked about endangerment by images like mass media, like television and magazines, I don't have to elaborate much, just turn on your TV set and you'll know what I'm talking about. So that has to be taken with caution but there are also other dangers. It's manifold, and some of it, a sense of reality and sense for the world out there, has been challenged by virtual realities. And it's not just television, it's the internet, it's digital effects, it's photoshop, and what can we trust.

KR: So it's also certain kinds of cinema?

WH: No. I wouldn't compare it to cinema; it's actually something that tries to encroach on our sense of dignified and new and exciting images which we should defend. It comes from all sort of sites including academia, but that's a minor event. I do not mean academia per se, I mean efforts by academia to overanalyze, vivisect poetry, literature, cinema, you just name it. The only form of art that is still resistant and cannot be tackled by it is music. You cannot speak in poststructural, postmodernist, post-whatever terms about music like that.[8] However, when you start to create some climate in some niches of academia, in overtheorizing things and just trying to only find structures—the structures of social behavior, structures inherent in history, structures inherent in psychology, to enforce it on literature, for example—it just doesn't do any good to any piece of literature, it does not do anything good to movies. Just try to get away from it, that's my advice, because the real wonder about cinema gets lost. The great love for poetry can be trampled, this flame that's somewhere there, you can trample it out and extinguish it easily. And that's a danger. And I like literature, or films, or music as something that can give you consolation. The poststructuralists will never accept a term like *consolation*.[9] My wife, who grew up in Siberia in a dictatorship, many books were forbidden and she as a fifteen-year-old had a secret copy of Bulgakov's *Master and Margarita* ([1928] 1967). The entire text, secretly, in longhand. And the schoolgirls would circulate these things around. And that's what we need. And that's what is real agitation, that is what is real reception of literature. The poststructuralists will stamp them out.[10] And we should be very, very cautious.

KR: It's the nightmare of our own lives, as academics, that we might be betraying the spirit of the thing that we care about.

WH: Not necessarily, as long as long as your students love literature. And as long as you guide them in loving cinema, poetry.

KR: I am interested in knowing whether you think that the university can do something to help nurture the reinvigoration of our images or whether you think that the structure of the university makes that very difficult to do.

WH: We should not speak summarily about university or academia because when you are a mathematician or you are in, let's say, you are in law school or you are in medical school, yes, sure, there has to be academic training. Even though some of the most interesting elements come in through people who come from a very different angle of thinking, and sometimes very unusual ones. But I have nothing against academia, I have nothing against universities. Thank god they exist. However, in the humanities, that's where it gets tricky. And that's why I'm always alarmed, and more alarmed than a few years ago. It's very alarming what is going on. I do not have a clear remedy. I hated school, I hate school so bad, and in particular my German literature classes. We were vivisecting Goethe's *Faust* for almost a year. And it was so bad, on a stupid, primitive, level. It was so unbearable that, up to today, I have not been capable of reading Goethe's *Faust*. Even in school, when I was only seventeen, they tried to stamp it out and tried to trample on my sense of poetry and sense of literature. And thank god I survived it. And I had very, very serious plans. Practical, serious plans to burn the school to the ground. And I'm not one of those Columbine type kids who opens fire, no, I would have done it at three at night when nobody would be close to the building. And this kind of aversion, and this kind of despair about the school system and the academic system, I still carry it in me. It would be silly to just rant against it without an argument.[11] But I think that the simplest, easy argument is, How does academia manage to create enthusiasm for literature, for poetry? And much of what is happening in literature, for example, I don't know how English literature is taught here or how film is taught here. I do not know. But how does it maintain, how would you maintain a kind of love and enthusiasm for cinema?

KR: Well, I appreciate your coming into this space, the university to talk with us.

WH: No, I don't have a recipe—I cannot be helpful because I cannot tell you how to teach a course. How do you, how do you manage to instill, a sense of love, for poetry . . . ?

KR: But some of this is helpful, and I'll be writing my lecture with your words in my ear. Anyway, I'd like you to say something about how you understand the difference between cinema and television, and also, you know, especially because you've just released a lot of your films on

DVD. Your documentary and shorts DVDs have just come out. And so I'm wondering how you feel people will experience your films differently if they're watching them at home, on their own or with a couple of people on a television screen. Or if they're watching them in the cinema, and how you feel about that.

WH: Let's not go too far into this. Early on in the early times, we had hopes that television would become an instrument of education, an instrument of culture, and of course it has not. I do remember when the second German channel ZDF was inaugurated in the 1960s. There were people who would deliver a speech, and part of the very first moment of ZDF was that they read the prologue of Goethe's *Faust*. There was the idea that we had created an instrument that would elevate the collective awareness for great culture for the general population. It did not. It just did not. It turned exactly the other way around. And now it has become exactly the common denominator, the most common, lowest denominator. However, television has a great advantage in certain ways. You do get a sense of what, for example, the collective preparedness, the collective expectations, what the collective dreams are all about. You have to study WrestleMania, and I keep saying Anna Nicole Smith, yes, because there's something momentous in these events.[12] Momentous in a way. It's very easy to dismiss television. The poet must not avert his eyes. That's my maxim. Not that you have to watch television all the time. And of course it has grave disadvantages. The biggest disadvantage in television nowadays is that it is completely market-driven. It's the sponsors, the companies, who finance television, but I do not blame Coca-Cola or Nike for destroying the flow of narrative. The flow of narrative is something we have seen for tens of thousands of years, cavemen sitting at the campfire and telling stories. And it's tens of thousands of years, and it's three, four thousand years of the high culture of literature, of novels, of narration in written form. And now it is somehow disrupted, the flow of narration. A gift, a human gift that distinguishes us from the cow and from the goose. It's such a wonderful gift that we have, and here comes a time of consumerism and of capitalism, and our way of life, which destroys a fundamental achievement of the human race. And this is one of the reasons why I do not work in commercials. Yes I could earn money, in doing commercials, and I could pay the rent. I do not do it. It's a little bit of a question of principle. I do not want to make a big moral issue out of it. It's not so much a moral issue, it's a question of how do we preserve a sense of story-telling.

KR: Do you see cinema as a place where we do collective dreaming?

WH: Yes. The collective dreams of the world are created in a way in movie theaters. And not when you are sitting lonesome in front of a TV set. You can't even laugh. Even if a film is very funny, you never laugh when you're all alone. And this is why TV stations in some of these sitcoms and other funny movies add laughter from the tape. To somehow cheat you out of the solitude of being alone and nobody laughs, but you hear the laughter, so you feel better.

KR: I wanted to ask you about comedy, because I was struck in *Encounters at the End of the World* by the roar of laughter when the image of the chimpanzee riding the goat appeared on the screen. It seemed like a one-liner joke and I'm interested in your relationship to comedy, because I think there are always comedic aspects in your films.

WH: There is a lot of humor, let's put it this way. I'm not into comedies, but many of my films have a lot of humor in them.

KR: Is it becoming more explicit? Do you think?

WH: In some of the films, yes, when you look at *The Wild Blue Yonder*, yes, it's very hilarious, there's a lot of humor. And when you see Brad Dourif as an alien, you know that, yes, he's the only authentic alien we can muster. And he's wonderful, and it's very funny. However, I know you only experience the laughter when you have a house with at least a hundred people in it. If it's only three people spread out in a theater, it is not a collective experience. And I make my mistakes. For example, in a very funny, humorous moment in *Encounters at the End of the World*, I make this mistake. A Polish scientist discovers in one single day three species, three new species of a single-cell creature. And they talk a little bit about it to scientists and then from off-screen they're saying, "well is this, is this a great moment?" Everybody laughs. You don't ask such a thing. Everybody laughs. The answer comes almost immediately, on asking, "is this a great moment?" And the scientist says, "Yeah. Yeah." And nobody hears it because everybody is still laughing so. My abilities to read an audience correctly like some of the great masters of comedy, such as Billy Wilder, have done, I don't have it in me. Yes, I can create a situation that is full of humor, but I do not read the timing of it, I make my mistakes.

KR: When you talked about Fred Astaire yesterday, you said that you loved him in spite of himself, because of his relationship to space and the movement of his body.

WH: Yeah, how he moves and how he dances.

KR: I wonder if, whether you'd liken it to slapstick comedy, and whether that early moment of cinema where it's so physical and so much about the movement of the body, and whether that interests you.

WH: It does, yes, but my only and lonesome favorite is Buster Keaton. I never got that much intrigued about Harold Lloyd or Charlie Chaplin, it's Buster Keaton. The kind of solitude of the man and the kind of stoic endurance against the quirks of fate. And of the objects around that are all an impediment to a human being.

KR: He belongs in your cast of characters.

WH: Yeah, and he's a wonderful, deep sort of figure and I truly love the man. But it's not that I'm such a great fan of these early slapstick movies and this jerky movement, the running police chases have never impressed me that much. But with Fred Astaire, it is somehow something else because it's so absolutely and crazily stylized. It is as remote from the real world as it can get.[13] And for only ten dollars you can remove yourself from reality as far as you can even imagine. And you just better watch a Fred Astaire movie. And him singing, "Don't Monkey with Broadway." And the way that they are dancing it is just phenomenal. And the face of Fred Astaire is enormously stupid, I've never seen a face that projects stupidity in such a bold way as he does. And the lines of dialogue and the song that they are singing are so phenomenally stupid, and still I love it. I don't know why. It is something very, very dear to my heart. When I even think about Fred Astaire, I become mellow.

KR: Critics sometimes describe you as, partly because of this desire to transcend, a Neo-Romantic and talk about the mysticism of your films and the spirituality of your films. It seems to me that I always find them to be in tension with what seems to be an equal fascination with the banal. So that in *Encounters at the End of the World,* you get the iceberg and the scale of the iceberg and the sense of a cathedral from under the water, but you also get the catastrophe of the Mr. Frosty machine breaking down in the South Pole and that these things coexist in the space of your films.

WH: I have to say that terms like mysticism or the spirituality of my films and all these things, I can only touch it with a pair of pliers. And Romanticism, well, that's always the disease of reviewers of my films because normally reviewers do not know much about Germany, they know about the Nazis and they know about the Romantics. Maybe sometimes Expressionism and Bertolt Brecht, and so they all of a sudden come up with the crazy idea that there's a Brechtian principle in my films, so it leaves me kind of baffled. But Romanticism is an important aspect of what does not constitute my cinema. It does not. When I speak, in Les Blank's film, *Burden of Dreams*, about nature and about the wildness and baseness and obscenity of nature, you cannot get a more contrary position toward a romantic view of nature than what I will give you. Or in *Grizzly Man* (2005), the kind of romanticizing, sentimentalizing of wild nature through Timothy Treadwell does not go uncontested for one moment.[14] I raised my voice and I have an ongoing argument with him. "Here I differ with Treadwell," my voice says.[15] There is one single exception and that is Caspar David Friedrich, the painter. But I like his way. He's all landscapes. Landscapes as an inner image, a human quality. The jungle in *Aguirre* (1972) is not a romantic jungle, but the jungle in *Aguirre* is a fever dream. The fever dream of some crazed man out there in the jungle in search of El Dorado. Yes, there is one, one small affinity [Friedrich], but otherwise my affinities go much, much earlier. Like, for example, Martin Luther, and here I'm speaking of his Bible translation. The language of his Bible translation, which is very, very deeply embedded in my sense of literature. Poets like Hölderlin, who was at the time of the Romantics although he's not a romantic poet. Kleist, who wrote some wonderful short stories and, and some dramas. Büchner, who wrote *Lenz*. If there is anyone here in the German department, force your students to learn it by heart. It's only thirty-five pages of prose text, but there is nothing more intense and nothing more beautiful, in my knowledge, within the German language. Such a wonderful and fine prose, and not a Romantic. Is Hemingway a Romantic? No. Is, Joseph Conrad a Romantic? No. Is Bruce Chatwin? No. So my affinities, my proclivities, are totally different. My aims are different, my sources of inspiration are different in literature, and of course much of it goes back to antiquity. I have started to go back to read texts that I was supposed to read in school. Now I read them. Latin, ancient Greek authors. And, for the sake mostly yes, sometimes, for the wonder of language and the wonder of the poetry they have in them. And sometimes for nothing but sheer consolation. In moments of deepest travail and tribulation I find consolation by reading the book of Job, in Luther's translation. And by reading Levi's *Second Punic War*. And it's only for the sake of consolation. Literature can do that, and music can do that as well. And, of course, religion, but I am not into religion anymore.

KR: We were talking today at lunch about the manly man. It seems to me that in your work there's a certain kind of masculinity that is totally different from the Hollywood hero, what you call real adventure. And you say that this real adventure has been lost.

WH: In a way, yes. I'm not a feminist and I'm not a macho either. The masculine image in Hollywood in the more collective mainstream, it's more the postpubescent kid-boys. Leonardo DiCaprio, who looks like a pubescent boy even though is probably thirty by now, or Brad Pitt, or you just name it, almost everyone. And the only last manly man out there is Clint Eastwood, but he comes from a stock of men that was Humphrey Bogart and Gary Cooper and John Wayne and Charles Bronson, Richard Widmark. So they are out of fashion, so probably the female dreams, the collective dreams, have significantly shifted and that's a very, very interesting thing. Ultimately, I do not want to see these postpubescent boy-men all the time in movies. It kind of doesn't feel right. It will shift. Hopefully, it will shift again to the more manly men. And it's very difficult for me, for example, to cast a new film that I'm planning if there has to be a manly man who at the same time is kind of fragile as well. That is the hardest to find and really difficult to cast it. It's not John Wayne, but a manly man like Humphrey Bogart, a man of complexity. A man like Marlon Brando, yes, a very manly man, and yet full of complexity. And, of course, it has shifted significantly, and it's interesting to observe what is emerging and what may be coming up next. I keep on wondering about it.

KR: You speak of the collective dreams of women perhaps shifting, and at times in your films you've looked very closely at female characters, like Fini Straubinger.[16] But, the attention of your filmmaking has been much more on male characters, and I wanted to maybe end by asking you why you think that you've so infrequently focused on female characters, is it something you have deliberately shied away from?

WH: I have no real clear answer to that, I don't. Ultimately, I don't know. But when you speak of male characters they are complex, complicated ones, and not the macho ones. When you look at Bruno S. in *Kaspar Hauser* (1974) or *Stroszek* (1977). No they, they're not that sort of John Wayne type, nor is Kinski, nor is Christian Bale in *Rescue Dawn* (2006).

KR: You've given us a whole new vocabulary of masculinity.

WH: Well, I have not thought about it, but it's nice that you say that because I wouldn't make a series of films toward some machismo or whatever. No, I'm not into that, but there is a certain manliness in some of them, yes. Sure, and a woman would not dream of hoisting a ship over a mountain in the Amazonian jungle. Women do not have that kind of dream. It's a fever dream of men. And these fever dreams are very, very known to me. I feel familiar with them. I feel comfortable with them, and I do the stories that I do understand. So it's fairly simple and fairly complicated because I am not looking at myself. And I don't want to analyze what I've done. I'm kind of cautious, but your observation is right. Undeniably. And in a way, I believe that Ingmar Bergman wouldn't be able to answer you why in almost all his films women are the leading central characters.

Notes

1. The context of the conversation was a screening of Herzog's new 2007 documentary film about scientists living in Antarctica, *Encounters at the End of the World.*

2. Coincidentally, Herzog has a role in the latest offering from the *Star Wars* franchise, a 2019 Disney series called *The Mandalorian*.

3. *The Wild Blue Yonder* is, along with *Fata Morgana* (1970) and *Lessons of Darkness* (1992), one of three films by Herzog often considered to be in the science fiction genre. It stars Brad Dourif as an alien condemned to live on earth and intercuts the alien's ramblings with footage from NASA and other sources.

4. *Little Dieter* is Herzog's celebrated biographical documentary of Vietnam War pilot Dieter Dengler and his travails as an escaped prisoner of war in the jungle. See the section "Black God, White Devil" in the essay.

5. Golder is a frequent collaborator of Herzog and directed a biographical documentary on Herzog called *Ballad of a Righteous Merchant* (2017).

6. *The Great Ecstasy of Woodcarver Steiner* is Herzog's biographical documentary of the ski-flyer Walter Steiner. See the section "Frontier Thesis" in the essay.

7. The reference here is to the accomplished photographer Lena Herzog, Herzog's spouse since 1999.

8. This is obviously false; music has been subject to postmodernist (and other post-) approaches for several decades and counting.

9. Herzog is here confused. The "consolation" that traditional postmodernists refuse is what Lyotard in *The Postmodern Condition* calls "the consolation of correct forms" (1984), that is, the slavish commitment to the authority of master narratives. Reversing and displacing these narratives such that they can live anew is the postmodern game, not refusing the human sentiment of consolation.

10. Herzog is walking on really thin ice here. Bulgakov, Bakhtin—all the heroes of *samizdat* literature circulating clandestinely with the *express intent* of displacing master narratives—these are the basic building blocks of what will consolidate in "the West," that is, 1960s Paris, as poststructuralism.

11. It would. The story of "vivisecting" *Faust* clearly resides as a sort of trauma in Herzog's consciousness. He's been telling the story as the *bête noire* standing in for *all humanities*, indeed "school," for decades. But the story, from beginning to middle to end, is simple to the point of banality: "I once had a bad teacher." From my anecdotal experience and those that I see from my colleagues around me, classes in film and literary studies rarely kill the spirit for literary reflection, "the wonder" before the work of art, in our students; quite the opposite. Herzog's films, of course, are exemplary in this regard.

12. WrestleMania is a US-based professional wrestling event produced by World Wrestling Entertainment. *The Anna Nicole Smith Show* was a pioneering celebrity-centered reality television show that ran for about a year beginning in late 2002.

13. Herzog has expressed appreciation for the opera form in similar terms. See the section "I'm planning something geographical. . . ."

14. Herzog here seems to be confusing a conventional, everyday notion of "romanticizing," as sentimentalizing, with the loosely coherent literary, philosophical, and artistic style of Romanticism. In other words, there is nothing un-Romantic about his comments on the obscenity of nature, which is a basic feature of the kind of sublime terror prevalent in Romanticism. See the section "The Small Voice of Conquest."

15. Timothy Treadwell is the protagonist of Herzog's documentary film *Grizzly Man*. A wildlife activist who was eaten by a grizzly bear, he left behind hours of video footage, some quite remarkable. Herzog inventively takes this footage and Treadwell's narration to enter into a sort of dialogic relation with the deceased activist.

16. Fini Straubinger is the deaf-blind activist at the center of Herzog's 1971 documentary *Land of Silence and Darkness*. See the section "Frontier Thesis."

Filmography

Herakles (1962)
West Germany: Werner Herzog Filmproduktion
Screenplay: Werner Herzog
12 minutes

Die beispiellose Verteidigung der Festung Deutschkreutz (*The Unprecedented Defence of the Fortress Deutschkreuz*) (1967)
West Germany: Arpa-Film, Werner Herzog Filmproduktion
Producer: Werner Herzog
Screenplay: Werner Herzog
Photography: Jaime Pacheco
Editor: Werner Herzog
15 minutes

Lebenszeichen (*Signs of Life*) (1968)
West Germany: Werner Herzog Filmproduktion
Producer: Werner Herzog
Screenplay: Werner Herzog
Photography: Thomas Mauch
Editor: Beate Mainke-Jellinghaus
Cast: Peter Brogle (Stroszek), Wolfgang Reichman (Meinhard)
91 minutes

Letzte Worte (*Last Words*) (1968)
West Germany: Werner Herzog Filmproduktion
Producer: Werner Herzog
Screenplay: Werner Herzog
Photography: Thomas Mauch
Editor: Beate Mainke-Jellinghaus
13 minutes

Massnahmen gegen Fanatiker (*Precautions against Fanatics*) (1969)
West Germany: Werner Herzog Filmproduktion
Producer: Werner Herzog
Screenplay: Werner Herzog
Photography: Dietrich Lohmann, Jörg Schmidt-Reitwein
Editor: Beate Mainke-Jellinghaus
12 minutes

Auch Zwerge haben klein angefangen (*Even Dwarfs Started Small*) (1970)
West Germany: Werner Herzog Filmproduktion
Producer: Werner Herzog
Screenplay: Werner Herzog
Photography: Thomas Mauch
Editor: Beate Mainke-Jellinghaus
Cast: Helmut Döring (Hombré), Paul Glauer (Erzieher)
96 minutes

Die fliegenden Ärzte von Ostafrika (*The Flying Doctors of East Africa*) (1970)
West Germany: Gesellschaft für Medizin und Forschung in Afrika, Werner Herzog Filmproduktion
Producer: Eleonore Semler
Screenplay: Werner Herzog
Photography: Thomas Mauch
Editor: Beate Mainke-Jellinghaus
Narrated by Wilifried Klaus
45 minutes

Behinderte Zukunft (*Handicapped Future*) (1971)
West Germany: Werner Herzog Filmproduktion
Producer: Werner Herzog
Screenplay: Werner Herzog
Photography: Jörg Schmidt-Reitwein
Editor: Beate Mainke-Jellinghaus
Narrated by Rolf Illig
42 minutes

Fata Morgana (1971)
West Germany: Werner Herzog Filmproduktion
Producers: Werner Herzog, Joschi Arpa
Screenplay: Werner Herzog
Photography: Jörg Schmidt-Reitwein
Editor: Beate Mainke-Jellinghaus
Narrated by Lotte Eisner
76 minutes

Land des Schweigens und der Dunkelheit (*Land of Silence and Darkness*) (1971)
West Germany: Werner Herzog Filmproduktion
Producer: Werner Herzog
Screenplay: Werner Herzog
Photography: Jörg Schmidt-Reitwein
Editor: Beate Mainke-Jellinghaus
Cast: Fini Straubinger (as herself)
85 minutes

Aguirre, der Zorn Gottes (*Aguirre, the Wrath of God*) (1972)
West Germany, Mexico, Peru: Werner Herzog Filmproduktion
Producers: Werner Herzog, Hans Prescher
Screenplay: Werner Herzog
Photography: Thomas Mauch
Editor: Beate Mainke-Jellinghaus
Cast: Klaus Kinski (Don Lope de Aguirre), Helena Rojo (Inez de Atienza)
95 minutes

Die große Ekstase des Bildschnitzers Steiner (*The Great Ecstasy of Woodcarver Steiner*) (1974)
West Germany: Werner Herzog Filmproduktion
Producer: Werner Herzog
Screenplay: Werner Herzog
Photography: Jörg Schmidt-Reitwein
Editor: Beate Mainke-Jellinghaus
Cast: Walter Steiner (as himself), Werner Herzog (narrator)
45 minutes

Jeder für sich und Gott gegen alle (*The Enigma of Kaspar Hauser*) (1974)
West Germany: Werner Herzog Filmproduktion, Zweites Deutsches Fernsehen (ZDF)
Producer: Werner Herzog
Screenplay: Werner Herzog
Photography: Jörg Schmidt-Reitwein
Editor: Beate Mainke-Jellinghaus
Cast: Bruno S. (Kaspar Hauser), Walter Ladengast (Professor Daumer)
110 minutes

Beobachtungen zu einer neuen Sprache (*How Much Wood Would a Woodchuck Chuck . . .*) (1976)
West Germany: Werner Herzog Filmproduktion, Süddeutscher Rundfunk (SDR)
Producer: Werner Herzog
Screenplay: Werner Herzog

Photography: Thomas Mauch
Editor: Beate Mainke-Jellinghaus
44 minutes

Herz aus Glas (*Heart of Glass*) (1976)
West Germany: Werner Herzog Filmproduktion
Producer: Werner Herzog
Screenplay: Herbert Achternbusch
Photography Jörg Schmidt-Reitwein
Editor: Beate Mainke-Jellinghaus
Cast: Josef Bierbichler (Hias), Stefan Güttler (Huttenbesitzer)
94 minutes

Mit mir will niemand spielen (*No One Will Play with Me*) (1976)
West Germany
Producer: Werner Herzog
Screenplay: Werner Herzog
Photography Jörg Schmidt-Reitwein
14 minutes

Stroszek (1977)
West Germany: Werner Herzog Filmproduktion, Zweites Deutsches Fernsehen (ZDF)
Producer: Werner Herzog
Screenplay: Werner Herzog
Photography: Thomas Mauch
Editor: Beate Mainke-Jellinghaus
Cast: Bruno S. (Bruno Stroszek), Eva Mattes (Eva)
116 minutes

Warten auf eine unausweichliche Katastrophe (*La Soufrière*) (1977)
West Germany: Werner Herzog Filmproduktion
Producer: Werner Herzog
Screenplay: Werner Herzog
Photography: Edward Lachman, Jörg Schmidt-Reitwein
Editor: Beate Mainke-Jellinghaus
Narrated by Werner Herzog
30 minutes

Nosferatu: Phantom der Nacht (*Nosferatu the Vampyre*) (1979)
West Germany, France: Werner Herzog Filmproduktion
Producer: Werner Herzog
Screenplay: Werner Herzog

Photography: Jörg Schmidt-Reitwein
Editor: Beate Mainke-Jellinghaus
Cast: Klaus Kinski (Count Dracula), Isabelle Adjani (Lucy Harker), Bruno Ganz (Jonathan Harker)
107 minutes

Woyzeck (1979)
West Germany: Werner Herzog Filmproduktion, Zweites Deutsches Fernsehen (ZDF)
Producer: Werner Herzog
Screenplay: Georg Büchner, Werner Herzog
Photography: Jörg Schmidt-Reitwein
Editor: Beate Mainke-Jellinghaus
Cast: Eva Mattes (Marie), Klaus Kinski (Woyzeck)
80 minutes

Glaube und Währung—Dr. Gene Scott, Fernsehprediger (*God's Angry Man*) (1981)
West Germany, France: Werner Herzog Filmproduktion, Süddeutscher Rundfunk (SDR), Sudfunk Stuttgart
Producer: Werner Herzog
Screenplay: Werner Herzog
Photography: Thomas Mauch
Editor: Beate Mainke-Jellinghaus
Cast: Gene Scott (as himself), Werner Herzog (narrator)
44 minutes

Huie's Predigt (*Huie's Sermon*) (1981)
West Germany, France: Werner Herzog Filmproduktion
Producer: Werner Herzog
Screenplay: Werner Herzog
Photography: Thomas Mauch
Editor: Beate Mainke-Jellinghaus
Cast: Huie L. Rogers (as himself)
41 minutes

Fitzcarraldo (1982)
West Germany: Werner Herzog Filmproduktion, Pro-ject Filmproduktion, Filmverlag der Autoren
Producers: Werner Herzog, Willi Segler, Lucki Stipetic
Screenplay: Werner Herzog
Photography: Thomas Mauch
Editor: Beate Mainke-Jellinghaus

Cast: Klaus Kinski (Brian Sweeney Fitzgerald—Fitzcarraldo), Claudia Cardinale (Molly), David Pérez Espinosa (Chief)
158 minutes

Ballade vom kleinen Soldaten (*Ballad of the Little Soldier*) (1984)
West Germany: Süddeutscher Rundfunk (SDR), Werner Herzog Filmproduktion, Zweites Deutsches Fernsehen (ZDF)
Producers: Werner Herzog, Manfred Nägele
Screenplay: Werner Herzog, Denis Reichle
Photography: Michael Edols, Jorge Vignati
Editor: Maximiliane Mainka
Narrated by Werner Herzog
46 minutes

Wo die grünen Ameisen träumen (*Where the Green Ants Dream*) (1984)
West Germany, Australia: Pro-ject Filmproduktion, Werner Herzog Filmproduktion, Zweites Deutsches Fernsehen (ZDF)
Producer: Werner Herzog
Screenplay: Werner Herzog, Bob Ellis
Photography: Jörg Schmidt-Reitwein
Editor: Beate Mainke-Jellinghaus
Cast: Bruce Spence (Lance Hackett), Wandjuk Marika (Miliritbi)
100 minutes

Gasherbrum—Der leuchtende Berg (*The Dark Glow of the Mountains*) (1985)
West Germany: Süddeutscher Rundfunk (SDR), Werner Herzog Filmproduktion, Zweites Deutsches Fernsehen (ZDF)
Producers: Manfred Nägele, Werner Herzog
Screenplay: Werner Herzog
Photography: Rainer Klausmann
Editor: Maximiliane Mainka
Narrated by Werner Herzog
45 minutes

Werner Herzog: Filmemacher (*Portrait Werner Herzog*) (1986)
West Germany: Werner Herzog Filmproduktion, TransTel
Producer: Lucki Stipetic
Screenplay: Werner Herzog
Photography: Jörg Schmidt-Reitwein
Editor: Maximiliane Mainka
28 minutes

Cobra Verde (1987)
West Germany, Ghana: Werner Herzog Filmproduktion, Zweites Deutsches Fernsehen (ZDF), Ghana Film Industry Corporation
Producer: Lucki Stipetic
Screenplay: Bruce Chatwin, Werner Herzog
Photography: Viktor Ruzicka
Editor: Maximiliane Mainka
Cast: Klaus Kinski (Francisco Manoel da Silva / Cobra Verde), King Ampaw (Taparica)
111 minutes

Les français vus par (*The French as Seen by . . .*) (one episode, 1988)
France, USA, Italy, West Germany, Poland: Centre National de la Cinématographie (CNC), Erato Films, France 2 (FR2)
Producer: Lucki Stipetic
Screenplay: Werner Herzog
Photography: Jörg Schmidt-Reitwein
Editor: Maximiliane Mainka
13 minutes

Giovanna d'Arco (*Joan of Arc*) (1989)
Codirected with Keith Cheetham
Italy, UK, Portugal, Finland: NVC Arts, BBC Television, La Sept
Producer: Fiona Morris
Screenplay: Temistocle Solera, Friedrich Schiller
Photography: Alan Beal, Mike Dugdale, David Gopsill, Martin Hawkins, Duncan McLaren, Keith Watts
Cast: Renato Brunson (Giacomo), Susan Dunn (Giovanna)
127 minutes

Wodaabe—Die Hirten der Sonne: Nomaden am Südrand der Sahara (*Herdsmen of the Sun*) (1989)
France, West Germany: Arion Productions, Canal+, France 2 (FR2) Werner Herzog Filmproduktion
Producers: Jörg Dattler, Patrick Sandrin, Werner Herzog
Screenplay: Werner Herzog
Photography: Jörg Schmidt-Reitwein
Editor: Rainer Standke
Narrated by Werner Herzog
52 minutes

Echos aus einem düsteren Reich (*Echoes from a Somber Empire*) (1990)
France, Germany: Films sans Frontières, Sera Filmproduktion, Werner Herzog Filmproduktion
Producers: Werner Herzog, Galeshka Moravioff, Walter Saxer
Screenplay: Werner Herzog
Photography: Martin Manz, Jörg Schmidt-Reitwein
Editor: Rainer Standke
Narrated by Werner Herzog
91 minutes

Cerro Torre: Schrei aus Stein (*Scream of Stone*) (1991)
Germany, France, Canada, Italy, Argentina, UK, South Africa: Sera Filmproduktion, Molécule, Films A2
Producers: Henry Lange, Richard Sadler, Walter Saxer
Screenplay: Hans-Ulrich Klenner, Walter Saxer, Robert Geoffrion
Photography: Rainer Klausmann
Editor: Suzanne Baron
Cast: Donald Sutherland (Ivan)
105 minutes

Jag Mandir: Das exzentrische Privattheater des Maharadscha von Udaipur (1991)
Austria, Germany: Neue Studio Film, Österreichischer Rundfunk (ORF), Zweites Deutsches Fernsehen (ZDF)
Producer: Wolfgang Rest
Screenplay: Werner Herzog
Photography: Wolfgang Dickmann, Rainer Klausmann, Anton Peschke
Editor: Michou Hutter
82 minutes

Filmstunde (1991–92)
Austria: Österreichischer Rundfunk (ORF)
Producer: Gerda Weissenberger
Screenplay: Werner Herzog
Photography: Karl Kofler
Editor: Albert Skalak
Narrated by Werner Herzog

Lektionen in Finsternis (*Lessons of Darkness*) (1992)
France, UK, Germany: Canal+, Première, Werner Herzog Filmproduktion
Producers: Paul Berriff, Werner Herzog, Lucki Stipetic
Screenplay: Werner Herzog
Photography: Paul Berriff, Rainer Klausmann, Anton Peschke
Editor: Rainer Standke

Narrated by Werner Herzog
54 minutes

Glocken aus der Tiefe—Glaube und Aberglaube in Rußland (*Bells from the Deep*) (1993)
Germany, USA: Werner Herzog Filmproduktion, Momentous Events
Producers: Ira Barmak, Lucki Stipetic
Screenplay: Werner Herzog
Photography: Jörg Schmidt-Reitwein
Editor: Rainer Standke
Narrated by Werner Herzog
60 minutes

Tod für fünf Stimmen (*Gesualdo: Death for Five Voices*) (1995)
Germany: Monarda Arts, Werner Herzog Filmproduktion, Zweites Deutsches Fernsehen (ZDF)
Producers: Werner Herzog, Lucki Stipetic
Screenplay: Werner Herzog
Photography: Peter Zeitlinger
Editor: Rainer Standke
Narrated by Werner Herzog
59 minutes

Die Verwandlung der Welt in Musik: Bayreuth vor der Premiere (*The Transformation of the World into Music*) (1996)
Germany: ARTE, Werner Herzog Filmproduktion, Zweites Deutsches Fernsehen (ZDF)
Producers: Ira Barmak, Lucki Stipetic
Screenplay: Werner Herzog
Photography: Jörg Schmidt-Reitwein
Editor: Rainer Standke
Narrated by Werner Herzog
90 minutes

Little Dieter Needs to Fly (1997)
Germany, UK, France: Werner Herzog Filmproduktion, Zweites Deutsches Fernsehen (ZDF), ZDF Enterprises
Producer: Lucki Stipetic
Screenplay: Werner Herzog
Photography: Peter Zeitlinger
Editors: Joe Bini, Glen Scantlebury, Rainer Standke
Cast: Dieter Dengler (as himself)
80 minutes

Höllenfahrten (*Hell Ride*) (1998)
Germany: Zweites Deutsches Fernsehen (ZDF)
Producer: Wolfgang Ebert
Screenplay: Werner Herzog
Photography: Peter Zeitlinger
Editor: Ellen Bader
45 minutes

2000 Jahre Christentum (*2000 Years of Christianity*) (1999)
Germany: Eikon Film, Zweites Deutsches Fernsehen (ZDF)
Producer: Lucki Stipetic
Screenplay: Werner Herzog
Photography: Jorge Vignati
Editor: Joe Bini
Narrated by Werner Herzog
125 minutes

Mein liebster Feind—Klaus Kinski (*My Best Fiend*) (1999)
Germany, UK, USA: Werner Herzog Filmproduktion, Cafe Productions Ltd., Zephir Film
Producer: Lucki Stipetic
Screenplay: Werner Herzog
Photography: Peter Zeitlinger
Editor: Joe Bini
Narrated by Werner Herzog
95 minutes

Wings of Hope (2000)
Germany, UK: Werner Herzog Filmproduktion, ZDF Enterprises, BBC Bristol
Producer: Werner Herzog
Screenplay: Werner Herzog
Photography: Peter Zeitlinger
Editor: Joe Bini
Narrated by Werner Herzog
65 minutes

Invincible (2001)
UK, Germany, Ireland, USA: Werner Herzog Filmproduktion, Tatfilm, Little Bird See
Producers: Gary Bart, Werner Herzog
Screenplay: Werner Herzog
Photography: Peter Zeitlinger
Editor: Joe Bini

Cast: Tim Roth (Herschel Steinschneider/Erik Jan Hanussen), Jouko Ahola (Zishe Breitbart)
135 minutes

Pilgrimage (2001)
Germany, UK: Werner Herzog Filmproduktion, BBC, Pipeline Films
Producer: Lucki Stipetic
Screenplay: Werner Herzog
Photography: Jorge Pacheco, Jörg Schmidt-Reitwein, Erik Söllner
Editor: Joe Bini
18 minutes

"Ten Thousand Years Older" (segment of *Ten Minutes Older: The Trumpet*) (2002)
Spain, UK, Germany, USA: Matador Pictures, Road Movies Filmproduktion, Atom Films
Producer: Lucki Stipetic
Screenplay: Werner Herzog
Photography: Vicente Rios
Editor: Joe Bini
92 minutes

Wheel of Time (2003)
Germany, Austria, Italy: Werner Herzog Filmproduktion, West Park Pictures Produktion, ARTE
Producer: Werner Herzog
Screenplay: Werner Herzog
Photography: Peter Zeitlinger
Editor: Joe Bini
Narrated by Werner Herzog
81 minutes

The White Diamond (2004)
Germany, Japan, UK: Marco Polo Film AG, NDR Naturfilm, NHK
Producers: Ira Barmak, Lucki Stipetic
Screenplay: Werner Herzog, Rudolph Herzog, Annette Scheurich
Photography: Henning Brümmer, Klaus Scheurich
Editor: Joe Bini
Narrated by Werner Herzog
88 minutes

Grizzly Man (2005)
Germany, USA: Lions Gate Films, Discovery Docs, Real Big Production

Producers: Kevin Beggs, Erik Nelson
Screenplay: Werner Herzog
Photography: Peter Zeitlinger
Editor: Joe Bini
Cast: Timothy Treadwell (as himself), Werner Herzog (as himself)
103 minutes

The Wild Blue Yonder (2005)
Germany, France, Austria, UK: Werner Herzog Filmproduktion, West Park Pictures Produktion, Tétra Média
Producers: Andre Singer, Lucki Stipetic
Screenplay: Werner Herzog
Photography: Henry Kaiser, Tanja Koop, Klaus Scheurich
Editor: Joe Bini
Cast: Brad Dourif (The Alien), Donald Williams (Astronaut Commander, as Captain Donald Williams)
90 minutes

Rescue Dawn (2006)
USA, Luxembourg: Metro-Goldwyn-Mayer (MGM), Top Gun Productions, Thema Production
Producers: Elton Brand, Harry Knapp, Steve Marlton
Screenplay: Werner Herzog
Photography: Peter Zeitlinger
Editor: Joe Bini
Cast: Christian Bale (Dieter Dengler), Steve Zahn (Duane)
120 minutes

Encounters at the End of the World (2007)
USA: Discovery Films, Creative Differences Productions, Discovery Channel
Producer: Henry Kaiser
Screenplay: Werner Herzog
Photography: Peter Zeitlinger
Editor: Joe Bini
Narrated by Werner Herzog
99 minutes

Bad Lieutenant: Port of Call New Orleans (2009)
USA: Millennium Films, Edward R. Pressman Film, Saturn Films
Producer: Stephen Belafonte
Screenplay: William M. Finkelstein
Photography: Peter Zeitlinger
Editor: Joe Bini

Cast: Nicholas Cage (Terence McDonagh), Eva Mendes (Frankie Donnenfield)
122 minutes

La Bohème (2009)
UK, Ethiopia: Sky Arts, English National Opera
Producer: Andre Singer
Screenplay: Giuseppe Giacosa, Luigi Illica
Photography: Richard Blanshard
Editor: Joe Bini
Cast: Peter Auty (Rodolfo), Mary Plazas (Mimi)
4 minutes

My Son, My Son, What Have Ye Done (2009)
Germany, USA: Defilm, Industrial Entertainment, Paper Street Films
Producer: Eric Bassett
Screenplay: Herbert Golder, Werner Herzog
Photography: Peter Zeitlinger
Editors: Joe Bini, Omar Daher
Cast: Michael Shannon (Brad McCullom), Chloë Sevigny (Ingrid)
91 minutes

Cave of Forgotten Dreams (2010)
Germany, USA: Creative Differences, History Films, Ministère de la Culture et de la Communication
Producers: Adrienne Ciuffo, Erik Nelson
Screenplay: Werner Herzog
Photography: Peter Zeitlinger
Editors: Joe Bini, Maya Hawke
Narrated by Werner Herzog
90 minutes

Happy People: A Year in the Taiga (2010)
Codirected by Dmitry Vasyukov
Germany: Studio Babelsberg
Producers: Werner Herzog, Christoph Fisser
Screenplay: Werner Herzog, Dmitry Vasyukov, Rudolph Herzog
Photography: Alexey Matveev
Editor: Joe Bini
Narrated by Werner Herzog
90 minutes

Into the Abyss (2011)
Germany, USA: Creative Differences Productions, Skellig Rock, Spring Films

Producers: Eric Nelson, Andre Singer
Screenplay: Werner Herzog
Photography: Peter Zeitlinger
Editor: Joe Bini
Narrated by Werner Herzog
107 minutes

Ode to the Dawn of Man (2011)
USA: Werner Herzog Filmproduktion
Producer: Werner Herzog
Screenplay: Werner Herzog
Photography: Werner Herzog
Editor: Maya Hawke
39 minutes

On Death Row (2012–13)
Austria, UK, USA: Creative Differences, Skellig Rock, Spring Films
Producers: Eric Nelson, Lucki Stipetic
Screenplay: Werner Herzog
Photography: Peter Zeitlinger
Editor: Joe Bini
Narrated by Werner Herzog
Eight episodes, 49 minutes each

From One Second to the Next (2013)
Germany, USA: AT&T, Verizon Communications, Sprint Mobile TV
Producers: George Sholley, Julie Collins
Screenplay: Werner Herzog
Photography: Peter Zeitlinger
Editor: Joe Bini
Narrated by Werner Herzog
34 minutes

Queen of the Desert (2015)
USA, Morocco: Benaroya Pictures, H Films, Raslan Company of America
Producers: Michael Benaroya, Cassian Elwes
Screenplay: Werner Herzog
Photography: Peter Zeitlinger
Editor: Joe Bini
Cast: Nicole Kidman (Gertrude Bell), James Franco (Henry Cadogan)
128 minutes

Into the Inferno (2016)
Germany, UK, Canada: Matter of Fact Media, Spring Films, Werner Herzog Filmproduktion, Momentous Events
Producer: Lucki Stipetic
Screenplay: Werner Herzog
Photography: Peter Zeitlinger
Editor: Joe Bini
Narrated by Werner Herzog
104 minutes

Lo and Behold: Reveries of the Connected World (2016)
USA: Saville Productions
Producer: Werner Herzog
Screenplay: Werner Herzog
Photography: Peter Zeitlinger
Editor: Marco Capalbo
Narrated by Werner Herzog
98 minutes

Salt and Fire (2016)
Germany, USA: Skellig Rock, Construction Film, Benaroya Pictures
Producers: Werner Herzog, Pablo Cruz
Screenplay: Tom Bissell, Werner Herzog
Photography: Peter Zeitlinger
Editor: Joe Bini
Cast: Veronica Ferres (Laura Sommerfeld), Michael Shannon (Matt Riley)
98 minutes

Meeting Gorbachev (2018)
UK, Germany, USA: Werner Herzog Filmproduktion
Producers: Svetlana Palmer, Lucki Stipetic
Screenplay: Werner Herzog
Photography: Yuri Burak
Editor: Michael Ellis
Cast: Werner Herzog, Michael Gorbachev
90 minutes

Bibliography

Academia Errante. 1963. *Lope de Aguirre descuartizado*. San Sebastián, Spain: Auñamendi.

Acosta Montoro, José. 1967. *Peregrino de la ira: Narración dramática sobre la aventura de Lope de Aguirre*. San Sebastián, Spain: Auñamendi.

Aguilera Skvirsky, Salomé. 2011. "Quilombo and Utopia: The Aesthetic of Labor in Linduarte Noronha's *Aruanda* (1960)." *Journal of Latin American Cultural Studies* 20, no. 3: 233–60.

———. 2017. "Realism, Documentary and the Process Genre in Early New Latin American Cinema." In *The Routledge Companion to Latin American Cinema*. Edited by Marvin D'Lugo, Ana López, and Laura Podalsky, 119–32. London: Routledge.

———. 2020. *The Process Genre: Cinema and the Aesthetic of Labor*. Durham, NC: Duke University Press.

Akomfrah, John. 2014. "The Politics of Mourning." Interview with Stoffel Debuysere. *Diagonal Thoughts*, June 24. http://www.diagonalthoughts.com/?p=2115.

Alpern, Stanley. 2011. *Amazons of Black Sparta: The Women Warriors of Dahomey*. New York: NYU Press.

Ames, Eric. 2009. *Carl Hagenbeck's Empire of Entertainments*. Seattle: University of Washington Press.

———. 2012a. "The Case of Herzog: Re-opened." In *A Companion to Werner Herzog*. Edited by Brad Prager, 393–415. Malden, MA: Wiley-Blackwell.

———. 2012b. *Ferocious Reality: Documentary According to Werner Herzog*. Minneapolis: University of Minnesota Press.

———, ed. 2014. *Werner Herzog: Interviews*. Jackson: University Press of Mississippi.

Anderson, John Lee. 2016. "An Isolate Tribe Emerges from the Rain Forest." *New Yorker*, August 8 and 15.

Araujo, Ana Lucia. 2007. "Political Uses of Memories of Slavery in the Republic of Benin." *History in Focus*. Issue 12. http://www.history.ac.uk/ihr/Focus/Slavery/articles/araujo.html#24t.

———. 2011. "Forgetting and Remembering the Atlantic Slave Trade: The Legacy of Brazilian Slave Merchant Francisco Félix de Souza." In *Crossing Memories: Slavery and African Diaspora*. Edited by Ana Lucia Araujo, Mariana Candido, and Paul Lovejoy, 79–103. Trenton, NJ: Africa World Press.

Ascárate, Richard John. 2007. "'Have You Ever Seen a Shrunken Head?': The Early Modern Roots of Ecstatic Truth in Werner Herzog's *Fitzcarraldo*." *PMLA* 122, no. 2: 483–501.

Barber, Stephen. 2014. *Performance Projections: Film and the Body in Action*. London: Reaktion.

Baroja, Pío. (1911) 2010. *Las inquietudes de Shanti Andía*. Mexico City: Porrúa.

Bataillon, Marcel. 1963. "The Pizarrist Rebellion: The Birth of Latin America." Translated by Nora McKeon. *Diogenes* 11, no. 43: 46–62.

Bay, Edna. 1998. *Wives of the Leopard: Gender, Politics, and Culture in the Kingdom of Dahomey*. Charlottesville: University of Virginia Press.

Beauducel, François. 2006. "À propos de la polémique '*Soufrière 1976*' . . ." *Institut de Physique du Globe de Paris*. Updated 2015. http://www.ipgp.fr/~beaudu/soufriere/forum76.html.

Beauducel, François, and Pascale Besson. 2008. "The Review of the 1975–1977 Eruption of La Soufrière de Guadeloupe (FWI)." Paper presented at the American Geophysical Union fall meeting, November 15–19.

Beckman, Ericka. 2012. *Capital Fictions: The Literature of Latin America's Export Age*. Minneapolis: University of Minnesota Press.

Beller, Jonathan. 2006. *The Cinematic Mode of Production: Attention Economy and the Society of the Spectacle*. Lebanon, NH: Dartmouth College Press.

Benelli, Dana. 1986. "The Cosmos and Its Discontents." In *The Films of Werner Herzog: Between Mirage and History*. Edited by Timothy Corrigan, 89–103. New York: Methuen.

Bereson, Ruth. 2002. *The Operatic State: Cultural Policy and the Opera House*. New York: Routledge.

Bernasconi, Robert, and Tommy Lee Lott, eds. 2000. *The Idea of Race*. New York: Hackett.

Bissell, Tom. 2006. "The Secret Mainstream: Contemplating the Mirages of Werner Herzog." *Harper's Magazine*, December, 69–82.

Bost, David. 1996. "Historians of the Colonial Period: 1620–1700." In *The Cambridge History of Latin American Literature*. Edited by Roberto González Echevarría and Enrique Pupo-Walker, 143–90. Cambridge: Cambridge University Press.

Brady, Emily. 2013. *The Sublime in Modern Philosophy: Aesthetics, Ethics, and Nature*. London: Cambridge University Press.

Briceño Picón, Adolfo. (c. 1890) 1994. *El tirano Aguirre*. In *Antología del teatro venezolano del siglo XIX*. Edited by José de la Cruz Uzcátegui. Mérida, Mex.: Dirección de Cultura del Estado.

Brown, Michael F. 1982. "Art of Darkness." *The Progressive*, August, 20–21.

Brown, Michael F., and Eduardo Fernández. 1991. *War of Shadows: The Struggle for Utopia in the Peruvian Amazon*. Berkeley: University of California Press.

Buci-Glucksmann, Christine. 1994. *Baroque Reason: The Aesthetics of Modernity.* New York: Sage.

Buck-Morss, Susan. 2000. "Hegel and Haiti." *Critical Inquiry* 26, no. 4, 821–65.

Buder, Emily. 2015. "'Reconquest of the Useless' Filmmakers on the Legacy of 'Fitzcarraldo' and Werner Herzog's Directing 'Problems.'" *IndieWire*, December 12. http://www.indiewire.com/2015/12/reconquest-of-the-useless-filmmakers-on-the-legacy-of-fitzcarraldo-and-werner-herzogs-directing-problems-45196/.

Bush, Andrew. 2012. "Remembering Faust in Argentina." In *Goethe's Faust and Cultural Memory: Comparatist Interfaces*. Edited by Lorna Fitzsimmons, 91–106. Bethlehem, PA: Lehigh University Press.

Canby, Vincent. 1977. "Film: Herzog's Pilgrims Hit the U.S. Road." *New York Times*, July 13.

Carvajal, Gaspar de. 1955. *Relación del nuevo descubrimiento del famoso rio Grande de las Amazonas*. São Paulo: Biblioteca Americana.

Carré, Valérie. 2007. *La quête anthropologique de Werner Herzog: Documentaires et fictions en regard*. Strasbourg, Fr.: Presses Universitaires de Strasbourg.

Carter, Erica. 2012. "Werner Herzog's African Sublime." In *A Companion to Werner Herzog*. Edited by Brad Prager, 329–55. London: Wiley.

Casement, Roger. 1904. *Report from His Majesty's Consul at Boma Respecting the Administration of the Independent State of the Congo*. London: His Majesty's Stationery Office.

Castellanos, Evencio. 1966. *El tirano Aguirre: Oratorio profano*. Caracas, Venez.

Chatwin, Bruce. 1980. *The Viceroy of Ouidah*. New York: Penguin.

———. 2015. "New Again: Werner Herzog." *Interview*, June 17. https://www.interviewmagazine.com/film/new-again-werner-herzog.

Christiansen, Rupert. 2009. "Werner Herzog Takes Opera into a Whole New Aria." *The Telegraph*. February 6. http://www.telegraph.co.uk/culture/music/opera/4540003/Werner-Herzog-takes-opera-into-a-whole-new-aria.html.

Cobb, Jasmine Nichole. 2014. "Directed by Himself: Steve McQueen's *12 Years a Slave*." *American Literary History* 26, no. 2: 339–46.

Corrigan, Timothy, ed. 1986. *The Films of Werner Herzog: Between Mirage and History*. New York: Methuen.

Cortés, Hernán. (1519–26) 2005. *Cartas de relación*. Mexico City: Porrua.

Crown, Daniel. 2009. "*Stroszek* and the Death of Ian Curtis." Posted in *Wonderchroma*, Accessed February 20, 2017. https://disordertc.wordpress.com/2015/05/17/stroszek-and-the-death-of-ian-curtis/.

Csicsery, G. P. 1985. "Ballad of the Little Soldier: Werner Herzog in a Political Hall of Mirrors." *Film Quarterly* 39, no. 2: 7–15.

Davidson, John. 1993. "As Others Put Plays upon the Stage: Aguirre, Neocolonialism, and the New German Cinema." *New German Critique* 60 (Autumn): 101–30.

———. 1994. "Contacting the Other: Traces of Migrational Colonialism and the Imperial Agent in Werner Herzog's *Fitzcarraldo*." *Film and History* 24, no. 3: 66–83.

———. 2012. "The Veil Between: Werner Herzog's American TV Documentaries." In *A Companion to Werner Herzog*. Edited by Brad Prager, 416–44. Oxford, UK: Wiley-Blackwell.

Dolkart, Ronald. 1985. "Civilization's Aria: Film as Lore and Opera as Metaphor in Werner Herzog's *Fitzcarraldo*." *Journal of Latin American Lore* 11, no. 2: 125–41.

Duhalde, Eduardo Luis. 1997. *Espejos rotos: El Che y Lope de Aguirre; La ética y los presupuestos de la violencia*. Buenos Aires: Aldaba.

Ebert, Roger. 1979. *Images at the Horizon: A Workshop with Werner Herzog*. Chicago: Facets Multimedia.

Edgerton, Robert. 2000. *Warrior Women: The Amazons of Dahomey and the Nature of War*. New York: Basic.

Elsaesser, Thomas. 1986. "An Anthropologist's Eye: Where the Green Ants Dream." In *The Films of Werner Herzog: Between Mirage and History*. Edited by Timothy Corrigan, 133–56. New York: Methuen.

———. 1989. *New German Cinema: A History*. New Brunswick, NJ: Rutgers University Press.

Enyutin, Victor. 2011. "Werner Herzog's *Stroszek* (1977)—A Surrealistically Comic Parable about European Escapees to American Freedom." *Acting-Out Politics*, June 19. http://www.actingoutpolitics.com/stroszek/.

Fabian, Johannes. 2014. *Time and the Other: How Anthropology Makes Its Object*. New York: Columbia University Press.

Fancelli, Agustí. 1989. "Werner Herzog dirige en Bolonia 'Giovanna d'Arco,' su tercer montaje lírico." *El País*, December 7. https://elpais.com/diario/1989/12/07/cultura/628988409_850215.html.

Fanon, Frantz. 1961. *The Wretched of the Earth*. New York: Grove.

Faudree, Paja. 2015. "Reading the *Requerimiento* Performatively: Speech Acts and the Conquest of the New World." *Colonial Latin American Review* 24, no. 4: 456–78.

Fay, Jennifer. 2013. "Werner Herzog and Preposterous War." *CR* 13, no. 1: 241–64.

Flinn, Caryl. 2004. *The New German Cinema: Music, History, and the Matter of Style*. Berkeley: University of California Press.

Foucault, Michel. 2003. *"Society Must Be Defended": Lectures at the Collège de France, 1975–1976*. Translated by David Macey. New York: Macmillan.

Franco, Jean. 1999. "High-Tech Primitivism: The Representation of Tribal Societies in Feature Films." In *Critical Passions: Selected Essays*, 181–95. Durham, NC: Duke University Press.

Frankfurt, Harry. 2005. *On Bullshit*. Princeton, NJ: Princeton University Press.

Fritze, Ronald. 1985. "Werner Herzog's Adaptation of History in *Aguirre, the Wrath of God*." *Film and History* 15, no. 4 (December): 74–86.

Galeano, Eduardo. 1971. *Las venas abiertas de América Latina*. Mexico City: Siglo XXI.

Gallant, Thomas. 1999. "Brigandage, Piracy, Capitalism, and State-Formation: Transnational Crime from a Historical World-Systems Perspective." In *States and Illegal Practices*. Edited by Josiah Heyman, 25–61. Oxford, UK: Bloomsbury Academic Press.

Galster, Ingrid. 2011. *Aguirre o la posteridad arbitraria: La rebelión del conquistador vasco*. Translated from the German by Oscar Sola. Bogotá: Universidad Javeriana.

Gandy, Matthew. 1996. "Visions of Darkness: The Representation of Nature in the Films of Werner Herzog." *Cultural Geographies* 3, no. 1 (January): 1–21.

García Márquez, Gabriel. 1970. *One Hundred Years of Solitude*. Translated by Gregory Rabassa. New Yorker: Harper and Row.

———. 2015. "Infidencias de García Márquez en Cannes." *Espectador* (Bogotá), 15 May. https://www.elespectador.com/noticias/cultura/infidencias-de-garcia-marquez-cannes-articulo-560619.

Gerbasi, Vicente. 1978. *El tirano Aguirre*. Caracas: Banco de Desarrollo Aguapecuario.

Goodwin, Michael. 1982. "Herzog, the Wrath of God." *American Film*, June, 36–51.

González, Betina, and Joshua Lund. 2012. "Mining the Tropics: Burton's Brazil and the History of Empire." *Qui Parle* 20, no. 2: 249–78.

Gordon, Richard. 2015. *Cinema, Slavery and Brazilian Nationalism*. Austin: University of Texas Press.

Gose, Peter. 1994. *Deathly Waters and Hungry Mountains: Agrarian Ritual and Class Formation in an Andean Town*. Toronto: University of Toronto Press.

Gosling, Maureen, and Les Blank. 1982. "Burden of Dreams." Booklet accompanying DVD.

Gow, Peter. 2016. "Jeronimo's Declaration of Independence: Piro Accounts of Slavery and Freedom." In *Freedom in Practice: Government, Autonomy and Liberty in the Everyday*. Edited by Moises Lino e Silva and Huon Wardle, 121–43. London: Routledge.

Grandin, Greg. 2011. "Reading *The Contours of American History* at Fifty." Introduction to *The Contours of American History*, by William Appleman Williams. London: Verso.

Gray, Andrew. 2004. *Mythology, Spirituality, and History*. Providence, RI: Berghahn.

Greene, Shane. 2004. *Customizing Indigeneity: Paths to a Visionary Politics in Peru*. Palo Alto, CA: Stanford University Press.

Guerrero, Ed. 2012. *Framing Blackness: The African American Image in Film*. Philadelphia: Temple University Press.

Hartman, Saidiya. 1997. *Scenes of Subjection: Terror, Slavery, and Self-making in Nineteenth-Century America*. Oxford: Oxford University Press.

Hauze, Emily. 2009. "Keyed Fantasies: Music, the Accordion and the American Dream in *Stroszek* and *Schultze Gets the Blues*." *German Life and Letters* 62, no. 1: 84–95.

Hazoumé, Paul. 1937. *Le pacte de sang au Dahomey*. Paris: Institut d'ethnologie de Paris.

Hegel, Georg Wilhelm Friedrich. 1837. *The Philosophy of History*. Translated by John Sibree. Kitchener, ON: Batoche.

Heringman, Noah. 2012. "Herzog's *Heart of Glass* and the Sublime of Raw Materials." In *A Companion to Werner Herzog*. Edited by Brad Prager, 256–80. Oxford: Wiley-Blackwell.

Hernández Cava, Felipe, Enrique Breccia, Federico del Barrio, and Ricard Castells. 1989–98. *Lope de Aguirre*. 3 vols. Vitoria, Spain: Ikusager; Barcelona: Edicions de Ponent.

Herzog, Werner. 1999. "Minnesota Declaration: Truth and Fact in Documentary Cinema." *WalkerArt*, April 30. http://www.walkerart.org/magazine/1999/minnesota-declaration-truth-and-fact-in-docum.

———. 2009. *Conquest of the Useless*. Translated by Krishna Winston. New York: Ecco.

———. 2014a. "Cobra Verde." Interview with Jean-Pierre Lavoignat. In Ames 2014, 100–105.

———. 2014b. "*Fitzcarraldo*: A Conversation with Werner Herzog." Interview with Bio Steinborn and Rüdiger von Naso. In Ames 2014, 59–81.

———. 2014c. Interview with Eric de Saint-Angel. In Ames, 2014, 47–51.

———. 2014d. Interview with Kraft Wetzel. In Ames 2014, 29–41.

———. 2014e. "South American Experiences: A Conversation with Werner Herzog on *Aguirre, the Wrath of God*." Interview with Peter Schumann. In Ames 2014, 12–17.

———. 2014f. "Werner Herzog: 'Like a Powerful Dream. . . .'" Interview with Noureddine Ghali. In Ames 2014, 18–23.

———. 2015. *Of Walking in Ice*. Minneapolis: University of Minnesota Press.

Herzog, Werner, and Karen Redrobe. 2007. *On the Ecstasy of Ski-Flying: Werner Herzog in Conversation with Karen Beckman*. Philadelphia: Slought, DVD.

Herzog, Werner, and Jonathan Cott. 1976. "Werner Herzog: Signs of Life." *Rolling Stone*, November 18.

Herzog, Werner, and Paul Cronin. 2002. *Herzog on Herzog*. London: Faber and Faber.

———. 2014. *Werner Herzog: A Guide for the Perplexed*. London: Faber and Faber.

Hoffmann, Hans-Christoph. 1966. *Die Theaterbauten von Fellner und Helmer*. Munich: Prestel.

Huertas Castillo, Beatriz. 2004. *Indigenous Peoples in Isolation in the Peruvian Amazon*. Copenhagen: IWGIA.

Huntley, Henry. 1850. *Seven Years' Service on the Slave Coast of Western Africa*. London: Thomas Curtley Newby.

Hurley, Andrew. 2007. "Whose Dreaming? Intercultural Appropriation, Representations of Aboriginality, and the Process of Film-Making in Werner Herzog's *Where the Green Ants Dream* (1983)." *Studies in Australian Cinema*. 1, no. 2: 175–90.

"Index *Index*." 1980. *Index on Censorship*, 9.2: 66–75.

Jay, Martin. 1993. *Downcast Eyes: The Denigration of Vision in Twentieth-Century French Thought*. Berkeley: University of California Press.

Johnson, Laurie. 2016. *Forgotten Dreams: Revisiting Romanticism in the Cinema of Werner Herzog*. New York: Camden House.

Jones, Kent. 2012. "Seconds." *Film Comment* 48, no. 1: 28–33.

Jos, Emiliano. 1927. *La expedición de Ursúa al Dorado: La rebelión de Lope de Aguirre y el itinerario de los "Marañones" según los documentos del Archivo de Indias y varios manuscritos inéditos*. Huesca, Spain: Campo.

Kant, Immanuel. 1914. *Critique of Judgment*. Translated by J. H. Bernard. London: Macmillan.

Kimmelman, Michael. 2008. "From Berlin's Hole of Forgottenness, a Spell of Songs." *New York Times*, December 24.

Kluge, Alexander, Edgar Reitz, and Haro Senft. 1988. "The Oberhausen Manifesto." *West German Filmmakers on Film: Visions and Voices*. Edited and translated by Eric Rentschler. New York: Holmes and Meier.

Koepnick, Lutz. 1993. "Colonial Forestry: Sylvan Politics in Werner Herzog's *Aguirre* and *Fitzcarraldo*." *New German Critique* 60 (Autumn): 133–59.

Köppen, Manuel. 2012. "Digeridoo, or the Search for the Origin of the Self: Werner Herzog's *Where the Green Ants Dream* and Bruce Chatwin's *The Songlines*." In *The Werner Herzog Companion*. Edited by Brad Prager, 356–70. London: Blackwell.

Kotnik, Vlado. 2013. "The Adaptability of Opera: When Different Social Agents Come to Common Ground." *International Review of the Aesthetics and Sociology of Music* 44, no. 2: 303–42.

Lastres, Juan. 1942. *Lope de Aguirre, el rebelde: Estudio histórico-psicológico*. Buenos Aires: El Ateneo.

Law, Robin. 1993. "The Amazons of Dahomey." *Paideuma: Mitteilungen zur Kulturkunde* 39: 245–60.

———. 2004a. "Francisco Felix de Souza in West Africa, 1820–1849." In *Enslaving Connections: Western Africa and Brazil during the Era of Slavery*. Edited by José Curto and Paul Lovejoy, 187–211. Amherst, MA: Humanity.

———. 2004b. *Ouidah: The Social History of a West African Slaving 'Port,' 1727–1892*. Columbus: Ohio State University Press.

Leppert, Richard. 2007. "Opera, Aesthetic Violence, and the Imposition of Modernity: *Fitzcarraldo*." In *Beyond the Soundtrack: Representing Music in Cinema*. Edited by Daniel Goldmark, Lawrence Kramer, and Richard Leppert, 99–119. Berkeley: University of California Press.

———. 2015. *Aesthetic Technologies of Modernity, Subjectivity and Nature: Opera, Phonograph, Film*. Berkeley: University of California Press.

Lévi-Strauss, Claude. (1956) 1977. "The Three Humanisms." *Structural Anthropology* 2: 271–74. Reprinted 1977.

———. (1955) 2012. *Tristes Tropiques*. Translated by John Weightman and Doreen Weightman. New York: Penguin.

López, Ana M., Mike Gonzalez, and Daniel Balderston. 2000. *Encyclopedia of Contemporary Latin American and Caribbean Cultures*. London: Routledge.

Madan, Aarti Smith. 2017. *Lines of Geography in Latin American Narrative: National Territory, National Literature*. New York: Palgrave.

Madan, Aarti Smith. 2013. "Werner Herzog as Double Translator: Thinking from Subalternity in *Aguirre, the Wrath of God*." *Dissidences* 5, no. 9: Article 3. https://digitalcommons.bowdoin.edu/dissidences/vol5/iss9/3.

Magaldi, Cristina. 2006. "Two Musical Representations of Brazil: Carlos Gomes and Villa-Lobos." In *Brazil in the Making: Facets of National Identity*. Edited by Carmen Nava and Ludwig Lauerhass, 205–28. New York: Rowman and Littlefield.

Mahar, William John. 1999. *Behind the Burnt Cork Mask: Early Blackface Minstrelsy and Antebellum American Popular Culture*. Urbana: University of Illinois Press.

Mampel González, Elena. 1981. *Lope de Aguirre Cronicas, 1559–1561*. Barcelona: Edicions Universitat Barcelona.

Maravall, José Antonio. 1976. *La cultura del Barroco: Análisis de una estructura histórica*. Barcelona: Ariel.

Mariátegui, José Carlos. 1928. *Siete ensayos de interpretación de la realidad peruana*. Lima: Minerva.

Martin, Michael, and David Wall. 2013. "The Politics of Cine-Memory: Signifying Slavery in the History Film." In *A Companion to the Historical Film*. Edited by Robert Rosenstone and Constantin Parvulescu, 445–67. London: Wiley.

Marx, Karl. 1972. *The Karl Marx Library*. Vol. 2, *On America and the Civil War*. New York: McGraw-Hill.

McCole, John. 1993. *Walter Benjamin and the Antinomies of Tradition*. Ithaca, NY: Cornell University Press.

McKain, Scott. 2015. "My Most Distinctive Thanksgiving (the One I Spent with Werner Herzog)." Posted in Spreaker. Accessed February 20, 2017. https://www.spreaker.com/user/scottmckain/my-most-distinctive-thanksgiving-with-we.

———. 2016. "The Thanksgiving I Spent with Werner Herzog." Accessed February 20, 2017. Posted in CreateDistinction. https://createdistinction.com/the-thanksgiving-i-spent-with-werner-herzog/.

Nagib, Lucia. 2012. "Physicality, Difference and the Challenge of Representation." In *A Companion to Werner Herzog*. Edited by Brad Prager, 58–79. London: Wiley.

Neira, Hernán, Juan Manuel Fierro and Fernando Viveros. 2006. "Lope de Aguirre: elementos para una teoría del mito de la conquista." *Estudios Filológicos*, 41: 145–63.

Nietzsche, Friedrich. (1873) 2008. "On Truth and Lies in a Nonmoral Sense." In *Truth: Engagements across Philosophical Traditions*. Edited by David Wood and José Medina, 14–25. New York: Wiley.

Norris, Renee. 2007. "Opera and the Mainstreaming of Blackface Minstrelsy." *Journal of the Society for American Music* 1, no. 3: 341–65.

Orum, Thomas. 2001. "The Women of the Open Door: Jews in the Belle Époque Amazonian Demimonde, 1890–1920." *Shofar* 19, no. 3: 86–99.

Oteiza, Antonio de. 1972. *22 notas sobre Lope de Aguirre*. La Coruña, Spain: Del Castro.

Otero Silva, Miguel. 1982. *Lope de Aguirre: Prínicipe de la libertad*. Caracas: Casa de las Américas.

Palma, Ricardo. (1872—1910) 2007. *Tradiciones Peruanas*. In the public domain. Project Gutenberg, http://www.gutenberg.org/ebooks/21282.

Páramo Bonilla, Carlos Guillermo. 2009. *Lope de Aguirre, o la vorágine de Occidente. Selva, mito y racionalidad.* Bogotá: Universidad Externado de Colombia.

Pardo, Isaac. 1957. *El tirano Aguirre: Estampas para una cantata*. Caracas: Revista Nacional de Cultura.

Parkes, Jason. With Julian Cope. 2008. "Herzog on Ian Curtis (and Lynch)." *Julian Cope Presents Head Heritage*, July 30. https://www.headheritage.co.uk/headtohead/unsung/topic/48706/flat/.

Pastor, Beatriz. 1992. *The Armature of Conquest: Spanish Accounts of the Discovery of America, 1492–1589*. Palo Alto, CA: Stanford University Press.

Pastor, Beatriz, and Sergio Callau. 2011. *Lope de Aguirre y la rebelión de los marañones*. Madrid: Castalia.

Peucker, Brigitte. 1984. "Werner Herzog in Quest of the Sublime." In *New German Filmmakers: From Oberhausen through the 1970s*. Edited by Klaus Phillips, 168–93. New York: Friedrich Ungar.

Polyani, Karl. 1966. *Dahomey and the Slave Trade: An Analysis of an Archaic Economy*. Seattle: University of Washington Press.

Posse, Abel. 1978. *Daimón*. Translated by Sarah Arvio. New York: Atheneum.

Prager, Brad. 2004. "The Face of the Bandit: Racism and the Slave Trade in Herzog's *Cobra Verde*. *Film Criticism* 28, no. 3: 2–20.

———. 2007. *The Cinema of Werner Herzog: Aesthetic Ecstasy and Truth*. London: Wallflower.

———, ed. 2012. *A Companion to Werner Herzog*. London: Wiley.

———. "Werner Herzog" (web page). *Oxford Bibliographies: Cinema and Media Studies*. Last updated September 25, 2018. doi 10.1093/OBO/9780199791286–0141.

Puar, Jasbir. 2015. "The 'Right' to Maim: Disablement and Inhumanist Biopolitics in Palestine." *Borderlands* 14, no. 1: 1–27.

Rama, Angel. 1984. *La ciudad letrada*. San Juan: Ediciones del Norte.

Ramos, Demetrio. 1958. "Lope de Aguirre en Cartagena de Indias y su primera rebelión." *Revista de Indias* 18, no. 73: 528–42.

Reber, Dierdra. 2016. *Coming to Our Senses: Affect and an Order of Things for Global Culture*. New York: Columbia University Press.

Rentschler, Eric. 1981–82. "American Friends and New German Cinema: Patterns of Reception." *New German Critique* 24–25 (Autumn—Winter): 7–35.

———. 1984. "How American Is It: The US as Image and Imaginary in German Film." *German Quarterly* 57, no. 4 (Autumn): 603–20.

———. 2014. "The Politics of Vision: Herzog's *Heart of Glass*." In *The Films of Werner Herzog: Between Mirage and History*. Edited by Timothy Corrigan, 159–82. London: Routledge.

Reyna, Ernesto. 1942. *Fitzcarrald: El rey del caucho*. Lima: P. Barrantes.

Ribeiro Sanches, Manuela. 2015. "Memory, Authenticity and (the Absence of) Ruins: Resonances between Werner Herzog and John Akomfrah." *Black Camera* 6, no. 2 (Spring): 94–111.

Rivera, José Eustasio. 1985. *La vorágine*. Caracas: Ayacucho.

Rocha, Glauber. 1965. *Uma estética da fome*. http://www.vermelho.org.br/noticia/319175–1.

Romero Rey, Sandro. 2008. "La ira de dios: Recuerdos de Klaus Kinski in Kolombia." *El Malpensante*, no. 86. https://www.elmalpensante.com/articulo/29/la_ira_de_dios.

Roselli, John. 1990. "The Opera Business and the Italian Immigrant Community in Latin America 1820–1930: The Example of Buenos Aires." *Past and Present* 127, no. 1: 155–82.

Rost, Andreas, ed. 1985. *Werner Herzog in Bamberg*. Munich: Kaltenecker.

Said, Edward. 1978. *Orientalism*. New York: Knopf.

———. 1993. *Culture and Imperialism*. New York: Knopf.

Sala, Gabriel. 1897. *Apuntes de viaje*: Lima: Imprenta la Industria.

Scheper-Hughes, Nancy. 1996. "Theft of Life: The Globalization of Organ Stealing Rumours." *Anthropology Today* 12, no. 3: 3–11.

Schultz, William Todd. 2013. *Torment Saint: The Life of Elliot Smith*. New York: Bloomsbury.

Schwarz, Roberto. 1973. "As idéias fora do lugar." *Estudos Cebrap* 3: 151–61.

———. 1992. "Misplaced Ideas." In *Misplaced Ideas: Essays on Brazilian Culture*. Translated by John Gledson. London: Verso.

———. 2001. *A Master on the Periphery of Capitalism*. Durham, NC: Duke University Press.

Sell, Michael. 2014. *Theatres and Concert Halls of Fellner and Helmer*. Cambridge, UK: Entertainment Technology Press.

Sender, Ramón. 1964. *La aventura equinoccial de Lope de Aguirre, antiepopeya*. New York: Las Américas.

Serier, Jean-Baptiste. 2000. *Les barons du caoutchouc*. Paris: Karthala.

Sheehan, Paul. 2008. "Against the Image: Herzog and the Troubling Politics of the Screen Animal." *SubStance* 37, no. 3: 117–36.

Sieff, Kevin. 2018. "An African Country Reckons with Its History of Selling Slaves." *Washington Post* online, January 29.

Simon, John. 1977. "German Measliness." *New York*, September 5, 70–74.

Singer, Alan. 1986. "Comprehending Appearances: Werner Herzog's Ironic Sublime." *The Films of Werner Herzog: Between Mirage and History*, Edited by Timothy Corrigan, 183–205. New York: Methuen.

———. 2012. *Herzog and Human Destiny: The Philosophical Purposiveness of the Filmmaker; A Companion to Werner Herzog*. Edited by Brad Prager, 566–86. London: Blackwell.

Snowman, Daniel. 2009. *The Gilded Stage: A Social History of Opera*. London: Atlantic.

Southey, Robert. 1821. *The Expedition of Orsua, and the Crimes of Aguirre*. Philadelphia: Hickman and Hazzard.

Spiegel Online. 1979. "Ein Gringo in Urwald." September 10. http://www.spiegel.de/spiegel/print/d-39909494.html.

Stevenson, Robert. 1973. *Foundations of New World Opera*. Lima: Ediciones Cultura.

Stewart, Rory. 2007. "Queen of the Quagmire." *New York Review of Books*, October 25,

Stiles, Victoria. 1989. "Fact and Fiction: Nature's Endgame in Werner Herzog's *Aguirre, the Wrath of God*." *Literature & Film Quarterly* 17, no. 3: 161–67.

Stone, Cynthia. 2005. "Aguirre Goes to the Movies: Twentieth-Century Visions of Colonial-Era Relaciones." *Chasqui* 34, no. 2 (special issue): 24–35. doi:10.2307/29742041.

Strickrodt, Silke. 2004. "Afro-Brazilians of the Western Slave Coast of the Nineteenth Century." In *Western Africa and Brazil during the Era of Slavery*. Edited by José Curto and Paul Lovejoy, 213–44. Amherst, MA: Humanity.

Survival International Review. 1979a. "Peru: Peruvian Indians Threatened and Imprisoned for Refusing to Collaborate with German Film-Maker, Werner Herzog." 4.3, no. 27: 28–29.

———. 1979b. "Peru: Werner Herzog and the Aguaruna Indians of Peru." 4.4, no. 28: 31–32.

———. 1981. "Werner Herzog Up to His Old Tricks with Peruvian Indians." 6.3, no. 35, and 6.4, no. 36: 110.

———. 1982. "Peru. Anti-Fitzcarraldo." 39–41, no. 42: 94–95.

Thomas, Hugh. 1997. *The Slave Trade: The Story of the Atlantic Slave Trade: 1440–1870*. New York: Simon and Schuster.

Torres, Carlos Arturo. 1989. *Lope de Aguirre*. Bogotá: Arango.

Trouillot, Michel-Rolph. 1995. *Silencing the Past: Power and the Production of History*. New York: Beacon.

Turner, Frederick Jackson. (1893) 1921a. *The Frontier in American History*. New York: Holt.

———. (1893) 1921b. *The Significance of the Frontier in American Society*. New York: Holt. Gutenberg edition available at http://www.gutenberg.org/files/22994/22994-h/22994-h.htm.

Uslar Pietri, Arturo. (1947) 2004. *El camino de El dorado*. Caracas: El Nacional.

Valle-Inclán, Ramón María del. (1926) 1987. *Tirano Banderas: Novela de tierra caliente*. Mexico City: Colihue.

Varese, Stefano. 2004. *Salt of the Mountain: Campa Asháninka History and Resistance in the Peruvian Jungle*. Norman: University of Oklahoma Press.

Vargas Llosa, Mario. 2008. *La casa verde*. Madrid: Punto de Lectura.

———. 2010. *El sueño del celta*. Madrid: Alfaguara.

Veblen, Thorstein. 1915. *Imperial Germany and the Industrial Revolution*. London: Macmillan.

———. 1923. "The Country Town." *Freeman*, July 11, 417–20; July 18, 440–43.

Vega Herrera, César. 2000. "La cabeza de Lope de Aguirre." In *Dramaturgia nacional 2000*. Edited by Sergio Arrau. Lima: Instituto Nacional de Cultura.

Villiers, Jacques de. 2012. "Myth, Environment and Ideology in the German Jungle of *Aguirre, the Wrath of God*." *Senses of Cinema* 63 (July). http://sensesofcinema.com/2012/feature-articles/myth-environment-and-ideology-in-the-german-jungle-of-aguirre-the-wrath-of-god/.

Von Trier, Lars, and Thomas Vinterberg. 1995. "The Dogma 95 Manifesto and Vow of Chastity." *POV* 10: 6–7.

Wahl, Chris. 2012. "'I Don't Like the Germans': Even Herzog Started in Bavaria." In *A Companion to Werner Herzog*. Edited by Brad Prager, 233–55. Malden, MA: Wiley-Blackwell.

Waller, Gregory. 1981. "*Aguirre, the Wrath of God*: History, Theater and the Camera." *South Atlantic Review* 46, no. 2: 55–69.

Wallerstein, Immanuel. 1976. "American Slavery and the Capitalist World-Economy." *American Journal of Sociology* 81, no. 5: 1199–1213.

Weidhauer, Friedemann. 2003. "From 'World Conspiracy' to 'Cultural Imperialism': The History of Anti-Plutocratic Rhetoric in German Film." In *The Terministic Screen: Rhetorical Perspectives on Film*. Edited by David Blakesley, 190–210. Carbondale: Southern Illinois University Press.

Weismantel, Mary. 2001. *Cholas and Pishtacos: Stories of Race and Sex in the Andes*. Chicago: University of Chicago Press.
Wilderson, Frank. 2010. *Red, White & Black: Cinema and the Structure of US Antagonisms*. Durham, NC: Duke University Press.
Williams, William Appleman. (1955) 1992. "The Frontier Thesis and American Foreign Policy." In *A William Appleman Williams Reader*, Edited by Henry Berger, 89–104. Chicago: Ivan R. Dee.
———, ed. 2011. *The Contours of American History*. London: Verso.
Zamora, Lois Parkinson (2006). *The Inordinate Eye: New World Baroque and Latin American Fiction*. Chicago: University of Chicago Press.

Films Discussed in the Essay

Allen, Woody. *Love and Death*, 1975.
Bauducel, Éric. *Tazieff/Allègre: La guerre des volcans*, 2015.
Blank, Les. *Always for Pleasure*, 2014.
Blank, Les. *Burden of Dreams*, 1982.
Blank, Les. *Werner Herzog Eats His Shoe*, 1980.
Bollaín, Icíar. *También la lluvia*, 2011.
Boorman, John. *The Emerald Forest*, 1984.
Bridges, James. *Urban Cowboy*, 1980.
Cabello, Ernesto. *Hija de la laguna*, 2015.
Chaplin, Charlie. *Modern Times*, 1936.
Chomsky, Marvin, et al. *Roots*,1977.
Cimino, Michael. *Heaven's Gate*, 1980.
Coogler, Ryan. *Black Panther*, 2018.
Coppola, Francis Ford. *Apocalypse Now*, 1979.
Corbijn, Anton. *Control*, 2007.
Eisholz, Lutz. *Bruno der Schwarze—Es blies ein Jäger wohl in sein Horn*, 1970.
Fleischer, Richard. *Mandingo*, 1975.
Fleming, Victor. *Gone with the Wind*, 1939.
Gaviria, Víctor. *La vendedora de rosas*, 1998.
Giral, Sergio. *El otro Francisco*, 1974.
Golder, Herb. *Ballad of a Righteous Merchant*, 2017.
González Iñárritu, Alejandro. *Babel*, 2006.
González Iñárritu, Alejandro. *Biutiful*, 2010.
Griffith, D. W. *Birth of a Nation*, 1915.
Gruber, Steff. *Location Africa*, 1987.
Guerra, Ciro. *El abrazo de la serpiente*, 2016.
Guerra, Ruy. *Os fuzis*, 1964.
Gutiérrez Aléa, Tomás. *La última cena*, 1976.
Herzog: See Filmography.
Hibbs, Jesse. *To Hell and Back*, 1955.

Jacopetti, Gualtiero, and Franco Prosperi. *Addio Zio Tom*, 1971.
Joffé, Roland. *The Mission*, 1986.
Jones, Chuck. *What's Opera, Doc?*, 1957.
Kluge, Alexander. *The Power of Emotion*, 1983.
Lang, Fritz. *Metropolis*, 1927.
Lockhart, Sharon. *Teatro Amazonas*, 1999.
Martel, Lucrecia. *Zama*, 2017.
McQueen, Steve. *12 Years a Slave*, 2013.
Morris, Errol. *Standard Operating Procedure*, 2008.
Nelson, Eric. *Dinotasia*, 2014.
Oppenheimer, Joshua. *The Act of Killing*, 2012.
Pereira dos Santos, Nelson. *Vidas secas*, 1963.
Pollard, Harry. *Uncle Tom's Cabin*, 1927.
Pontecorvo, Gillo. *Burn!*, 1969.
Pressman, Sam. *Reconquest of the Useless*, 2015.
Rakich, Andy. *Tears of God*, 2007.
Robbins, Tim. *Dead Man Walking*, 1995.
Rocha, Glauber. *Antonio das Mortes*, 1969.
Rocha, Glauber. *Deus e o diabo na terra do sol*, 1964.
Saura, Carlos. *El Dorado*, 1988.
Sayles, John. *Men with Guns*, 1997.
Spielberg, Steven. *Amistad*, 1997.
Tarentino, Quentin. *Django Unchained*, 2012.
Von Trier, Lars. *Manderlay*, 2005.
Weisenborn, Christian and Erwin Keusch. *I Am My Films*, 1979.
Weisenborn, Christian. *I Am My Films, part 2: 30 Years Later*, 2010.
Winding Refn, Nicolas. *Valhalla Rising*, 2009.
Winterbottom, Michael. *24 Hour Party People*, 2002.
Wood, Sam, and Edmund Goulding. *A Night at the Opera*, 1935.

index

Achebe, Chinua, 154
Addio Zio Tom, 143
Adjani, Isabelle, 95, 180
Aguilera Skvirsky, Salomé, 129–30, 138, 165
Aguirre, der Zorn Gottes, 2, 4, 5, 9, 10, 95, 98, 152, 175, 190–91n18, 230; actors in, 11–12; budget for, 17; chaos at start of, 11; comparisons to *Signs of Life* and *Even Dwarfs Started Small,* 33–34; DVD version of, 188n7–8; form-content logic of hardship in, 17–18; frontier thesis of, 51–88; as Herzog's breakthrough film, 12; historical points of reference to, 40–41; historical setting of, 28–33, 62–63; human psychology explored in, 38–40; indigenous figures in, 41–42, 193n41; interpretive key in last part of, 47–48; kabuki battle scenes in, 42–44; landscape as character in, 18–22; language of excess in, 20–22; monkeys in, 10, 49–50, 84; opening scenes of, 13–17; other films on same topic as, 190–91n24; pessimism in, 54; plot of, 12–13; political climate of Peru and, 46–47; political critique in, 45–46; small voice of conquest in, 10–50; Spanish empire explored in, 34–38; territorialization and sovereignty in, 44–45; in trilogy, 140–41
Akomfrah, John, 170
Allègre, Claude, 97
Allende, Salvador, 47
Alvarado, Velasco, 60
American Dad, 2
American dream, the, 75
American society: capitalism in, 56–57, 71–74; frontier era in, 64–73, 86–87, 198n70; Herzog's portrayals of, 87–88, 195–96n56, 196n57
Ames, Eric, 8
Amistad, 153
Amnesty International, 120, 205–6n118
Apocalypse Now, 101
Arcadio Buendía, José, 48
Atkins, Chet, 63, 70, 78, 82
Auch Zwerge haben klein angefangen, 25–26

Bad Lieutenant: Port of Call New Orleans, 179, 181
Bakhtin, Mikhail, 134
Bale, Christian, 180–81, 232
Ballad of a Righteous Merchant, 7
Ballad of the Little Soldier, 147
Behinderte Zukunft (*Handicapped Future*), 55
Bell, Gertrude, 182
Beller, Jonathan, 173
Bells from the Deep, 178
Berlin International Film Festival, 23
Bierbichler, Josef, 181
Birth of a Nation, 143, 216n174
Bissell, Tom, 59
Blank, Les, 103, 120, 124, 126, 130, 134, 230
Bogart, Humphrey, 231
Bohorquez, Huerequeque Enrique, 100
Bokassa, Jean-Bédel, 144
Bollaín, Icíar, 121
Bonanza, 67, 87, 198n70

Boondocks, The, 2, 179
Boorman, John, 121
Bowie, David, 180
Brando, Marlon, 85, 231
Brecht, Bertolt, 230
Bronson, Charles, 231
Brown, Michael F., 135–36
Browning, Tod, 146
Bruno der Schwarze—Es blies ein Jäger wohl in sein Horn, 196–97n62
Burden of Dreams, 103, 120, 124, 126, 134, 136, 142, 230
Burn! 143, 153
Burns, Ken, 179

Cage, Nicholas, 179, 180–81
capitalism: American, 56–57, 71–74; in *Cobra Verde*, 161–68; de Souza and, 149–51; Eurocentrism and, 128, 162–63; in *Fitzcarraldo*, 104–5, 113–14; slavery and, 161–68; in *Stroszek*, 71–83
Cardinale, Claudia, 100, 180
Carmen, Eric, 98
Carré, John le, 120
Cartas de relación, 46
Carty, Linda, 186
Caruso, Enrico, 101–3, 105–6, 108, 122–23
Cave of Forgotten Dreams, 180
Cerro Torre: Schrei aus Stein (*Scream of Stone*), 99
Chaplin, Charlie, 229
Chatwin, Bruce, 152, 180, 230
Churchill, Winston, 182
Cimino, Michael, 101
Cinema of Werner Herzog, The, 10
classroom films, 55
Cobra Verde, 5, 10, 23, 179, 181; capitalism explored in, 161–64; criticisms of, 153–57; de Souza portrayed in, 149–50, 158, 214–15nn168–69, 217–18n182; narrative structure of, 140–41; plot of, 141; production problems of, 142–43; racism explored in, 153, 158–60, 161; scenes set in Africa in, 168–74, 218n183; sexual violence in, 160; as slavery film, 143–51, 158–68; in trilogy, 140–42
Colbert, Stephen, 33
Cold War cultural politics, 40–41, 87
Companion to Werner Herzog, 6
Conquest of the Useless, 7, 120
Conrad, Joseph, 230
Cooper, Gary, 231
Coppola, Francis Ford, 101
crisis of the image, 133–34
Critique of Judgment, 18
Curtis, Ian, 84

Dafoe, Willem, 180
Dead Man Walking, 184
de Aguirre, Lope. See *Aguirre, der Zorn Gottes*
Dengler, Dieter, 147–49
de Souza, Francisco Félix. See *Cobra Verde*
DiCaprio, Leonardo, 231
Die grosse Ekstase des Bildschnitzers Steiner (*The Great Ecstasy of Woodcarver Steiner*), 53, 56, 223
Die Verwandlung der Welt in Musik: Bayreuth vor der Premiere (*The Transformation of the World into Music*), 93
Dinotasia, 180
Django Unchained, 143, 153
documentaries by Herzog, 6, 55–57, 177–80, 184–87, 212–13nn156–57
Doktor Faust, 93, 94
Domingo, Plácido, 110
Dourif, Brad, 180
Dylan, Bob, 85

Eastwood, Clint, 51, 231
Echoes from a Somber Empire, 144
El abrazo de la serpiente, 121
El otro Francisco, 153
Elsaesser, Thomas, 127–28
Emerald Forest, The, 121
Encounters at the End of the World, 177, 221–22, 228
Enigma of Kaspar Hauser, The, 21, 53, 54, 58–60, 66, 232
Enyutin, Victor, 77–78
Ernani, 102, 105
Eurocentrism, 128, 157–58, 162–63, 209–10n138

Even Dwarfs Started Small, 26–27, 33–34; capitalist modernity examined in, 41; pessimism in, 54
excess, language of, 20–22

Faith and Currency, 57
Fata Morgana, 17, 144, 179
Faust, 226, 227
Feldman, Douglas, 178–79
Ferres, Veronica, 180
Fitzcarrald, Carlos Fermín. See *Fitzcarraldo*
Fitzcarraldo, 4, 5, 9, 56, 98, 152, 179, 223; capitalism explored in, 104–5, 113–14; critical and public reaction to, 119–20, 124–27, 205–6nn117–18, 211–12n148; as dossier of products, 120, 124, 128–29; drums-*versus*-opera scene of, 122–24; geography of, 115–17; God and creation in, 138–39; as Herzog's best-known film, 94–95; historical setting of, 107–14; indigenous communities oppressed in, 134–39, 207n125; opera and, 106–14, 131–32, 204n106, 204n109, 206–7n121; performances in, 100–101; plot of, 101–14; political critique in, 129–30, 145–47; process genre in, 129–30; production problems of, 121–22, 124–25, 207–8n126; rubber industry portrayed in, 114–18, 128, 131–33, 144, 204n108; scene of fabrication in, 128, 131; simultaneous subtlety and obviousness in, 133–34; story behind, 90–92; in trilogy, 140–41
Fitzgerald, Brian Sweeney, 94
Foucault, Michel, 175
Franco, James, 180
Franco, Jean, 124
Fratta, Robert, 186

Galeano, Eduardo, 45, 109, 133
Ganz, Bruno, 95, 180, 181
García Bernal, Gael, 180–81
Gardel, Carlos, 148
Gasherbrum (The Dark Glow of the Mountains), 99
Gebrauchsfilm, 55
Gein, Ed, 85–86
German Romanticism, 19, 54–55, 188–89n11, 230
Giovanna d'Arco, 93
Glaube und Währung: Dr. Gene Scott, Fernsehprediger (God's Angry Man), 56–57
God and creation, 138–39
Goethe, Johann Wolfgang von, 226, 227
Golder, Herb, 223
Gone with the Wind, 143
Gorbachev, Mikhail, 180
Gori, Pietro, 108
Great Ecstasy of Woodcarver Steiner, The, 53, 56, 223
Grito de Dolores, 35
Grizzly Man, 6, 21, 98, 176–77, 230
Gruber, Steff, 142
Grupe, Norbert, 181
Guerra, Ciro, 121
Gutiérrez Aléa, Tomás, 164

Handicapped Future, 146
Happy People: A Year in the Taiga, 179
Hartman, Saidiya, 171
Heart of Glass, 21, 53, 54, 59, 60–61, 98, 181
Heaven's Gate, 101
Hegel, G. W. F., 157–58, 171, 215–16nn171–72
Hemingway, Ernest, 85, 230
Hernani, 105
Herzog, Werner, 89; autobiographical films of, 7; classroom films of, 55; desperate solitary rebels of, 52–53; diversity of work by, 179–80; documentaries of, 6, 55–57, 177–80, 184–87, 212–13nn156–57; earliest work of, 23; interviews of, 174–75, 219n186, 221–32; introduction to, 1–10; later works of, 174–87; lost appeal of films by, 180; New German Cinema and, 1, 3, 52, 194–95n50; opera and, 92–94; pessimism of, 53–54; political themes in films of (*see* political themes); process genre and, 129–30, 209n133–34; prominent actors in films by, 180–81 (*see also* Kinski, Klaus); self-reference in films of, 175–79; themes in scholarly work on, 3–7

Herzog on Herzog, 8
Hill, Norman, 83, 155
Hittscher, Paul, 100
Howard, Ron, 175
How Much Wood Would a Woodchuck Chuck, 56, 74, 93
Hugo, Victor, 105
Huie's Predigt, 57

I Am My Films, 7
I Am My Films, Part 2, 7
Il Guarany, 111
In Cold Blood, 185
Into the Abyss, 4, 6, 146, 182, 184
Into the Inferno, 98, 178
Invincible, 180

Jameson, Frederic, 10
Jara, René, 175
Jimerson, Michael, 186
Joy Division, 84

Kant, Immanuel, 18
Keaton, Buster, 229
Kérékou, Mathieu, 142–43
Kidman, Nicole, 180–81
Kilmer, Val, 180
Kinski, Klaus, 2, 11, 13, 66, 140, 177, 178, 181, 232; in *Aguirre,* 49–50, 51; in *Cobra Verde,* 142–43, 151, 158, 162; as Dracula, 100; in *Fitzcarraldo,* 112, 124, 125–26, 128, 130–31, 137; *My Best Fiend* and, 16–18, 120, 176, 208n126; in *Nosferatu,* 95
Koepnick, Lutz, 130
Köppen, Manuel, 154

La casa verde, 111
Lachman, Ed, 96
Land des Schweigens und der Dunkelheit (*Land of Silence and Darkness*), 53, 55
landscape as character, 18–23
language and capitalism, 57–59
La Soufrière—Warten auf eine unausweichliche Katastrophe, 95–96, 178; crew of, 96; story of, 96–100
La última cena, 153
Lawrence, T. E., 182
Lebenszeichen. See *Signs of Life*
Lee, Spike, 175
Leppert, Richard, 102, 103, 105, 113, 121
Lessons of Darkness, 6, 98, 147, 212–13nn156–57
Lewgoy, José, 165
Lewis, Damian, 180
liberalism, modern, 52
Little Dieter Needs to Fly, 6, 147–49, 223
Lloyd, Harold, 229
Lo and Behold: Reveries of the Connected World, 6, 182
Lohengrin, 93
Luther, Martin, 230, 231

magical realism, 109, 110–11
male characters in Herzog's films, 199n74
Manderlay, 153
Mandingo, 143, 153
Manon, 122
Martel, Lucrecia, 34
Marx, Karl, 71, 127, 128, 140, 161–62
Master and Margarita, 225
Mattes, Eva, 61, 66, 181
Mauch, Thomas, 142
May, Karl, 69
McKain, Scott, 74, 84
McNee, Malcolm, 176
Milam, Blaine, 186
mirages, 47–48
Mission, The, 153
Murnau, F. W., 95, 99
Musk, Elon, 182
My Best Fiend (*Mein liebster Feind*), 7, 16, 18, 21, 120, 126, 176, 179, 207–8n126
My Son, My Son, What Have Ye Done? 180–81

Nabucco, 108
Nagib, Lucia, 154
Native Son, 185
Nazi Germany, 4, 136, 146, 148–49, 230
Neira, Hernán, 37
Nelson, Erik, 179–80
neocolonialism, 120
New German Cinema, 1, 3, 52, 194–95n50

Nicholson, Jack, 180
Nietzsche, Friedrich, 33
Nosferatu: Phantom der Nacht (*Nosferatu the Vampyre*), 23, 53, 54, 95, 99
novela de la selva, 128
Nugkuag, Evaristo, 90

Of Walking in Ice, 7
On Death Row, 4, 178–79, 182, 184–87
One Hundred Years of Solitude, 48
opera: *Fitzcarraldo* and, 106–14, 131–32, 204n106, 204n109, 206–7n121; Herzog's interest in, 92–94; *La Soufrière* and, 98–99; modern, 106–7
oppression of indigenous communities, 134–39

Páramo Bonilla, Carlos, 46
Pérez Espinosa, David, 124, 181
pessimism, 53–54
Philosophy of History, The, 157
political themes, 3–7, 182–84, 187n3; in *Aguirre,* 34–38, 45–46; in *Cobra Verde,* 143–49; in *Fitzcarraldo,* 129–30, 145–47
Prager, Brad, 10, 19–20, 130, 154–58
Pressman, 121
process genre, 129–30, 209n133–34
Puar, Jasbir, 166

Queen of the Desert, 178, 182, 184

Rama, Angel, 44
Rancière, Jacques, 10, 134
Reber, Dierdra, 133
Reconquest of the Useless, 121
Redrobe, Karen, 221–32
Refn, Nicolas Winding, 34
Rescue Dawn, 178, 181, 232
Review of the Civil Administration of Mesopotamia, 182–83
Reyes, Alfonso, 171
Ribeiro Sanches, Manuela, 154
Rick and Morty, 2
Rogers, Huie, 57
Rogue Film School, 175, 219n186
Roots, 143, 153, 158
Roselli, John, 107
Roth, Tim, 180
Routier, Darlie, 186

Salt and Fire, 98, 177–78, 180–81
Saxer, Walter, 101
scene of fabrication, 128, 131
Schleinstein, Bruno, 61, 66, 178, 181, 232
Schmidt-Reitwein, Jörg, 96
Schroeter, Walter, 105
Schumann, Peter, 45
Schwarz, Roberto, 112, 159
Scorsese, Martin, 175
Second Punic War, 231
self-reference in films of Herzog, 175–79
Sevigny, Chloë, 180
sexual violence, 160, 216n174
Shannon, Michael, 180–81
Signs of Life, 2, 17, 23–26, 27–28, 33–34, 42, 146, 178, 179; capitalist modernity examined in, 41; pessimism in, 54
Singer, Alan, 10
slavery, 216–17nn175–76; in *Cobra Verde,* 143–51, 158–68; film genre on, 143–49; Hegelian philosophy and, 157–58, 215–16nn171–72
Spaghetti westerns, 187–88n5
Spence, Connie, 186
Spiel im Sand, 23
Star Wars, 222
Steiner, Walter, 181
Straubinger, Fini, 147, 231
Stroszek, 51, 53, 56, 58–59, 153, 179, 200n80, 200–201nn82–84, 232; capitalism explored in, 71–74; as celebration of America, 87–88, 195–96n56, 196n57; claustrophobia portrayed in, 66–67; crew problems while shooting, 83–84; final sequence of, 84–85; frontier society explored in, 60–61, 64–73, 86–87; Herzog's circumspection in, 85–86; historical setting of, 62–63; as hybrid production, 61–62; plot of, 63–70
Sykes, Mark, 183

También la lluvia, 121
Tazieff, Haroun, 97
Ten Thousand Years Older, 139

Terry, Sonny, 179
Third Reich, 4, 136, 146
Tirano Banderas, 35
Tocqueville, Alexis de, 64
Tod für fünf Stimmen (Death for Five Voices), 93
Treadwell, Timothy, 176–77, 230
Trump, D., 107
Turner, Frederick Jackson, 51, 64–65, 70–72
12 Years a Slave, 143, 153, 158, 216n173
Twilight of the Gods, 98

Uncle Tom's Cabin, 143, 153

Valhalla Rising, 34
Valle-Inclán, Ramón María del, 35
Vargas Llosa, Mario, 111
Vázquez, Francisco, 10
Veblen, Thorstein, 71–73, 85
Venas abiertas de América Latina, 45, 109
Verdi, Giuseppe, 101–2, 105
Viceroy of Ouidah, The, 152
Vietnam War, 136, 146, 147–48

Wade, Ralph, 81
Wagner, Richard, 98
Walker Art Center, 176
Wayne, John, 231, 232
Werner Herzog: A Guide for the Perplexed, 8
Werner Herzog Eats His Shoe, 7
Werner Herzog: Filmemacher, 7
Werner Herzog: Interviews, 8
Where the Green Ants Dream, 146–47
White Diamond, The, 98, 180, 182
Widmark, Richard, 231
Wild Blue Yonder, The, 6, 178, 179, 222, 228
Williams, William Appleman, 65
World War II, 4, 136, 146, 148–49
Woyzeck, 53, 54

YouTube, 7

Zabriskie, Grace, 180
Zahn, Steve, 180
Zama, 34

Joshua Lund is a professor of Spanish at the University of Notre Dame. He is the author of *The Mestizo State: Reading Race in Modern Mexico* and *The Impure Imagination: Toward a Critical Hybridity in Latin American Writing*.

Books in the series Contemporary Film Directors

Nelson Pereira dos Santos
Darlene J. Sadlier

Abbas Kiarostami
Mehrnaz Saeed-Vafa and Jonathan Rosenbaum

Joel and Ethan Coen
R. Barton Palmer

Claire Denis
Judith Mayne

Wong Kar-wai
Peter Brunette

Edward Yang
John Anderson

Pedro Almodóvar
Marvin D'Lugo

Chris Marker
Nora Alter

Abel Ferrara
Nicole Brenez, translated by Adrian Martin

Jane Campion
Kathleen McHugh

Jim Jarmusch
Juan Suárez

Roman Polanski
James Morrison

Manoel de Oliveira
John Randal Johnson

Neil Jordan
Maria Pramaggiore

Paul Schrader
George Kouvaros

Jean-Pierre Jeunet
Elizabeth Ezra

Terrence Malick
Lloyd Michaels

Sally Potter
Catherine Fowler

Atom Egoyan
Emma Wilson

Albert Maysles
Joe McElhaney

Jerry Lewis
Chris Fujiwara

Jean-Pierre and Luc Dardenne
Joseph Mai
Michael Haneke
Peter Brunette

Alejandro González Iñárritu
Celestino Deleyto and Maria del Mar Azcona

Lars von Trier
Linda Badley

Hal Hartley
Mark L. Berrettini

François Ozon
Thibaut Schilt

Steven Soderbergh
Aaron Baker

Mike Leigh
Sean O'Sullivan

D.A. Pennebaker
Keith Beattie

Jacques Rivette
Mary M. Wiles

Kim Ki-duk
Hye Seung Chung

Philip Kaufman
Annette Insdorf

Richard Linklater
David T. Johnson

David Lynch
Justus Nieland

John Sayles
David R. Shumway

Dario Argento
L. Andrew Cooper

Todd Haynes
Rob White

Christian Petzold
Jaimey Fisher

Spike Lee
Todd McGowan

Terence Davies
Michael Koresky

Francis Ford Coppola
Jeff Menne

Emir Kusturica
Giorgio Bertellini

Agnès Varda
Kelley Conway

John Lasseter
Richard Neupert

Paul Thomas Anderson
George Toles

Cristi Puiu
Monica Filimon

Wes Anderson
Donna Kornhaber

Jan Švankmajer
Keith Leslie Johnson

Kelly Reichardt
Katherine Fusco and Nicole Seymour

Michael Bay
Lutz Koepnick

Abbas Kiarostami, Expanded Second Edition
Mehrnaz Saeed-Vafa and Jonathan Rosenbaum

Lana and Lilly Wachowski
Cáel M. Keegan

Todd Solondz
Julian Murphet

Lucrecia Martel
Gerd Gemünden

Werner Herzog
Joshua Lund

University of Illinois Press
is a founding member of the
Association of University Presses.

Composed in 10/13 New Caledonia
with Helvetica Neue display
by Lisa Connery
at the University of Illinois Press
Manufactured by Sheridan Books, Inc.

University of Illinois Press
1325 South Oak Street
Champaign, IL 61820-6903
www.press.uillinois.edu